# MUGGED BY REALITY

# MUGGED BY REALITY

The Liberation of Iraq and
the Failure of Good Intentions

## JOHN AGRESTO

ENCOUNTER BOOKS
NEW YORK

First edition published in 2007 by Encounter Books, an activity of Encounter for Culture and Education, Inc., a nonprofit, tax exempt corporation.

Encounter Books website address: www.encounterbooks.com

Manufactured in the United States and printed on acid-free paper.

The paper used in this publication meets the minimum requirements of ANSI/NISO Z39.48-1992 (R 1997)(Permanence of Paper).

FIRST EDITION

Library of Congress Cataloging-in-Publication Data

Agresto, John
    Mugged by Reality: The Liberation of Iraq and the Failure of Good
    Intentions/John Agresto
        p. cm.
        ISBN 1-59403-187-8
        1. Postwar reconstruction—Iraq    2. Iraq war, 2003–
    3. Education—Iraq    I. Title.
    DS79.769.A37 2007
    956.7044'3—dc22
    2006026428


10   9   8   7   6   5   4   3   2

*For Ali al-Hilfi and Jim Mollen,*
*both of whom died for Iraq.*

# Table of Contents

**Preface**  ix

**One**  **Going**  Why we are there. Why I was there.  1
What we hoped to accomplish. "Neoconservatism"
and democracy. Democracy and Terror. Religion
and Terror.

**Two**  **Daily Life**  Conditions as I found them. Of life  25
in the Green Zone. Of safety and security. Iraqi
culture, American culture, common culture.

**Three**  **Truth, Facts, and Lies: Five Aspects of Culture and**
**Character**  Truth, Facts, and Lies. Stories and  41
Lessons. Death Goes to Pick the Finest of All.
Getting Iraqis to Fight. An Assassination Attempt
and a Kidnapping.

**Four**  **Higher Education, Politics and Religious**
**Totalitarianism**  Politics, fanaticism, and the  71
universities. Conditions before and after the war.
Difficulties with the Minister. Fears and hopes.

**Five**  **Bringing Iraq To Democracy**  Democratizing a
non-democratic country. Effects of both tyranny
and socialism on character. Democracy and the  97

necessary character of citizens. "Cultural
Insensitivity," or American ignorance as to what
makes its own democracy work.

**Six**    **Education and Democracy**    Reflections on    **121**
higher education and political liberty.

**Seven**    **"All Assistance Short of Actual Help"**    What    **139**
we did and, especially, what we failed to do.
Funding failures and the failures of misplaced
priorities.

**Eight**    **Soldiers**    How the US military saved the day,    **155**
and also how it lost it.

**Nine**    **Reality Often Astonishes Theory**    American    **171**
Ideals and the Failure of Good Intentions. What we
did right, what we did wrong, and what we might
learn from it all. The death of Ali. Hopes for the
future, and fears.

**Acknowledgments**    **195**

**Index**    **197**

# Preface

This book covers my experiences in Iraq during the formative and transitional time from 2003 to 2004. The period was formative, because it was right after the war in 2003 that we set out our plans for the pacification and democratization of Iraq, established governing structures, and slowly, slowly laid plans for reconstruction. Formative also because we put in place "policies" (if that is the right word) such as not resisting looters, not paying attention to what was called "Iraqi on Iraqi crime," not policing the streets or cleaning up neighborhoods, and not re-arresting the criminals that Saddam had freed and armed in anticipation of our invasion.

The period was transitional because it was during this time that the insurgency picked up momentum and learned to destabilize the occupation by terrorizing Iraqis as much as attacking Americans. The period was transitional, also, because some of our counter-insurgency tactics then began to tilt the opinion of ordinary Iraqis away from seeing us as liberators and more toward seeing us as occupiers, occupiers whose motives now seemed ever more unclear. A chapter such as the one entitled "Daily Life" is not in this book to be merely historical or, worse, quaint. Its purpose is to show that there was a time, a time now gone, when Americans in Iraq could sit with students in their cafeterias and talk about exchange programs, meet with professors to discuss an upcoming conference, go buy rugs unescorted in the marketplace, or sit and have ice cream with locals at a corner store. But that was during the transition, and now that time is past.

To try to understand why this all has been lost, to see what was inevitable and what might have been prevented, is why this book was written.

▲▼▲

I find myself in the position of having spent close to a year in Iraq working with some extraordinary individuals—Americans and Iraqis as well as Italians, Brits, and Czechs—individuals who gave their best in hopes of rebuilding Iraq. Some gave their lives. And I have to say that I think most of it has turned out to be for naught.

But by "most" I do not mean "all," and therein lies the rub. There are still things that only America or the "multinational force" under our leadership can do that prevent our full disengagement. It was our forces that captured Saddam and eliminated his two sons; it was we who had both the intelligence capacity to track down Zarqawi and the air power to kill him. Our presence helps shelter the government and its personnel from attack, retards the foreign insurgency, and may even, to a lesser extent, moderate indigenous Shiite-Sunni militia activity. Moreover, much of the building and rebuilding of the infrastructure of Iraq is still carried out under American direction and with American funds. Contrary to so much of the banter one hears that points to America as the irritant in Iraq (claiming that if only we would leave, then Iraqis would come together to build a united and peaceful nation), the truth is that our leaving would not give peace a chance, but would give anarchy, mayhem, and full-scale civil war its best chance.

Perhaps the strangest part of the current debate over our continued engagement in Iraq is that both sides are close to holding the same position. The Administration is eager to point to any number of so-called successes—two national elections, a new constitution, some working civic projects, a growing Iraqi civil defense force—and declare that as these items take root,

America and American forces can begin to step down. The Administration's opponents read the same news stories but see the events in Iraq as indicative of a country in disarray if not civil war, a bloody nation with a dysfunctional government, a people indifferent to our liberation of them and indignant at our continued presence; they think it's high time for America to pull back. The difference is not so much in the goal—disengagement—as in whether to call it a failure and come home or call it a success and come home. Oddly, sadly, tragically, it may be a failure from which we cannot so easily come home, at least not completely. That situation—the need for continued American support for both security and development under seriously adverse conditions—may well be the worst of all possible worlds. It may also be the real world.

▲▼▲

As I was preparing to leave Iraq in the early summer of 2004, the Defense Department sent around a memo asking those of us on the ground to jot down a paragraph or two on "lessons learned." The thought that anyone could summarize anything of value in a few sentences struck me as preposterous. What did we not foresee? What was inevitable? What did we not understand? Why did we not understand it? What did we do right? Where did we go wrong? Each of these categories demanded investigation, demanded an *analysis,* not just a few words or, worse, a few fingers pointing at random trying to attach blame.

So this book is an attempt to understand what it was that we were hoping to do in Iraq, why it was important, where we succeeded, where we came up short, and, above all, *why.*

Today there are no end of books and essays purporting to "explain" how we went wrong. But most of them seem, to me, to be thin and superficial. If only we had done *this* differently or *that* differently, all would have been better. "If only we had more troops"—to give the one example we hear constantly. Well, not unless we had intentions of using them differently. Not unless we intended to enforce security, shoot looters, spread troops out along thousands of miles of borderland, and act as neighborhood policemen. Without a change of policy, more men would only have meant more targets and more casualties. And more troops killing more Iraqis and seizing and destroying more property would almost certainly have made all matters worse. Yes, in some cases, for some purposes, more soldiers would have helped. But it would not have fixed the problem without a change in vision and in policies.

Perhaps, we are told, the problem was we "disbanded the army" and de-Ba'athified too thoroughly—that we removed too many administrative elements of the former regime who alone could have held the country together. Perhaps. But that would have meant keeping in power people feared and hated by those who suffered most under Saddam and whose loyalties we most needed on our side. Were we willing to trade the support of Sistani or other Shi'a to keep former Ba'ath party functionaries at work? Were we willing to risk the pacification of the country by keeping in armed power those we so recently fought to kill? Or should we have reconscripted the Shiites in Saddam's army, who rationally deserted at the first opportunity? Besides, in places like Mosul we didn't de-Ba'athify as we did elsewhere, we didn't fire all the army officers or eliminate their pensions, but still Mosul often rivaled Ramadi as a haven for the insurgency and anti-Coalition activity. We often say that hindsight is twenty-twenty, but not when we look back through simplistic and muddled lenses.

It's an historic American trait to look for one cause of all our woes and blame that one thing. Or perhaps find the person at fault and hold him responsible. I'm sorry—if we want to understand what has happened in Iraq, we have to be smarter than that.

It seems we love not only the simple explanation but also, looking ahead, the simple solution. Are the separate militias a problem? Well, why not dismantle them and "integrate" their men into the national civil defense force? What a great idea! But then we realize that, having put on the uniform of Iraq, insurgents somehow forgot to shed their loyalty to this ethnic group or that religious sect. So now militiamen still torture and kill their Iraqi opponents, but they do it wearing Iraqi uniforms and under the authority of the general government. And the killings go on. (Not to put too fine a point on it, but it is as if we decided that the way to stop gangland murders in Chicago in the Thirties would have been to deputize Al Capone as an FBI agent. Then for sure he would have forsworn his past and been on the side of good government, no? Maybe we were brighter back then.)

Is the murderous and fanatical Muqtada al-Sadr a problem? Well, let's try asking him "to join the political process." Doesn't that sound nice? Then, when he wins a fair number of seats in the national assembly, holds the balance of power in the selection of a new prime minister, and is granted ministry positions, we do all we can to block his choice and deny him power.

We live off the hope that people will change from murderers and fanatics into middling politicians competing for votes rather than ideologues hungering for power or souls. So we repeatedly misunderstand the character of fanaticism, and misunderstand that there are certain issues of religion or nationality that drive some people to demand power and not seek accommodation. We put our faith in diplomacy, thinking that if we could only communicate better, talk more, or really understand the other side's point of view, then concessions will develop and all will improve. We seem to look upon democracy as some kind of magic—an alchemy that changes fanatics into politicians, ready to truck and bargain and compromise their views to get ahead. This shows how quick we are to think the best of people, think the best of the "democratic process," think that communication and understanding will bring people together, as if, deep down, we're really all on the same side and all want the same things. So we constantly delude ourselves, and think that because it's hopeful, maybe it will someday be real.

As I will repeatedly argue in this book, it was not America's lack of awareness of "Iraqi culture" or "the character of the Middle East" that harmed the mission so much as our amazing incomprehension of human nature, our blindness to the power of fiercely held notions of religion and morality and honor, our misunderstanding of all that real democracy entails, and our

ignorance of the damaging effects of tyranny on a people's outlook and character. Yes, America was mugged by a reality that
was sometimes opaque, a reality hidden, in a sense, behind a
Middle Eastern veil. But it was also mugged, sorry to say, by a
reality of human nature, human needs, and human passions
painted in the boldest colors and hidden right before its eyes.

Perhaps I could summarize it this way: We are in danger
of losing all we hoped to accomplish in Iraq because we haven't
a clue as to how to be an effective occupying power. But that
sentence contains within it a dozen ingredients, all of which
require thought and examination. What did we not know about
the preconditions for establishing democracy in a fractured
country, or what did we not know about the public consequences of fiercely held private religious beliefs? These are just
two major questions in this book.

Again, that we as a nation knew less than we should about
the "culture" of the Middle East may well be true, but not terribly instructive. While the Left often prattles on about the
necessity to be sympathetic to another people's culture, it's often
excruciatingly unclear as to just which culture, in this case which
Iraqi culture, we needed to absorb more thoroughly—Iraqi culture in its modern, secular manifestation? Its religious but tolerant side? Its fanaticism? Its desire to be modern? Its desire to
be closed, xenophobic, and medieval? Culture is important.
Culture is often determinative. But culture is rarely either mono-
lithic or stagnant. And Iraqi culture was, at the start of the war,
varied, multi-stranded, and, most importantly, fluid. As we shall
see, our problem was our inability to understand and promote
those parts and aspects of the culture that were modern, democratic, and liberal and deflect those parts that were fanatical,
repressive, and antagonistic.

So when I argue that those who carried out this endeavor
were "mugged by reality," I'm not particularly saying that they
were mugged by the strangeness of a foreign culture or taken aback
by customs that took them by surprise. The problems were far
deeper than that. What was truly serious is that America and American foreign policy were blind to so many basics—blind, for
instance, to what happens to the character of people who live in

a state of dependency and fear for three decades. Blind to how raw human nature becomes when stripped down to its elements by a vicious and unrelenting tyranny. Blind to the natural need people have to belong to something that gives order and direction to their lives. Blind to what it means to confront individuals who love eternal life so passionately that this life is as nothing. We spouted, and still spout, fortune cookie platitudes about democracy and freedom without much serious thought given to what might be needed to bring democracy and liberty together and make them effective and alive in the real world. We talked about bringing democracy, freedom, and prosperity to a long subjugated nation—and had no idea of how idle and vain such talk was without the will, first and foremost, to protect and secure persons and property. We were blind to the notion that security precedes freedom—precedes even the *hope* of freedom. We thought we could give liberty without order, and we were dead wrong.[1] Above all, America has been blind to how fierce, bloody, and barbaric serious religious passions can be. In our more easy-going and secular ways, we forget the immense power, the joy, that comes with doing God's will and preparing a place for yourself in paradise, even when it involves sacrificing your life—or killing others.

▲▼▲

I was in charge of helping to rebuild Iraq's system of higher education. I hope I can do justice in these pages to all that we tried to do and actually did. But I have to admit that so much of what we worked to do has not survived. Yes, Ba'ath Party ideology

---

[1] I will have occasion throughout this book to take to task any number of liberal shibboleths, platitudes about culture and democracy and religion that ill served us in Iraq. But this particular foolishness regarding liberty and order—that (as I've heard it said) "a people who prefer security to freedom deserve neither"—is actually a right-wing silliness that is not only foolish but dangerous. Without order and security, without police on the streets and criminals behind bars, the enjoyment of all rights and liberties is constantly at risk. To think we could have introduced democratic liberty to Iraq without the absolute restoration of law and order was to embark on a fool's errand. One would have thought conservatives knew this since, to give a small example, they so vociferously defend the right to bear arms—i.e., the right to be personally secure in our homes and in public.

and courses on the social philosophy of Saddam are gone. Yet in their place are sectarian strictures and codes of orthodox behavior as rigorous as anything Saddam could have imposed, with compliance enforced by beatings and death.

To speak only about higher education, we have a fairly rough idea of how many professors have been killed. In 2005 alone, one report has 296 professors and staff members murdered, including eighty from the University of Baghdad alone.[2] The number of Iraqi scholars and professors who have fled the country is surely well over a thousand. When the figures finally are collected for 2006, I imagine they will be substantially higher.

There had been killings of professors and university administrators from the start of liberation up until the time I left in the summer of 2004—perhaps three dozen in all. My sense was that virtually all of them were killed for political reasons since they were by and large Ba'athist functionaries. But now the situation under the new "democratic" dispensation is different: Led most often by students and backed by local Shiite militias and brigades, this is simply the execution and exile of the intellectual class, a class more secular and rational than the new sectarian forces will allow.

I have no figures on how many students, women as well as men, have been beaten, killed, or forced to abandon the university, but without doubt the number is now in the thousands. And the number of teachers and physicians killed is quickly approaching that of university professors.

Hasan, one of our translators and a person you will soon meet in this book, summed it up most poignantly in a few recent letters from Baghdad:

----

[2]*The Chronicle of Higher Education,* "Iraq's Intellectuals are Marked for Death," June 29, 2006. Exact figures are, to be sure, extremely hard to come by. And some, as these above, include staff and university administrators along with professors. If we turn to pre-collegiate education, the Ministry of Education in Iraq recently declared that 311 teachers and 64 students under the age of twelve were killed simply in the four months preceding March 2006, with over 400 schools attacked.

A near total eclipse of the heart & soul is the reason for not writing. As you're concluding from what you gather, nothing is going in the right direction. Deterioration is the master of the scene.

[W]e're living in unbelievably unbearable circumstances. Everything is worse than the day before: infrastructure, services, security, even hope! I don't need to elaborate. What you gather from the media is only a fraction of reality....Nowadays women are afraid of going outdoors unless for an absolute need ... but most must wear veils as a precaution from a sudden harassment by a stupid degenerate, claiming to implement religion....To top it all, we have a curfew extension, so now we should be home sunset till 6 A.M., just like domesticated farm animals!

Our feelings & reaction have become numb....To wrap it up, wasn't I right [back in 2004] about sitting down & watching [TV] with a drink in hand, hoping to live another day with our limbs and head where they were the day before?![3]

Each time there's a newly elected government, we in America hope for a new beginning, hope for some semblance of peace, security, and the protection of basic rights. But the sad facts speak for themselves.

▲▼▲

The sadistic brutality of the former regime was well known. The sadistic brutality of the current insurgency and even of those who wear the uniform of the Iraqi army are now equally well known. Today, more journalists have been killed in Iraq than in any other war in history. Stopping school busses in order to take out children of the "wrong" sect and killing them barely makes the news. And while the beheading and mutilation of American contractors in Fallujah in 2004 created an understandable furor and the siege of the city, it was only because it was the beginning of how many subsequent beheadings and mutilations? Only the most sickening acts seem to make a lasting impression on us today, as when two young American soldiers are tortured and dismembered beyond recognition, or nine heads are found in fruit boxes in Baghdad.

---

[3]From two letters, dated March 5 and June 17, 2006.

Although I now believe that the situation in Iraq is disastrous, the reader needs to know that I began with the view that there were both valid humanitarian as well as serious geo-political reasons—defensible reasons—for the liberation of Iraq from Saddam. It is because I believe we had valid and defensible humanitarian and democratic objectives that I take so seriously what I fear is fast becoming both a failure and a tragedy. It is because I also believe we had valid national and international objectives that I now worry that a war that was fought with American treasure and blood is about to be won by Iran.

▲▼▲

Education, religion, culture, and democracy. These—not troop strength or the correct levels of de-Ba'athification policies—are the most important issues we needed to understand in order to fashion intelligent policies in Iraq. We still need to understand them if we have any hope of salvaging anything from this venture. I've attempted to give each issue its separate due, as well as to do justice to their interconnections. But two—democracy and the pervasive power of religion—need to be highlighted here before we start.

I do believe it's true that we have brought democracy to Iraq. And it's possible that, in time, it may evolve into a decent and free government. But it is hardly that today. It's a democracy the likes of which not one of us in this country would consent to live in for a day. Yes, it is a democracy. It has elections; it has majority rule; it even has a constitution. But not all democracies, as I will argue later in this book, are good. And so long as we muddle about in foreign affairs thinking that "democracy" by itself is a fine thing, we will have no way of stopping some of the most illiberal, tyrannical, fanatical, and internationally dangerous states from arraying themselves against us and others, propping themselves up with the argument that they were *elected*. I for one would hardly be comforted by knowing that terrorist mayhem or global destabilization was the result of a popular vote rather than the decree of an oligarch or the whim of a self-appointed thug. Elections do not, in themselves, confer legitimacy, or make malevolent acts acceptable.

We know this, and yet we don't. We propose elections in the Palestinian Authority, and encourage all parties to take part. Yet when a militant Islamist terror organization, Hamas, wins a decisive victory, we fluctuate between downplaying their radicalism ("they won because they were against Fatah's corruption") and simply denying their legitimacy and right to govern. It's a strange policy that encourages democracy worldwide, yet works against its results.

Still, I'm not overly concerned with any supposed inconsistency. A terrorist government is illegitimate no matter whether it was appointed, was anointed, was elected, or rules by ancient and prescriptive right. Rather, my worry is that, by making "democracy" the cornerstone of our current foreign policy, we make the spread of fanaticism and terror more, not less, likely.

Let me stay on this point for a while. In Chapter V, I try to be clear about why the establishment of the kind of constitution and democracy Iraq now has is hardly the kind of democracy one might have hoped for. It is hardly a democracy conducive to moderation, liberty, peace, or the protection of rights. Arguably, however, while a turbulent and repressive democracy might be a disaster for the nation in question, it might not seem to rise to the level of international concern. But it does. In so far as we have made the promotion of "democracy" the centerpiece of our foreign policy, we may well be in the process of promoting both the establishment of extremism and religious immoderation within a country and the empowerment of terror internationally. All too often—in Algeria in 1991, in Iran with the election of Ahmadinejad, in the Palestinian Authority with the election of Hamas, just to name the most obvious examples—extremist factions have come to power democratically; in other places—Lebanon and (sorry to say) Iraq spring to mind—Islamic extremists have achieved a secure hold on a large measure of political power, all democratically, all through elections. Moreover, in a free election, the Muslim Brotherhood would grow powerful if not victorious in Egypt, the Saudis would almost certainly cast their ballots for a virulent form of Islamic extremism, and Pakistan could easily become the first pro-Al-Qaeda/Taliban state with nuclear weapons. If anyone thinks that terror somehow becomes acceptable or "legitimate" because it was elected into power in this or that state, that person has a rather odd notion of what it takes to legitimate evil. And to say that we simply have to support democracies and then hope for the best is a policy that can only be labeled wrong-headed and destructive.

I argue throughout this book that the establishment of liberal democracies, democracies that respect human dignity and individual rights, *is* in the long-range interest of both America and the international community. But not all democracies are liberal democracies, no matter what our hopes. And any regime that works to impose its ideology or sectarian orthodoxy abroad has no claim on our respect, no matter how many elections it holds or how many constitutions it writes. There is no magic in the word "democracy" that makes a terrorist state acceptable.

Finally, the reason why the promotion of "democracy" in general (rather than liberal democracy in particular) makes the spread of fanaticism and terror more likely is that we are today witnessing a world-wide revival of Islamic fanaticism the depth of which has probably not been seen in centuries. It's an extremism that has the capacity to capture the imagination of the young, provide convincing answers to many of the best educated, and give comfort and promise to the masses. Islamic extremism is, in many places, a democratic, popular, mass movement.

I find this hard to write, but it is increasingly true: because Islamic fanaticism is quickly becoming a mass movement, capturing the hearts and minds of people in pivotal and powerful states world-wide, the more we promote a simple-minded view of "democracy," the more we will find ourselves promoting and empowering the most war-like, imperial, and destructive ideology since Stalinism and Fascism.

▲▼▲

When we began our incursion into Iraq, we had high hopes. The establishment of a mild Islamic state, free, prosperous, and tolerant, would be a model of liberal democratic life in the region. It would encourage the progressive elements in Iran and, by its example, increase the possibility of liberalizing others. In its aftermath, however, we have seen the election of a firebrand fanatic hot in pursuit of nuclear weapons in Iran, the election of Hamas in Palestine, the emboldening of Hezbollah, and growing political power of Iranian-style religious extremism in Iraq itself.[4]

In this age, we are all, all of us, seduced by hope but mugged by reality. And the pre-eminent reality of the day is a religious fanaticism, self-assured, unafraid of death, unafraid of killing, medieval in its outlook yet armed with powerful modern weaponry, growing in its mass appeal and able to co-opt democratic forms and elections.

---

[4]Iraq's current ties to Iran are many, deep, and significant. The Ayatollah Sistani is, is as most people know, Iranian by birth, Iranian by religious training—he still retains his Iranian citizenship in preference to accepting Iraqi citizenship. The Islamist Dawa party, the Supreme Council for the Islamic Revolution (SCIRI), and SCIRI's military wing, the Badr Brigade, all came to Iraq, especially to southern Iraq, from Iran—as did over a hundred thousand displaced Iraqi Shi'a, Iranian operatives, and armed subsidiaries of Iranian intelligence. As George Packer points out, rather than speak of Iranian "influence" in Basra and southern Iraq, it might be more correct to speak of Iranian "occupation." And the various Iranian religious parties were the agents of this occupation.

Iran has been responsible for sending money, men, and materiel into Iraq, and is almost certainly responsible for the increased lethality of IEDs and other weapons currently in use by anti-Coalition forces. Indeed, perhaps the most virulent of the anti-Coalition, anti-American gangs, Muqtada al-Sadr's party and its Mahdi army, are armed, often trained, and heavily funded directly by Iran.

Politically, these Iranian-connected Shiite religious parties are the nucleus of the current ruling coalition, the United Iraqi Alliance. Prime Minister Maliki is from this Alliance, which includes not only Dawa (Maliki's party) and SCIRI, but also five ministers from Sadr's party and one minister from the Iranian-bred "Iraqi Hezbollah," all elected democratically. Already the current leaders in the new Iraq have made it clear that in any armed contest between America and Iran, they would support and supply Iran.

I believe it to be substantially true that we fought the war but Iran may soon win it, but with the following crucial addendum: It is Iran not as a political state but as a *religious* state that is now succeeding. The Shiite fanaticism that rules Iran is a trans-national phenomenon. It exists the way "Christendom" once contained within it various countries and regions. Expansion of this rule, and armed opposition to this rule, is what fuels the religious/civil war now raging in Iraq. The worry of course is that soon there will be the rule of Shiite theocrats, under the guise of democratic forms and elections, ruling a large swath of the Middle East, from Iran through Iraq through south Lebanon.

Democracy may well be, as de Tocqueville argued, the irresistible wave of the future. But the combination of popular rule with a religious fanaticism world-wide in its scope will make the last century—which also combined mass ideology with massive destructive force—seem almost tolerable by comparison.

# ONE

# Going

I had been in Iraq a short while when one of the Iraqis who worked for the Coalition, a young man named Ali, asked me for a favor. He and I had gotten to know one another fairly well. He had been making inquiries about scholarship possibilities in America and had somehow managed to irritate my assistant who was putting the scholarship program together, so he always came by late at night to talk with me after my assistant had gone to bed or gone down to watch a movie.

He was trained as a pharmacist and had actually worked as a pharmacist's assistant before liberation. But with the coming of the Coalition he signed up to work as a bookkeeper with KBR—Kellogg, Brown and Root—a part of Halliburton and the people who fed us all each day. His English was extraordinarily good and his French almost better, though he did not like talking French all that much, not being a particular fan of the French lately. We would chat about nothing in particular. I would ask him about student life and the study of pharmacy. He would tell me the story of his family, about his mother's illness, and about his sisters, whom he clearly loved more than anything else in the world.

This was the favor: his younger sister had just started college and even though she was enrolled in one of the better universities in Baghdad, she was in a field in which she had no interest. She had wanted to study computer science, but her college entrance exam grades were not good enough. So she was destined to spend the next four years becoming a mini-expert in something she was quickly growing to despise. Could I put pressure on the university to let her switch to computer science?

Though I had the august title of Coalition Provisional Authority Senior Advisor to the Ministry of Higher Education and Scientific Research, he and I both knew that this was something even I could not do. The qualifying exam you took at the end of high school pretty much determined what fields you could enter, and entering a field above your grade was flatly impossible. Iraq is a society of strict rules, moderated only by family connections and the pay-off, and those avenues were both unavailable in this case.

There was one way around that might work, however. Almost every university in Iraq ran what they called "night school." These were classes that started later in the afternoon, were a bit laxer in their requirements, and for which tuition is charged. All of higher education in Iraq is public and free, except for these afternoon and evening classes. So I called the vice president of one of Baghdad's best universities and first asked if Ali's sister could transfer there, switching her concentration up to computer science. I was given the anticipated and fairly paternal lecture as to how and why such a thing was impossible. Still, he asked why I was concerned.

"She is the sister of a guy who gave up a career in pharmacy to work for the Coalition," I answered, "so I thought I would lend a hand."

"No," he said; the answer was still no.

Then I suggested that she be allowed to enroll in the evening classes.

"But it's getting late in the year; she may flunk. Besides, there's a tuition fee for the night school," he countered.

Not knowing her from Eve's cat, I still replied, "I don't think that will be a problem. I know her brother and she comes from a very smart family, and I'm pretty sure the family can pay."

"OK. Have her come by tomorrow and talk to me."

I did not see Ali for a few days and pretty much put the whole episode out of my head. The call took less than five minutes and Ali deserved a good deed for putting his life on the line to work with us. When I finally did run across Ali, he told me that his sister was accepted in the night school and was the happiest person he knew. He then added that he had been thinking about me and about his boss over in KBR, whom he very much liked, and that he had decided to change his life. He had decided he would start becoming "an American." I clearly didn't have a clue about what he meant, so he tried to explain.

"Yesterday I stopped for a man begging on the street and I gave him lots of money. And before that I saw a mother having a hard time with little children, trying to get them to school, so I gave the whole family a ride to the school. See, I'm becoming an American."

"OK, I'll bite. How does this make you an American?"

"Everyday I will try to do something good for someone I don't know, like you did for my sister. That's all."

▲▼▲

I tell this story in part to introduce Ali, and in part to help explain why I—and virtually everyone I knew in Iraq—volunteered to go to Iraq. Clearly, we, as civilians, did not go to find weapons of mass destruction or to capture Saddam. Nor did we go to make money, profit from the war, or cash in on the peace. Our goals were both smaller and grander.

Smaller, because each of us had one sector, one area, in which to do our work. I had the Ministry of Higher Education and Scientific Research; others had Health, or Culture, or Justice, or Oil, or Youth and Sport. Each of us worked as the representative of Ambassador Paul Bremer, the "Administrator" of Iraq, as he was so unassumingly titled; and each of us was asked to work with the newly appointed ministers (twenty-five in all) in helping to get each sector of Iraq functioning once again. We had only modest staffs—my office never exceeded twelve people, including three translators and three Iraqi exiles who came back sporadically from the UK or US to help. Nor did we have budgets. We were there as "advisors," doing our best to help our ministers and our ministries get on their feet, make connections to the world outside, build up their internal organizations, and move the sector and the country ahead.

This was the small reason each of us had—to help fix a piece of Iraq in a sector where we each had some competence. But this desire to help "fix" something hardly makes sense without some understanding of the larger picture. I think I speak for all of us when I say we were there for grander reasons, reasons that had everything to do with, as Ali would say, "being American."

I should, however, just speak for myself: I have spent my whole adult life in higher education. I've been a professor at a number of colleges and universities; I was the chief administrative head and for a while chief policy head of a Federal agency; and I was for eleven years president of St. John's College in Santa Fe, New Mexico, a small, well-regarded liberal arts college.

So when I was asked, first by a close friend and university administrator and, next, by the Defense Department, if I would help shore up Iraqi higher education, I never thought about it twice. Even though all of us who went were aware of the obvious dangers, I knew from the minute the issue was raised that I would say yes.

I said yes for personal, educational and, to be sure, political reasons as well. I had never been in the military and I thought this call now might be a reasonable way to serve. I also had an inkling that this would be a never-to-be-repeated adventure and, of course, it was. And, sappy as it might sound, I knew I was pushing sixty, and did not have that many years left to do some good. Besides, I knew I had enough experience in the classroom, in government service, and in academic administration to be of some help.

But central to my accepting this assignment were political reasons, larger reasons. I was, from the start, a believer in the war. From the beginning, I defended our motives and objectives in this venture. Nonetheless, the reason for writing this book is not to defend the war but to analyze the justifications for that continuing conflict and, in comparison to that justification, to measure our results. Sorry to say, in the most crucial areas, I do not believe we have succeeded in accomplishing what we set out to do. Indeed, despite my defense of the war and our high hopes for its success, I now believe that American foreign policy and American interests are in a worse position than if we had never ventured down this path.

Still, I do not intend for this to be a catalogue of errors as much as an analysis of what we did right, where we went wrong, and, above all, *why*. What is it that America did not understand that led it, at so many junctures, to choose the worse policy alternative rather than the better? What is it that we did not know not only about Iraq but also about *ourselves?*

I hope I fairly show in this book those places where we succeeded and why. Nonetheless, throughout this war, fooling ourselves—fooling ourselves with optimism, with hope, with "happy talk" as we called it in Baghdad, and with a blindness to the character of our enemies, blindness to the character of the Iraqis we liberated, and blindness to America's own limitation as a liberating power—was and remains the real problem. Unless we understand why America did not succeed in achieving its grand goals, we will not only fail to salvage what we can over the next few years in Iraq, but we also will fail again if ever we attempt another similar venture in the Middle East, and perhaps with even more dismaying results.

Nevertheless, were you to think that this book will be yet another critique of American "unilateralism," or of the illegitimate extension of American power, or a conventional attack on the US for throwing its weight around for the benefit of Big Oil, Halliburton, Israel, or whatever the view of the month happens to be, I'm afraid you will be disappointed. Neither do I support the notion that our mistakes all stem from some singular and glaring error, because we were unwilling to "put more boots on the ground," or because we hastily disbanded the Iraqi army, or because we "failed to seal the borders," or any of the other pat explanations favored by so many pundits. Odd as it will seem, this is a critique of America's involvement in Iraq from what will appear to be a more conservative than liberal or left perspective. That means, oddest of all, that this is a conservative critique of conservatism gone astray.

▲▼▲

I know that many, both here and abroad, think of the war as founded on a lie, seizing on the fact that no chemical, biological, or nuclear weapons of mass destruction have been uncovered. Of course, for this we should all be grateful. How many thousands of Americans would have died on the battlefields of Iraq if Saddam possessed and deployed such weapons? If the weapons existed and were used, the Administration would have been vilified for sending our soldiers into sure, painful, gruesome death. I, for one, could not have been happier that the weapons were gone.

Nevertheless, those of us who went to Iraq understood that our mission had very little to do with discovering any such weapons. While the Administration may have had to highlight the issue of WMDs in its presentations before the UN and other international bodies (these organizations clearly had scant interest in other issues), finding and destroying such weapons was not something I or most of the civilians and soldiers I worked with in Iraq ever thought central to our going.[1]

Two other issues were far more important to all of us who went: assisting and freeing a people who had suffered under an

---

[1]Saddam played a very interesting game regarding his weapons of mass destruction that has been far too little commented on: The international community strongly suspected he still had had biological and chemical weapons since we know he used them in the war against Iran and against the Kurds over a decade earlier. Even France, Germany, and Russia assumed he had such weapons during the buildup to the war. Yet, it now seems clear, he did not have them, at least not at the ready. So, why would Saddam not admit to not having them, and thus put the world's mind at rest? Because by not having any weapons to be found, he knew he could keep the international community from decisively calling him an outlaw and acting on that understanding; yet, by leading the world to think that he just might still have them hidden but at hand, he could keep his neighbors at bay and maybe even the US and Great Britain, who would probably think twice about invading a country possessed of such weapons. The ploy only partly worked.

oppression that combined tyranny with sadistic, psychopathic brutality; and finding an alternative, long-range, but perhaps permanent way of helping to ameliorate the threat of international terrorism.

Enough has been written and catalogued about the brutality of Saddam's regime that I needn't add much to it here. I should note, however, that it differed essentially from virtually all the other great tyrannies of the twentieth century. It was not a tyranny driven by a particular ideology. It was not based on notions of Aryan racial purity or the ultimate success of Marxist-Leninism, and only in part on visions of national glory. Nor was it a religious autocracy. While there were elements of religious fervor in the activities of the regime, and there were particular religious views it knew needed to be suppressed, it was, by and large, a secular, non-ideological, non-religious tyranny. It was closer to the very personal tyranny of, say, an Idi Amin than to the rule of a Hitler or Stalin or Mao.

It was, in that sense, more like the great despotisms of the age before Modernity, where the ruler ruled for the satisfaction of his personal, idiosyncratic, and often debased and degenerate desires. This is important to understand from the outset. First, because we have to understand that totalitarianism can come in many guises, following many banners—ideological, religious, racial, national, personal, and secular. In the complexity of world affairs, there is no single enemy of human dignity, liberty, and democracy, and so no single way to set all matters right.

More importantly for our purposes, however, was the fact that, since Iraq was a personal tyranny, there was no underlying nationalism that had to be overcome in winning the war, no ideology that needed to be countered, and (it was thought) no surging religious sentiment that would strangle the growth of personal and political liberty. Since it was Saddam's tyranny, not the tyranny of race or sect or idea, what we saw, or thought we saw, was a people not wholly different from us—more secular than most Middle Eastern nations, controlled in politics but left more or less alone in the daily matters of life, a nation more modern, more progressive even, than many of its neighbors. We warred against Iraq not because it was the nation furthest from us but because it was, in many ways, the *closest* to us of all the antagonistic states in the Middle East. In our common understanding, all that would be needed to have liberty and democracy succeed in that sad nation was to take the lid off.

I hasten to add that to say that the regime and its brutality were non-ideological or non-religious takes nothing away from its horrors. It may actually mean that often the tortures were the worse for being more personal: they were tortures not carried out in the name of some grand vision or ideal, nor tortures carried out "efficiently," but tortures often done for the pleasure of Saddam and his sons. And often, I believe, *by* Saddam and his sons, whose love of cruelty seems to have been endless. Of Uday it was repeatedly said, for example, that he took little pleasure in his daily and multiple rapes unless the woman or girl bled.

But it still might be argued that neither the threat of weapons of mass destruction nor the brutality of a regime against its own and neighboring peoples is cause for armed intervention. If Hitler had not attacked our allies and declared war against us, would we have fought Germany simply to stop the murder of the Jews? I would think yes, though I am sure there are many who would come down on the other side. Intervention in Bosnia? In Rwanda? In Haiti? We intervene, often too late; yet we do intervene, sometimes simply on humanitarian grounds. This is what my friend, Ali, saw us doing when he said he would try to become an American. Still, were compassion and humanitarianism the only grounds for our intervention, even with torture and mass murder in view, I would think prudence would dictate extreme caution. More and greater reasons were needed than the fact that Saddam was bad.

Let me see if I can help us understand these further reasons by going back to why we non-contractor civilians thought it right to go, for it makes no sense to speak of success or failure without first knowing why it was we were involved in Iraq in the first place.

To speak of our involvement in Iraq in simply a humanitarian vein does small justice to the complexity of motivations involved. But let me connect our ideas to an event: To many, our going had something to do with the sight of Saddam's statue being toppled in Firdos Square and jubilant Iraqis kicking it and beating it with their shoes. Although I might later see in that event things that were not evident that April, no one reading this book should doubt that Americans—at least the Americans I had the privilege of working with in Iraq—saw the liberation of a people from despotism and their entrance into freedom as something they themselves wanted to be part of and to contribute to. That is, it was not simply deposing a tyrant, or humanitarianism understood as helping people with health or schooling or material things that were our fundamental concerns; it was that higher understanding of humans as our equals in the hope of possessing, finally, rights, dignity, and freedom that motivated not virtually but *absolutely* every American I knew in Iraq.

I know there are some very fine Americans, conservative like me, who view the liberation of others into freedom as no doubt a good thing, but essentially none of our business. "We" are our only valid concern; "they" are not our concern unless their actions substantially affect us. Besides, wars are risky business, and, once begun, have a way of confounding the best of planners. Moreover, the law of unintended consequences is a universal law, and no one, not even the most brilliant, can know everything he sets in motion by so monumental an act as war. Prudence is not simply a conservative predilection; it is a human virtue, disregarded at our peril. Great nations often need to fight great wars; but they should only do so *in extremis,* and only when their own freedom, safety, security, or vital national interests are in the balance. "Idealism" is a fool's errand, for the realist knows that, in this world, no good deed does go unpunished.

To respond, as President Kennedy did, that we should pay any price, bear any burden, or meet any hardship in order to assure the success of liberty seems both stirring and insufficient. But, as we all had in mind as we went to Iraq, to accomplish two great things at once—to help secure the liberty of others while at the same time undermining the advance of fanaticism and terror—is hard to categorize as simply "idealistic." It seemed, at least in the spring and summer of 2003, a prudent and "realistic" way of promoting our own security and safety.

Let me be as clear as possible about our national motives here as I understand them. As individuals, many Americans went to Iraq for the sake of Iraq itself—to help a people who had suffered so fiercely under dictatorship to enjoy the benefits of freedom and prosperity. Whether in civilian clothes or military uniform, these people's first impulse was and remains other-directed and humanitarian.

But most of us went to Iraq not for Iraq's sake but for America's. Yes, if there were weapons of mass destruction, they would need to be removed; yes, if there were Al-Qaeda links, they would need to be broken. A grander self-interest was at work in all this, but a self-interest nonetheless: The coming of freedom and democracy and prosperity and stability to Iraq would be a world-changing event, an event of inestimable value to us and the free world. As I will soon explain in greater detail, a free, prosperous, and stable Iraq had the potential to change the political future of the whole Middle East, and change it for our benefit.

We tend these days to lose sight of this grand interest of ours in all our chatter over not finding weapons of mass destruction. But America's enemies haven't lost sight of what we hope to achieve there, otherwise they wouldn't be dying so desperately to see us fail. No, America's real interest is not and was not in capturing Iraq's oil or in scattering its weapons; it was in changing the very character of the Middle East.

I will, fairly soon, lead us through many of the reasons we fell so short of achieving our aims as I understand them. But still it has to be said that, far from being simply "idealistic," the war in Iraq grew out of some rather hard-nosed and realistic calculations. With a democratic Turkey as a potential part of the European Union to the north, with an Afghanistan freed of the Taliban and Al-Qaeda, and with a free Iraq on the other side of Iran and neighbor to a smaller, worried Syria, our hope of controlling and ultimately defeating Terror rises. With the fall of Saddam we would soon have the potentially richest Islamic country in the region now on the side of liberty, toleration, and economic growth. As with the other nations we helped liberate across the globe in the last fifty years, America would have a strong ally, strategically placed. We would have, in other words, a far more potent partner against terror than any other Islamic country in the region, and a force more powerful than soldiers, planes, and ships.

Let no one mistake our motives: Yes, we did it in part for them; but we did it in even greater part for us.

We have to be clear from the outset that this was not a war of us against Islam, though our enemies are now hard at work to portray it as such. If it had been a war against Islam, freeing and empowering an Iraq made up of 90 percent Muslims would have verged on the idiotic. Rather, our judgment was that the establishment of a free, peaceful, prosperous, and tolerant *Muslim* state in the heart of the Middle East would be as much an ingredient in the War on Terror as capturing Bin Laden or killing Zarqawi or suppressing the Taliban or destroying Al-Qaeda.

It is now more likely the case that the "paleo-conservatives" who counseled non-intervention were right, and we "neo-conservatives" who saw the liberation of Iraq as part of America's long-term national interest were wrong. It is not simply the goodness of the ends but a comprehensive understanding of the necessary and appropriate means, and the will to employ them, that makes the difference between success and failure.

Nevertheless, given all this, forgive me if I am hesitant to join in the chorus of commentators, usually on the left, who now find it easy to call our venture in Iraq a "mistake." If "mistake" implies mistaking our goals, or having irresponsible intentions, then the war was not a mistake. But if mistake implies an inability fully to understand not the ends but the means, if it implies not knowing exactly what to do, when to do it, or even how to do it, then mistakes were made aplenty. Good intentions do not ensure success, and nice guys often do finish last. In that sense, looking at our failures of execution rather than of aim, I now have no hesitation in stating that we should not have undertaken the war.

▲▼▲

As was said above, the great desideratum was to turn Iraq from our enemy to our friend in the War on Terror. A liberal and prosperous Iraq would have little interest in serving as a promoter of terrorists. It would have no reason to be a nursery of anti-Israeli activity. It could serve as a model for the liberal and democratic forces simmering under the surface in Iran. Along with a free and democratized Afghanistan, an Iraq that was tolerant, democratic, prosperous, and liberal would serve both as a model to reformers in other Muslim states and as an antidote to the worst aspects of Islamic radicalism and anti-Western hatred. Such, at least, was the goal.

It may seem odd at first view, but it is nonetheless true, that while liberal democratic nations might and often do wage war against their ideological enemies—liberal democracies have fought both hot and cold wars with Fascist and Communist states, for example—they rarely if ever wage war against each other. No matter how furious we Americans might get with France or Germany, invading a democratic Germany or bombing France is simply beyond anything we could ever imagine. Is Australia likely ever to attack Austria, or Poland Israel? What two nations have ever had a border as long, as historic, or as peaceful as that between Canada and us? No, the more nations become members of the "club,"' so to speak, of free nations, the more those nations act more or less peacefully toward one another, no matter how serious their differences.

While there were more things that stood in the way of a stable, free, and democratic Iraq than American policy makers realized, Iraq seemed, as I've noted, the most *potentially* liberal democratic country in all the Middle East. As I mentioned, it was not a nation governed by a racial, religious, or ideological regime. It was not, in other words, a nation that, like Nazi Germany, needed to be broken in order to be fixed. It was, moreover, among the most seemingly secular of Muslim countries, and thus a seemingly strong counter to religious fanaticism. Additionally, the liberation and empowerment of women was widespread and deep-rooted in most parts of the country. Both of these—the liberation of women and the secularization of Iraqi society—were things Saddam did. In part because of the loss of so many young Iraqi men in the long war with Iran, and no doubt in part because Saddam recognized their equal talent and usefulness, women, secular women, were in positions of authority in many sectors of Iraqi life. Unlike, say, Afghanistan, women in Iraq were professors, doctors, lawyers, professionals of every sort. Nor was there regular or overt discrimination against religious minorities—Christians worshipped freely in all parts of Iraq and even anti-Semitism seemed far under the surface, if there at all. While I heard any number of anti-Palestinian comments in my months in Iraq, I heard and saw nothing that looked like anti-Jewish hatred until close to the end of my stay, when it boiled to the surface of some the more fervent and devout Islamic groups.[2]

It was this more secular and tolerant face of Iraqi society that gave those who wished for democratic liberty in Iraq substantial hope. I am not one who believes that Islam is, in all its manifestations, the enemy of the West. I know enough Iraqis who are both Muslims in good standing and totally liberal, tolerant, capitalist in their economic outlook, and democratic in their political leanings. At the university level I met scores of devout Muslims, Shi'a and Sunni alike, who were completely on the side of intellectual openness and freedom of inquiry for everyone in all areas. I have lived with Kurds, who are both Muslim and highly Westernized. And I met many Iraqis who were simply secular, whose friends were Arab and non-Arab, Sunni and Shi'a and Christian, for whom Islam was part of their

---

[2]There's an odd fringe of American political opinion that goes from left to right that sees the war as fought at the behest of Israel, concocted by Jewish neoconservatives in support of Israeli interests. I think this, along with the view that we went to Iraq to capture its oil, is both simplistic and false. As in the Israeli strike on Iraq's nuclear facilities in 1981 and as we did in Afghanistan, Israel tends to deal with its political enemies in more direct and less grandiose and roundabout ways. Besides, Iran and Syria, not Iraq, were and remain Israel's most serious enemies. I have no way of verifying it, but it's colorful enough to repeat, that the former Israeli Prime Minister, Benjamin Netanyahu, when asked about the wisdom of attacking Saddam, replied that with all the truly dangerous regimes in the Middle East that needed to be destroyed, why was America wasting its time by going after Tony Soprano?

cultural matrix, their heritage, but not a deep part of their spiritual lives, much less their political lives. If this were not true, if Iraq were made up only of single-minded Islamic radicals bent on imposing their doctrines and worldview on the rest of the globe, then liberating Iraq to be an ally in the war on terror would not simply have been foolish but lunatic. This is because, while there are elements of Islam that are not the enemies of the West, Islamic fundamentalism in its more radical formulations is indeed the enemy.

That seems a hard, almost shameful thing to write. We have grown, in the West, to have such a benign view of religion, all religion, that, to most of us, merely to say "religion" is to talk about something good by nature. We want, when we see evil being done in the name of faith, to call it a perversion of religion. Bad things can be perpetrated by "cults," or by fanatics who use religion for their own purposes, but not by anything truly "religious." The "true" Islam, we seem always to want to say, is surely peace-loving, merciful, benign, charitable, loving ... for that's what we think religions are "supposed" to be. So those that are bloodthirsty, intolerant, fanatical, or destructive must be cults, perversions of the true religion, false religions.

I, for one, am not prepared to tell any other faith what is authentic to that faith and what is false. I am not about to say that tolerant Islam is authentic while militant and severe Islam is false. But I do know that there are some parts of the Muslim world that are open to the principles of liberty and equality and toleration and democracy, and parts that are not, and I need not put myself in a position of having infallibility of religious judgment to say which parts are true to their faith and which parts are not.

The reason to put aside all abstract discussion of truth and falsity in someone else's religion is that we have to understand simply that some beliefs and much of today's religious fervor can be and often is the enemy of democracy, equality, and liberty in the world today. We have to admit that virtually all the most catastrophic events of the last three decades—the wanton bombings, the suicide attacks, the beheadings, the shooting of children—were done by those devoted to their God, loyal to their faith as they understood it, and secure in the hope of the promised rewards of the afterlife. Honest devotion to certain religious beliefs has taken the place of tyranny, nationalism, and ideology as today's impetus for terror and even genocide.

It used to be said that with the Death of God, all things would be permitted, even the most supposedly vicious and immoral. After all, with no all-seeing and just law-giver, who would there be to denominate right from wrong and, above all, who would reward the good and punish the wicked? But now the opposite seems increasingly true: *With God* all things are now possible, at least to some. For today we hear that God so strongly demands a particular notion of justice that he permits all things—be it the targeting of innocents, the blowing up of women and children, even public beheadings—to rout the Americans, eliminate Israel, and punish Muslim apostates. In some places, it is this devotion, this complete love of a peculiar God, that has now become the root of all evil.

To go back for a second, I think it is understandable why Americans view religion so highly. I think it's true to say that we Americans tend to see religion as almost always a force for good in the world. This is why, as I've said, we want evildoers to be part of a "cult" and not really religious believers. This is why we talk of their religion, Islam, as being "hijacked" by this or that leader whenever we hear about calls for a holy war or see hostages taken in Iran or hear the name of God invoked to bless murders, tortures, or mass killings. We think religion is supposed to teach brotherhood, liberality, toleration, love of our neighbors, and peace. We look at ourselves and see how Christianity has so forcefully commanded us to love our neighbors, to sacrifice and be of service to others, to turn the other cheek, and to stifle our worst habits of self-interest and selfishness. And we inherited from Protestant Christianity a healthy respect for freedom, self-reliance, and not a little skepticism of authority. All these teachings have been of enormous use to us in our life together as a people, and we know it. Because of that, in large measure, we have tended to see religion simply as a good. Naively we ask, "Don't all religions preach brotherly love and peace?"

Well, no. The history of the West is a history full of flay-ings and burnings and tortures as horrific as beheadings, and often done in the name of religion. The doctrine that all governments must be subservient to the Church, or that a person's belief was not a matter of private conscience and private choice but could justly be compelled, or that error had no right to exist, or that those who persisted in error deserved death—these were sentiments common to both Protestant and Catholic Christianity for ages. Despite all that we might point to in the Gospels regarding peace and love and charity and brotherhood, we should never forget the bloody nature of Christianity before it was beaten down by its own religious wars and then tamed by the Enlightenment.

But our history, the history of the taming of the sanguinary nature of Christianity by Modernity in its many forms, is not particularly Islam's history, though, as I said, I had the pleasure of working with many Muslims who were pushing in that direction. In dealing with Islam as a whole we cannot be blinded into thinking that they're just like us, only with a few different beliefs here and there. We should not forget that Islam is the only one of the great monotheistic religions still untamed by the Enlightenment or European rationalism or theories of liberal capitalism.

We should bear in mind that what a person believes in shapes his or her outlook and activities more, I dare say, than his socio-economic class, or her sex, or his ethnic roots, or her race. Somehow, we seem to have gotten it into our heads, especially in the higher realms of education, that a person is the outcome of the interplay of class, race, and gender when, in the real world, most people are pushed or pulled by the demands of their basic human nature and by the moral horizon they see before them. And that horizon is, in towns, villages, and cities across the globe, shaped more by the teachings of religion than any other factor. This is why the establishment of a tolerant, liberal, and democratic state in the heart of the Middle East, moderating the demands of religious extremism, was one of our highest hopes, as well as the greatest fear of the jihadists and radical Islamists.

I do not believe for a moment that poverty causes terror. We in the West should put aside the deceitful dreamings of Marxist ideology and stop looking for material causes for ideological or religious feelings. People rarely kill others because they are poor; more rarely do they kill themselves because of their poverty. But they do kill themselves and others because of what they themselves believe. And if people believe that others are infidels, or are leading their neighbors and children to eternal damnation, or are simply opposing God's will, then terror might become justified to them. As I will repeat in other parts of this book, terrorists are sometimes poor and uneducated; other times they are rich and hold Ph.D.s. Terror is a function of one's beliefs and passions, one's moral horizon, not one's poverty.

Yet, while terror may not have a material cause, it may have, in part, a material solution. What moved Christianity in the West from its history of bloody, intersectarian warfare to something far more pacific and mild over the last few centuries? In part, of course, warfare was *beaten* out of it. Each side in the Christian wars of the seventeenth and eighteenth centuries suffered more losses than they wished to recount. In part, also, it was because the partisans of toleration and peace could find strong threads of mercy and forbearance in the basic texts of Christian life and in the person of Christ Himself. But we should not forget that the West began, in the seventeenth and eighteenth centuries, philosophically to reformulate our understanding of what a good person might look like: no longer was it the religious firebrand working for the universal conquest of God's kingdom as much as the person who worked hard, produced goods and services for his fellow men, cared for the material needs of his family and children, respected the rights of others, and minded his own business. We managed to make respectable a concern for the things of this world more than for the things of heaven. We even managed to say, in our own most public documents, that the purpose of government—that is, the purpose of our banding together collectively—was not to save our souls or promote the Kingdom of Heaven, but to protect our rights, our liberties, our property, and our own pursuit of happiness. We managed to turn our eyes from up to down—from heaven towards the things of this world—and we managed to get our religion to support that new gaze. Henceforward, prosperity honestly achieved would be no sin, hard work would be a virtue, and protecting the rights and liberties of all a near-religious command.

In sum, that's what I meant when I referred to Christianity being "tamed" by the Enlightenment. Religion now finds itself in the position of moderating the self-interest Modernity made respectable, if we even think about religion at all. Religion is no longer the cause of our fighting one another; we now ask people what they do for a living rather than what god they believe in. And we have, by doing all this, turned the democratic, capitalist West into a place of prosperity and plenty unimaginable to ages past.

If you wish to find the single, most important "neoconservative" rationale for the liberation of Iraq and the connection between that liberation and the War on Terror, it is in what I have written above. If Iraq could be buttressed as a free, tolerant, democratic nation with a system of free enterprise that would turn the attention of all citizens, but especially of the spirited younger generation, toward a concern with respecting the rights of all to enjoy the things of this world, to get ahead materially and financially, to be more concerned with work than with doing justice as their faith explained it to them, we would have made a major advance in the safety of the West and the peace of the world.

An acquaintance of mine said to me a while back that our goal in Iraq was to get Iraqis to go to the mall instead of the mosque. Perhaps. But it at least was the goal of getting them to visit the mall on their way home from the mosque. Liberal democracy is not the enemy of religion, but it does seek to undermine the intolerant, autocratic, and fanatical aspects of religion that, over time, virtually all faiths have had.

Sadly, more stood in the way of achieving this goal in Iraq than was realized at the start. On our side, to begin with, was the fact that Iraq was already a multi-religious, generally tolerant, diverse, and pluralistic society. It had emancipated women and respected their rights to property, educational advancement, and engagement in professional life far more than many other countries in the region. And Iraqis were natural traders who had no contempt for either the marketplace or moneymaking. What we failed to realize was how even the more moderate and less fanatical versions of Islam still see their version of sectarian truth as more important than general religious toleration, how natural the desire to impose orthodoxy by law on the heterodox is to most men, how resistant to philosophical modernity certain parts of the Islamic faith would be,[3] and, at the extreme, how virulent, how savage, the response of the religious zealots and fanatics—who knew exactly what we were trying to accomplish in Iraq—would be. But more on all of this in the pages to come.

All this means, of course, that far from being a "diversion" in the War on Terror, the liberation of Iraq was, in conception, a central, vital, major part of that very war. If proof be needed, just look at the terrorist war being waged in Iraq today—to drive us and our allies out, to destabilize and destroy any non-fanatic and free government, and to kill all those who collaborated or supported the Coalition or moderate and democratic

---

[3]This is not to say that the "conversion" of Christianity from its theocratic and absolutist tendencies was easy. It took centuries to get the major branches of Christianity to accept the rule of secular states, or the universal rights of conscience and religious liberty. Nor can we overlook the fact that toleration may, in part, depend on a peculiarly Protestant *theological* refinement: That men are saved by faith, but faith cannot be coerced and remain faith. (See John Locke, *A Letter Concerning Toleration*.) Happily for us in the West, today even the Catholic Church easily speaks the language of rights.

Despite an easy connection to some ideas developed through the Protestant Reformation, it's been argued that all the raw ingredients for the development of toleration and modern natural right were embedded, in nascent form, in the gospel teachings: equality, universal brotherhood, mercy rather than force, peace rather than the imposition of will ... all these have their origins in aspects of the New Testament. I have spoken to a number of devout Muslims who say the same is true of the Koran. Nonetheless, while in following Christ the Christian is imitating a person of whom it could be said was meek and humble of heart, Mohammed was a warrior leader, indeed, a leader who himself participated in battles and beheadings. For a Christian to imitate his founder (can one imagine Christ beheading anyone?) has to be different than for a Muslim to imitate his. This has to make the conversion of that faith into a supporter of democratic liberalism and toleration substantially more problematic than it was for Christianity.

Iraqi government in any way. The tragedy of our situation is that, despite all the missteps and miscalculations and all the lives lost, to leave now may well be worse—both for Iraq and for us—than if we had never acted in the first place.

▲▼▲

For a long time after 9/11, the news journals, in referring to the terrorists, seemed fixated on the question "Why do they hate us?" It's a bit of an odd question, for it seems to suggest that the reason for the hatred is somehow our doing—that we are hated because of something wrong about us, or wrong that we have done. It's also an odd question since I cannot envision others who have been attacked—as we were in 2001—naturally asking that question. (Do American Indians ask it? Do Jews ask it about Nazis? Do African-Americans ask it about the KKK? I tend to doubt it.) But there may be a value in answering the question as posed. Perhaps we *are* hated because of who we are—as well as because of who they are.

If the analysis I gave a few pages back is more or less correct, then at least one reason we are hated is because our desire to act for the liberation of all people strikes at the heart of the most radical elements of Islam. We are—for our sakes as well as theirs— the bearers of Modernity. And modernity entails personal liberation, a respect for the dignity of all individuals and the equality of both sexes, a toleration of differences, and a latitudinarianism towards all religious beliefs. "But it does me no injury," Jefferson could say, "for my neighbor to say there are twenty gods or no God. It neither picks my pocket nor breaks my leg." Such a sentiment is the part of Modernity the fanatic imagines God despises most. That is, the very thing we most prize and that we most seek to propagate is the thing that the terrorists most hate.

In seeking the causes of terror, let me go back to a sentence I used before. I said that most people are pushed or pulled by the demands of their basic human nature and by the moral horizon they see before them. And that horizon is shaped more significantly by the teachings of religion than any other factor. But, while I think the religious element is the core ingredient of modern terror, it is not the only ingredient.

We sometimes hear it said that our "power" causes resentment in the rest of the world. I wouldn't doubt that throwing our weight around causes problems in parts of old Europe, perhaps elsewhere, but that's not exactly what I saw in Iraq. Indeed, the opposite was true. It was our lack of power—our inexplicable inability to get things moving, to stop the looters and vandals, to find the troublemakers and punish the terrorists—that led to our being held in contempt by so many Iraqis. The worst part of the aftermath of the war was that we did not show how powerful we were, but the very opposite; we showed how inept we were. We couldn't protect the Iraqis; we could only, sometimes barely, protect ourselves. We couldn't restore electricity or oil production in the face of simple looting or more serious sabotage. We couldn't fix the sewers or even get drinkable water to flow into the Green Zone. We proved that we had immense destructive power, but little constructive power. If we had that power, there is no doubt the Iraqis would have respected us more. "We thought you Americans had the wand of Moses in your hands," one of the most decent and pro-American Iraqis once said to me, "but now we know you don't." It's our lack of power to keep even the smallest Iraqi safe that the insurgents are showing the Iraqi people every day. It's the terrorists' power to hem in the Coalition and any new Iraqi government and frustrate their plans that they repeatedly present to the Iraqis. It's not our power that elicits scorn; it's our lack of it.

But there may be a way in which our power, our supposed invincibility—at least our military invincibility—might have engendered hatred. There is, at the level of our basic human nature, a rather perverse love of equality, a commonplace but still nasty desire to see the high laid low, to see Goliath fall, to see the mighty brought to the level of everyone else. I remember, going back fifty years, how slogans and sayings shaped the outlook of the old neighborhood where I grew up. And the sayings were always ones of equality: "Birds fly high, but they come down," "The bigger they are, the harder they fall." I saw much the same aspect of our common nature in Iraq. Despite each individual's own love of power, prestige, and position, when it came to others, there was joy in watching the mighty crumble.

I even think, in looking back at the toppling of Saddam's statue, in seeing people decapitating it and hitting it with their shoes, that what seemed to me a great expression of freedom over tyranny may actually have been, in part, the expression of a more basic human trait—joy at the fall, at the humiliation, of the powerful and mighty. (Surprisingly, I heard many Iraqis after the capture of Saddam demand not his execution but his continued humiliation—I can't tell you how many told me that what they'd really like to see is Saddam put in a zoo and Iraqis be given the power to throw things at him as he cowered behind bars.[4]) One lesson learned was that you cannot always expect thanks from those you have helped liberate. They are both embarrassed at their inability to have failed, for thirty-five years, in doing the job themselves, and jealous of and unhappy with the power that finally brought it about.

If true, this means that we are in an unwinnable situation when it comes to earning the respect, of "winning the hearts and minds," of ordinary Iraqis. We are envied for our strength and held in contempt for our weakness. Of the two, however, I think the more serious was our weakness.

In reflecting further on human nature and anti-Americanism, or human nature and the causes of Terror, I need to point us towards one thing more. It often seemed that, while the religious fanatic was sincere in his beliefs, especially when his belief included the dream of rivers of honey and wine and the comfort of virgins, there were times it did not. There were times when religion seemed to be the excuse or, more exactly, the *avenue* through which other passions could be released and satisfied.

---

[4]We should avoid thinking of this as merely a quaint trait, however. While the desire to see our opponents humiliated may well be intrinsic to our basic human nature, part of our understanding of what it means to be civilized is to repress and control this natural desire. Yet far too many Iraqis I met honestly saw capture and humiliation of an opponent as natural, and often associated it not with savagery but with justice. Consider our response to the mutilation and display of the American contractors that precipitated the first battle of Fallujah. We saw the humiliation connected to the public desecration of fellow citizens as vile, but no Iraqi I knew saw it that strongly. Indeed, they were generally far more concerned about our military response than they were to the cause that compelled us to take action.

For example, in September of 2004, after the beheading of one of their American hostages, the terrorists addressed themselves to President Bush: After referring to him as "a dog," they said, "Now you see before you people who love death just as you love life. Killing for the sake of God is their highest wish. Getting to your soldiers and allies are their happiest moments. And cutting the heads of the criminal infidels is implementing the orders of our lord."

What lies right below the surface of clear religious belief seems to be an even deeper love of blood and the thrill of death. A dozen sordid passions live here: the joy of humiliation, akin to the natural desire to see the high brought down; the love of power; a love of seeing others suffer; a joy found in the degradation, despair, destruction, and death of others. We sometimes talk glibly about *schadenfreude,* joy at the misfortune of others. But evident in a statement like the one cited above are emotions, passions, on a far more horrific scale. At the deepest level, these are what it means to be barbaric, and not fully human, at least not civilized human.

These are passions that religion has often, though not always, sought to channel into a finer and more spiritual direction. Animal, not human sacrifice. Or, self-sacrifice, not the sacrificing of others. Or, in the ultimate Christian mystery, God sacrificing himself for men so that men will not kill in order to offer up other men to God. Yet here we see passions incited by religious faith, exacerbated by religion, or perhaps simply passions that find religion a ready vehicle for their expression. What is striking about this aspect of Terror is not its seriousness and determination, or its sense of religious duty, but its joy. This is the face of Terror smiling.

Again: Why do they hate us? The question assumes not only that the fault is in us but also that the question is answerable by a rational response. But hatred is all too often not rational—and, in the case of terrorism, seems least rational of all. There is a psychological-religious frenzy involved here, a passion, a savage intensity, and an insanity impervious to all argument.

I wrote out these reflections because I do not want us to oversimplify the problem of Terror or the nature of evil. What we are up against in the world is not a movement born of poverty, or even born of resentment. It's not a movement solvable by something as political as resolving the Israeli-Palestinian dispute. It's a movement born of a number of diverse, strong, and often fierce and sordid feelings and passions. Its roots lie in a fear of Modernity, a hatred of Modernity, a particular and passionate view of God's commands, a hatred of our power, a contempt for our shortcomings, a perverse view of equality, and, deepest down, a barbarism that gives both religious satisfaction and joy. It is a barbarism we cannot reason with or deflect into other more constructive channels. We can only confront and defeat it.

Yet still the question recurs: But *how?*

# TWO

# Daily Life

It was the beginning of September 2003. The first Senior Advisor for Higher Education and Scientific Research, Andrew (Drew) Erdmann, had already returned from Iraq to take up a position in the White House, at the National Security Council; his deputy, Lieutenant Colonel Steve Curda, was pretty much holding down the mission in Baghdad alone. Joseph Ghougassian, who had been the American Ambassador to Qatar in the 1980s and who would be one of my deputies in Iraq, and I met with Drew in Washington to pick his mind about the situation there and what we would be expected to do. That, and one quick conference with Curda when he came to DC for a series of meetings, was pretty much the only orientation or introduction any of us had to the situation in Iraq before we left—on September 11, 2003, two years exactly after the attack on the World Trade Towers.

We flew from Washington to Texas, where we caught a 747 converted to military use into Kuwait. In Kuwait we acclimated ourselves to the weather—it was 110 degrees and fierce at midday—and we practiced one thing repeatedly: how to put on our gas masks. Yes, even as late as September, almost half a year after our troops entered Iraq, it was still assumed that the possibility of a chemical attack was real. From Kuwait we flew into Baghdad on a C-130, an immense cargo propeller plane left over from the days of Viet Nam. The plane corkscrewed straight down into Baghdad airport in an attempt to avoid enemy rockets, leveling out just a few hundred feet above the tarmac. It was an airborne adventure I had the misery of experiencing a few more times over the coming year.

There were twenty-five ministries in Iraq and, therefore, twenty-five of us "Senior Advisors." In addition to Higher Education, there was a ministry of Education that covered all primary and secondary schooling, as well as such ministries as Oil, Electricity, Justice, Transportation, Youth and Sport, Foreign Affairs, Interior, Planning, and so on. Thus, every major "sector" of the Iraqi government had a ministry to govern it, and we senior advisors were acting in the place of the various ministers until the Governing Council (about which more later) in coordination with Ambassador Bremer named an Iraqi minister to each post. Drew functioned his whole time there—from about May till September—as the de facto minister of higher education for all Iraq. In my case, the minister was named just a few days prior to my arrival in Baghdad. This meant that I would actually be, as my title suggested, the "senior advisor" to the ministry and its new minister and not, as Drew had been, acting as the minister himself.

Each senior advisor's office had an international staff to help with daily work. Some were rather large, with perhaps two dozen staffers. Some, like Culture or Youth and Sport, were small, like us. Curda was leading the staff of three translators, plus three Iraqi ex-pats who had been hired by the Pentagon to be "advisors" to the operation, an Italian working to bring the universities up to speed in computing, a Czech working on scholarships to European universities, and one other American, Jim Mollen. Jim, a civilian who had been picked up by the State Department to work in Iraq, was there to put together a special State project: to set up video teleconferencing centers at five major Iraqi universities to connect their classrooms with universities here in the States. It was a very fine idea, and Jim and Diego, the Italian, visited each of the universities, helped select the appropriate room to dedicate to the project, and interviewed the people who would keep the project up. Needless to say, by the time Jim was killed over a year later, the video teleconferencing project hadn't started. I doubt if it's started yet, or is even on the table.

The American senior advisors had all been reviewed and appointed by Presidential Personnel working in the Pentagon. The intelligence, dedication, and hard work of almost all the advisors belied their political appointments. Leslye Arsht and Williamson Evers in (basic) Education, Rodney Bent in Finance, Mounzer Fatfat in Youth and Sport, Jim Haveman and Robert Godwin in Health, Daniel Rubini in Justice, and Susan Johnson in Foreign Affairs could not have been more intelligent or more dedicated.

We senior advisors all met together every morning (except Sunday) at 7:30 A.M. with Jessica LeCroy, Bremer's executive assistant. The meetings would always begin with someone from the military reporting on the events of the previous day—number of hostile incidents, how many casualties the Coalition had suffered, any foreseeable threats in the day or two ahead. We'd then talk over common problems or matters of common interest and be out by 8, when Bremer himself had a meeting of senior advisors from the "more important" sectors—Interior, Transportation, Defense, Oil, Electricity—that Bremer thought he needed personally to keep an eye on daily.

On the one hand, it was fine not to be invited to these obviously more important meetings, since those of us in civil affairs and the "softer" sectors could work within our ministries without constant micromanagement. Bremer trusted us to do the right thing without daily supervision, and, by our own lights, we did. But on the other hand, it was also painfully clear that Oil and Electricity and Defense were the important sectors, the indispensable sectors, and we were not. Of course, it would be a tragedy if education suffered or the universities closed or clinics and hospitals ransacked, but not as big a disaster as if the oil ceased to flow or electricity was disrupted or the insurgency grew. At least it could so be argued. Still, it was odd that the ministries that I think were most successful during my time in Iraq—us, Education, Health, Youth and Sport—were the ones most neglected by the front office.

### Danger

Everyone back in the States assumed that life in Baghdad was one of constant danger. Then again, they also assumed that all of Iraq was, after the war, little but a pile of charred rubble. Both notions are wrong. Indeed, to speak of the second first, while there were surely bombed-out buildings hit during Shock and Awe, these were mostly governmental buildings or military fortifications that needed to be taken out to prosecute the war. Some of these buildings were reduced to rubble, often lying next to structures of no military value still standing and operable. The precision of the bombing at the start of the war was, in all honesty, amazing. No, the real damage done to the infrastructure of Iraq came after the end of the war, during the looting.

But wasn't it very dangerous? Yes and no. Yes, a sniper killed a soldier connected to our office shortly before I arrived. He and a few other soldiers were with Curda at the University of Baghdad. The soldier, SPC Jeffrey Wershow of the Florida National Guard, left his buddies to go to the cafeteria to get a drink. He was shot in the head and died. His assailant, said to be a Yemeni and not an Iraqi, was never found. But in all the months I was in Iraq—and those of us in the office went to the University of Baghdad as well as everywhere else almost every day—not one of us was lost.

While many Coalition soldiers were killed during the course of the fighting, the newspapers reported that only one US civilian—a contractor working on a reconstruction project—had died in the months before I deployed. This was the summer of 2003, when lack of air conditioning killed thousands upon thousands of elderly French people during a severe European heat wave. It seemed, off hand, that one might take a greater risk by summering in Paris than working in Baghdad.

Still it was clear that the risks were there, and one had to be exceptionally careful—less so within the Green Zone itself, of course, but more so when venturing out.

Perhaps the worst place to be at any time was the eight-mile road that runs from the airport into Baghdad. It may seem impossible, but for a nation that could strike exact targets with missiles fired from thousands of miles away, the United States could not secure this vital stretch of road. The highway is bordered by Ba'athist neighborhoods with people still loyal to Saddam and with Sunni mosques that openly preach death to the invaders. Still it was my understanding that rather than seem heavy-handed, we decided not to displace people from their homes and neighborhoods after the war, even if they were clearly potential enemies. So we operated our main supply line and personnel transport road, in a sense, openly behind enemy lines, and we suffered the consequences daily.[1]

After our spiral flight into Baghdad, Ghougassian and I met Steve Curda at the airport and he escorted us into the Green Zone. We had, for this trip as well as for so many others over the next few months, very heavy security: A humvee in front of our car with well-armed soldiers and a guy manning the machine gun on the roof. The exact same thing behind our car. And, in my car, two shooters with long guns in the back seat, Curda driving with a pistol on his lap, and me, unarmed in the passenger seat, with flak jacket and helmet, scanning the rooftops on my side for snipers. We went out this way for all the weeks that Curda remained with us since he still hurt over the loss of SPC Wershow. As soon as Curda went back to the States, however, we made other arrangements.

These "other arrangements" were clearly against policy. But they had become, by this time, a necessity. The military made it obvious that it didn't relish its job as babysitters for Coalition civilians, escorting us from one meeting to another while they waited for hours outside in clear view as we met with deans and professors within. Besides, traveling with the military

---

[1]The same odd restraint was apparent when the Rashid Hotel was attacked by rockets fired from a nearby park. When a number of senior advisors asked why the park wasn't closed, we were told by a highly placed State Department official that the park was enjoyed by Iraqi families and it might make enemies out of friends if we closed down their park. Sorry to say, when American moderation is perceived as American weakness, America loses.

not only put them at risk, it made us greater targets. Half the people in my office were Iraqis, and I could pass for an Iraqi so long as I kept my mouth shut. So we traveled with our translators in their cars, unarmed, without flak jacket or helmet, with me usually up front, window down, and always, always, without a seatbelt. No matter how Iraqi you might look, wearing a seatbelt was a dead giveaway, so to speak, that you were American. Of course, the chance of getting killed in Baghdad in a car crash is incredibly high—with the coming of liberation, what side of the road you drive on seems to have become a matter of personal preference—but we still chanced it rather than risk a bullet. In any event, the best way to travel was in one of our translator's eleven-year-old Oldsmobile with velvet seat covers. That *had* to be Iraqi.

Assuming someone intent on killing us was always watching, each day we varied our route as we went out. We always varied our times as well. We would never tell anyone, not even the Minister or a university president, when exactly we'd arrive— "between ten and one" was always accepted.

Our Iraqi friends worried about us as much as we worried about ourselves. Once, at the end of Ramadan, the president of one of the universities invited our whole office to his private club to break the fast. The manager who was setting up the banquet, looking at the occasion and the number, said that he assumed some Americans would be joining in the party. Upon hearing those words, the president simply cancelled the party.

I said above that we were relatively safe within the Green Zone, but only relatively. Starting around the Christmas of 2003, mortars and rockets started to hit the Green Zone with fair regularity, usually at night, usually between 8 P.M. and midnight. Whenever they landed, an alarm would sound and we all scurried to the basement. At least at first. Soon it became clear that there was no use going to the basement *after* the bombs hit— and they never hit repeatedly since that would make their firing position known to the US warplanes patrolling overhead. Since there was no warning as to when they might hit, you couldn't wait for a warning siren and then take cover: The sirens went off *after* the bombs fell.

The real danger, however, was not sitting in our offices in the Palace, but having a mortar hit our trailers with us in our beds. We lived in what could best be described as metal construction trailers, perhaps about thirty feet long by twelve feet wide. Each was divided into two small rooms, with two people per room, with a very small shower and sink in the middle. There was no desk, no chair, and no privacy. Since no real work could be done in these graceless tin cans, I and all the other senior advisors I knew were always at work by 6:30 or 7 and still at our desks at midnight or 1 A.M. Even though high sandbag walls ran up and down the rows of trailers, which surely were some protection, if a mortar hit near you, you were just dead.

The Palace where we all worked was a far safer place to be. After the first Gulf War, we were told, Saddam was so fearful of being bombed by the Americans that he reinforced the roof and ceilings of the Palace with metal and concrete. He did a fine job of it, too. A few days before I was to come home, a rocket scored a direct hit on the roof of the Palace, pretty much just above my head. It knocked some cornices off the building, and blew out the windows (*out,* not *in,* as we had expected), but no one was hurt. It was a damn good palace.

To this day I do not know if we took risks we should have been careful to avoid, or if we should have been braver and done more. Members of the office staff were out in what became known as "The Red Zone" every day. Some went to the Ministry, others to the universities. We had work to do, and it couldn't all be done from behind a desk. And part of our job was socializing—having tea with the Ministry staff, taking the translators out to lunch, having dinner at the houses of Iraqi friends, going to a wedding, visiting the sick or those who had been shot, sitting with students in the cafeteria, walking this or that campus with a dean. Some of it, like going out for ice cream in downtown Baghdad or shopping for bargains on oriental rugs, was no doubt stupid. Mounzer Fatfat, the Senior Advisor for Youth and Sport, and I even went into the poorer neighborhoods to visit Iraqi pigeon flyers on their roofs, have a soft drink, and admire their birds. (Both Mounzer and I flew pigeons as kids—he in Lebanon, me in Brooklyn. But that's another whole book.) I'm sure we could have been more careful. But we had a mission to accomplish, a mission that involved both building institutions and building relationships, and it couldn't be accomplished by hiding. Still, it was rather disconcerting to drive by a beggar on the street with a cardboard sign around his neck that read in Arabic, "Will Kill for Money."

Often we'd be in a situation where it was hard to know how to be cautious. Once Jim found himself with two other Americans at a dead stop in a Baghdad traffic jam. All of a sudden a young boy comes up to the car and, pointing, starts yelling "Americans! Americans in this car!" He clearly was hoping that someone would come forward and roll a grenade under the vehicle. And even though they were fully armed, there was nothing Jim and the others could do but wait for the jam to break up and then drive off quickly. Diego found himself in a similar situation at the very end of our stay when, while driving alone at night from the Italian Embassy into the Green Zone, two cars tried to drive him off the road. One came up right behind him and the other tried pushing him off the road from the left. Without even turning his head, Diego fired at the car on his left with the pistol he had on his lap. The car spun around and hit the guardrail, and Diego sped off as the insurgents in the chase car went over to help their comrades. If he had not managed this, I am morally certain that Diego would have been paraded before the Al-Jazeera cameras, then beheaded.

It should also be remembered that, while soldiers were daily targets, and, after a while, Iraqis became targets of the insurgents as well, we civilians were more often in danger accidentally than deliberately. Remember also, it wasn't until March of 2004—three months before the Coalition Provisional Authority was to "dissolve"—that the first non-contractor civilians connected to the CPA were captured and killed. That was when Fern Holland, who was working on women's rights out of Hillah, and Robert Zangas were both murdered.

Of all the non-Iraqis in the office there was no doubt that Jim, Dana (the young woman from the Czech Republic who worked on scholarship programs), and the ever-irrepressible Diego, were the most daring of us all. Dana lived under Czech protection at a local hotel and commuted in every morning.

Jim hated living in the trailers and either lived with Diego or moved from fleabag hotel to fleabag hotel to avoid suffocating in the Green Zone. And Diego got himself a very handsome apartment right in Baghdad, with his own generator and a satellite TV hookup that brought in five hundred channels, all so he could watch Italian news programs.

Perhaps one incident might give you a picture of Baghdad life, with all its dangers as well as its charms. Jim and Dana had discovered a very upscale small restaurant in Baghdad. It was open late, served beer and wine at all hours, and had the best Lebanese-style food anywhere. So four of us—Dana, Jim, Diego, and I—decided to go there one sparkling clear night in December. As we walked in we realized we were the only people in the whole place. We ordered a round of beers and a few appetizers. From the back corner of the room a well-dressed man, who we guessed was the manager, slowly walked over to our table. "You Americans?" he asked in a none-too-pleasant voice. Well, Jim and I were, so we said so. Diego, not to confuse matters, declared himself an American as well. Dana insisted she was Czech, but that didn't seem to mean much to the man. (Actually, when she said she was "Czech" he responded, puzzled, "Chick?" To have played around and insisted that she was a Czech chick would have only made matters worse, so Dana relented and agreed, "Yes, Chick.")

Satisfied that we were at least mostly Americans, he walked over and said something under his breath to the only other person in the room, the piano player. With that, as carefully as he could, the piano man began to play "New York, New York." He then played and replayed every Sinatra song he could remember. It was a great evening.

The four of us were supposed to go back to the same restaurant for New Year's Eve, but Jim was delayed in coming back from a trip, so the three of us celebrated in the Green Zone. That night, just around midnight, the driver of a white Toyota Corolla blew himself up outside the restaurant. Eight people died (including three Americans) and thirty-five were wounded.

▲▼▲

While sleeping conditions were miserable and the security situation unattractive, I have to admit the food was exactly to my
liking. Not Iraqi food, particularly.[2] Iraqi lamb, rice, and egg-
plant are fine, but not as exciting as eggs with grits and bacon,
or chicken fried steak, or ham hocks and greens, or Southern
fried chicken. Kellogg, Brown and Root supplied us all our food,
and they did a fine job of it. We ate with the soldiers in the dining room in Saddam's palace, with its gilt and geometric ceiling and half-paneled walls. Soldiers, I learned, need a fair number
of calories to get through the day. So, every day, for four meals
a day, it was like eating Billy-Bob's grandma's cooking in a road-
side shack in the hills of Georgia—except, of course, for the gilt
ceiling and half-paneled walls.

▲▼▲

I cannot believe that Baghdad was ever an attractive city. Perhaps it was before Saddam, but even that seems to me doubtful. In any event, behind the ugly concrete "Jersey barriers" that
shield shops and hotels and even homes from suicide bombers,
there are brutally unattractive concrete buildings. Thanks to
Saddam, Baghdad is a fortress town with good-sized buildings
that look something like a cross between 1960s Soviet-style
design and the worst of American project architecture. Even the
fanciest private homes (and there was no shortage of private
wealth in Saddam's day, especially for top Ba'ath party functionaries and favored businessmen) were a hodge-podge of
cement and limestone, combining every known expensive style
together into one totally incoherent and unattractive whole.
The villa that Ambassador Bremer took over as his private residence was particularly intriguing: with its pillars and rotun-

---

[2]Generally, you'll be happier in Iraq if you ask what, exactly, a menu item
might mean before you order. For example, who would think that "mixed
grill" sometimes means "including lambs' testicles"? But some things you
will simply have to get over, like worrying who just used your plate or drank
from your glass—the one that still has someone else's yogurt in it when the
waiter refills it and gives it now to you. For all their medical sophistication, it
would seem that the germ theory of contagion has yet to make an impression on some parts of Iraqi culture.

das, it seemed like what I imagine a million-dollar caretaker's house at an upscale California pet cemetery might look like. But most people in Baghdad lived in the mile after mile of drab apartment buildings and high-rises, or in two- and three-story walk-ups over shops along the many commercial streets.

As I mentioned, we worked each day in Saddam's "Presidential Palace," also once known as the Republican Palace. It's the one that had the four great heads of Saddam at the corners. The inside was, at the same time, both spectacular and shoddy. Beautiful marble balustrades soared two and three stories, but they would collapse if you leaned on them too hard. Marble was everywhere, generally mismatched. And there were long halls with hundreds of crystal chandeliers, which those who said they knew claimed were only clear plastic. The palace had swimming pools, acres of palm trees, cabanas, fountains, and gilt bathroom fixtures. It also had an amazing room, as large as an auditorium, that had glorious military murals painted on the walls, including one of ballistic missiles being fired, presumably at Israel or the US. It was in this room that Saddam had his gold and velvet "throne," plus all the shorter gilded chairs and sofas for his minions to sit on. It had the look of very expensive whorehouse furniture. Rumor had it that this was the room where Saddam would call together members of his party and the armed forces, sometimes to reward the most loyal of his men with money or a Mercedes, sometimes to shoot a person to death with his own hand. Often, I gather, a person didn't know which it was until he stood before Saddam and heard from him his fate. Rumor also had it that some so shook with fear that they had heart attacks when they heard their names called. Ironically enough, when I first arrived, this death-room had been turned into the Coalition's chapel.

Although there were a few civilians who hunkered down in their trailers in the semi-protection of the Green Zone, most of us went out almost every day. Some went to their Ministries; some visited their public works projects, their schools, or their courthouses. In our office, we divided our time between our Ministry, the universities, and all the half-business, half-social occasions that I mentioned before and that are part of every functioning cooperative operation. Everything from visiting a sick (or shot) Iraqi acquaintance to late evenings at home with our translators and their families all built a bond of trust and friendship between the Iraqis whom we were there to support and us civilians. As I will attempt to explain later, because we were given so little to offer in terms of money or material support, because in the end all we could offer was advice and guidance, it was clear that the friendship was genuine. They had little to give us and we had less, in material terms, to offer in return.

I say that the Green Zone was only semi-protective. This was not only because mortars and rockets could easily be fired from across the Tigris, but also because the Zone encompassed a few square miles of residences surrounding the Palace that were home to thousands of ordinary Iraqis. Or, perhaps, not so ordinary, since Saddam certainly made sure that those who lived near where he lived were of no danger to him. So, it would not be uncommon to see children of Saddam's supporters standing by the side of the road, smiling, and holding up his picture as we drove by.[3] Given the rings of security around the perimeter of the Zone, getting a bomb in is difficult. But piecing one together with wire and batteries and garage door openers already within the Green Zone would be easier, and almost undetectable. This, not having a mortar make a direct hit, was always our biggest worry.

Needless to say, little effort was made to relocate the Iraqis who lived within the Zone. This was, after all, their home. As I've tried to point out, not knowing when to be tough and, as in the first battle of Fallujah, not knowing when to be careful rather than ruthless, plagued the operation from the start. Power, rationally used, would have cost us little and gained us much.

---

[3]More often, of course, children would just stand there and wave. Some people I knew were heartened by this, as if their waving meant that we had won the battle for hearts and minds. All I know was that little kids are likely to wave at anything, whether humvees with soldiers in them or garbage trucks.

But timidity on one side and rashly throwing our weight around on the other cost us plenty.[4]

▲▼▲

## Living and Working with the Iraqis

Putting all its dangers aside, living and working with Iraqis was comfortable and even familiar. Our three translators could have been any three guys we worked with back home. They were our main entry into understanding the thoughts, joys, and fears of Iraqis more generally.

Imad,[5] who, in his thirties, was the youngest of the three, was also the quietest and most private. A religious man, taking Iraq from Saddam and giving it to his fellow Iraqis seemed to him almost a religious duty. Although he was glad we were there, and was dedicated to working closely with us, he looked forward to the day when we would be gone and Iraq governed itself.

Suhail, a Christian Arab, was the exact opposite of Imad— bubbly where Imad was serious; outgoing and generous where

---

[4]For example, it would be hard to overestimate the damage done to the success of our operation by the response the Marines made in the first battle of Fallujah after the four contractors were killed and mutilated. Military emotion in the face of this barbarism knew no bounds, but in vindicating their deaths, we used force so seemingly irrationally that it was we who were forced to retreat. The killing of Fallujans seemed so indiscriminate, and hundreds died without the perpetrators being brought to justice; the Governing Council—including our closest friends on the Council— unanimously voted its outrage; Iraqi public opinion began to turn in favor of our withdrawal despite the insurgency; and too many average Arab Iraqis increasingly viewed us with a mix of hatred leavened with contempt that made our work there all the more difficult. So, we conducted a hasty retreat from Fallujah, handing the operation over to former Saddam loyalists who themselves quickly collaborated with the insurgency, which all led to a second policy disaster. The rational use of force is both necessary and appropriate, but emotional and irrational use of force is always and everywhere disastrous.

[5]None of the ordinary Iraqis who appear in this book appears under his or her own name. This is painful for me, since I want to honor them. But the situation for them is already too dangerous.

Imad was reserved; inquisitive, even nosy, where Imad was respectful, and terrified of what would become of Christians and "collaborators" if Iraq ever fell to an extremist Islamic majority. He loved freedom, toleration, peace, and calm, and was, of all Iraqis I knew, the most hesitant about Iraq's free democratic future. Of the three, Suhail was the one most desperate to be Americanized, most hopeful to come to the States and live freely, and most seriously upset at our leaving without him. Physically, despite the fact that he was short, broad, and round-faced, he had the strength of a bear. He could grab a knife blade in his hand and snap it if he had to, and has. He had a beautiful, petite wife and two happy children, both with his character. He would do anything for us, especially if it smacked of adventure. Conversely, he'd be hard to pin down if all the day promised was work.

Finally, there was Hasan. A secular Muslim trained as an architect, Hasan had been educated by the Jesuits when they still had their prep school in Baghdad.[6] Cultured, diplomatic, acutely perceptive, and amazingly mathematical, he may also have been the most well educated Iraqi working for any office in the CPA. He was, however, totally latitudinarian in his tastes: He would be sitting at his desk, working over the Ministry's budget submission, mumbling either some Shakespeare or some lines from Joyce Kilmer under his breath, while listening to Blondie sing "The Tide Is High" over and over and over on his cassette radio.[7] Jim and I would drive over to his house every now and then for dinner with him and his wife, where there were two things you could always count on—as much beer and

---

[6]"TheAmericanJesuitFathers," as he would respectfully refer to them, as if it were all one word.

[7]*They say that life is a highway and its milestones are the years,*
 *And now and then there's a toll-gate where you buy your way with tears.*
 *It's a rough road and a steep road and it stretches broad and far,*
 *But at last it leads to a golden Town where golden Houses are.*
 —"Roofs" by Joyce Kilmer
  Hasan said he memorized this in high school, in hopes of winning the annual "elocution contest." Every year he tried, and every year he came in second. He knew this was unfair, since he was the best English speaker in the school, but the Fathers probably did it on purpose, to keep him from being

scotch as you might want, and the Fashion Channel on the television.[8]

I say all this not to characterize or caricature anyone, but to help us understand how familiar, how regular, how "un-foreign" many an ordinary Iraqi, even an ordinary religious Iraqi, is to an ordinary American. Compatibility, of course, was attenuated the more uneducated or religiously extreme the Iraqi might be. It was as if you could put Iraqis on a continuum, with enemy political Ba'athist extremists at one end, antagonistic or fanatical Islamic radicals at the other, with the more or less secular, more or less religious Iraqis, occupying the broad middle. It was this broad middle that we in the Coalition had to find ways of supporting, this moderate center that we had to help bring to positions of power and authority in Iraq. Sorry to say, as I will argue later in this book, it was exactly in this area where America fell short.

Nonetheless, despite cultural differences and religious differences, despite thirty years of brutality and tyranny, despite thirty years of an economic arrangement that promoted privilege, dampened initiative, encouraged dependency, and undercut any ethic of work as we understand it, it was still apparent that there was and is a common humanity we all saw and understood in each other. Imad's love of country; Suhail's love of peace, devotion to his family, and desire for freedom; Hasan's friendship towards us and his overwhelming respect for those who once did great things for him—all these were universal character traits that all of us understood. As I hope to make clear in subsequent chapters, it is this interplay of nature and culture, of what's common about us and what's different, and what it is we need desperately to understand about both, that helps give shape to this book.

---

too prideful. I think, for as often as he repeated this poem, Hasan knew that it was both about his life and Iraq's as well.

[8]Everyone has TV in Baghdad, and the Fashion Channel is a major attraction. With dozens of flimsily dressed women parading before you in your living room, it was as close to soft-core porn as you could easily get in Baghdad. Ah, the fruits of liberation.

# THREE

# Truth, Facts, and Lies: Five Aspects of Culture and Character

## Truth, Facts, and Lies

A short time after my arriving in Baghdad, Ambassador Bremer called all the newly appointed Ministers to a meeting in the Green Zone, in the Convention Center. This was my first time in the Convention Center, a sprawling Saddam-built complex just across from the ill-fated Rashid Hotel.

I had spoken with Dr. Zeiad, the new Higher Education minister, about the meeting a few times over the previous days. I arrived early, fully expecting to escort him in, perhaps introduce him to Bremer who I knew had not yet met him. Zeiad didn't show. The Senior Advisors were to sit directly behind the Ministers, and I sat behind an empty chair. Zeiad was one of only two or perhaps three ministers out of twenty-five who failed to show.

Later that day, Lieutenant Colonel Curda, who had been my predecessor's deputy and was functioning as mine as well, went with me to the ministry to see what was wrong. We sat down with the Minister and, in a solemn and hushed way he told us what happened to him the night before: It was late at night when there was pounding on his door. He went down dressed in his bedclothes and when he went to the door, in pushed American soldiers, guns pointed at him. They threw him to the floor, stepped on his chest, put a rifle to his head, ransacked his house, terrorized his wife and children—and then left without apology or explanation. He was, needless to say, far too shaken up, far too terrorized by this event, to make it to a meeting with Ambassador Bremer or anyone else that day.

I took the story at face value; Curda didn't believe a word of it. In a day or two Curda had tracked down the army patrol that had been in the Minister's neighborhood that evening. Yes, they had gone, armed, to the Minister's house. Here's what they said: While patrolling the neighborhood, they saw a group of men with guns standing outside a house. It was the Minister's house and the men were his security team. The soldiers went up to the men, disarmed them, inspected their weapons cards, found out it was the house of a new minister and these were his guards. The weapon cards were in order, the men were rightly there, and the soldiers gave them their guns back. They then knocked on the door, told the Minister why they were there and what they had done. Told him everything was in order. And they left.

When I told this version of events to the Minister, he denied it vehemently and may have even embellished the original story further. But when I told him that I had the names of the soldiers who had conducted the raid and would demand a formal, written apology, he immediately softened—It was all right; surely a mistake; no apology was necessary; probably just best forgotten. It was then I was certain that Curda was right and the army story, which clearly had the ring of truth to it as opposed to the Minister's tale, was the true version. While the Coalition military was and is capable of doing some inexplicable and needlessly damaging acts, invading the house of a new minister and terrorizing him and his family for no reason seemed beyond extraordinary.

This happened, as I said, very soon after I arrived in Iraq, but this kind of episode, the telling of stories of the worst kind, would be repeated over and over. For example Suhail, one of the translators, told us about the chairman of one of the science departments at Al-Mustansiriya University who had dared to take down a Shiite banner that was put up for an Islamic holy week and that had stayed up long after the event. Soon after removing the banner, while walking down one of the arcades on the university grounds, he was attacked by a band of radical students and had his throat slit. He was dead, having died right there on campus, outside his classroom.

Weeks later I repeated this story to someone who knew the professor—indeed, who had seen the professor on TV just the night before. Yes, he had done something that greatly annoyed the radicals. Yes, he knew he was in real trouble and he had been threatened. Yes, he was no longer teaching classes and would be transferred to another post for his own safety. But, no, he wasn't dead. He wasn't even hurt.

When we told this to my translator, he simply said, "I told you he was in big trouble. See, very big trouble."

"But he's not dead, Suhail. He may be in 'big trouble,' but no one ever slit his throat." "Yes, big trouble. See, just like I told you."

▲▼▲

I once caught myself saying that I didn't think I had ever been told the truth by any Iraqi, not even once. But that's wrong. I have been told the truth by Iraqis probably as often as by anyone else. The problem is, however, I may never have been told the *facts*.

The truth is important to Iraqis. They live their lives by the truth as they see it; they even govern their lives by the truth as their religion presents it and are willing to stake their eternal lives on its veracity. But, despite our view that the two are intimately related, to Iraqis and perhaps to all in the Middle East, truth and facts are different things.

Let's go back to the tall tale told by the Minister. Did the American army push its way into his house, throw him to the floor, step on his chest, point a gun at his head, and ransack his house while terrorizing his family? Probably not. Did soldiers come to his door, perhaps get him out of bed, tell him what the situation was, and inadvertently scare the wits out of him and his family? Probably so. And that's the truth that underlies the story. The truth was that soldiers came to his house. That so terrified him that he was too shaken up to go to any meeting the next day. To underscore that truth, to exemplify it, to make it real to Curda and me, he told a story. The story, the "facts" he told, weren't true, but there was a real truth that the new story made alive—more alive than any simple recitation of the facts would have managed.

▲▼▲

There are three things I think I've learned from these episodes. First, no matter how detailed, no matter how plausible, you should take nothing told you by an Iraqi at face value. Not that the story is false, but, rather, that *there might be a truth trying to be told that isn't obvious,* a truth that has only a passing relation to the facts being recounted. This is, after all, the land of Scheherazade and *The Arabian Nights,* of story-telling and fable and myth. You may be being told a different truth than the one you think you are hearing, a truth hidden under an exquisitely detailed, and fully fabricated, tale.

Second (and here's the perpetual academic in me coming out), I had always thought that those who insisted on taking the Bible literally had a hard case to make. Now I think their case impossible. Creation was managed in six twenty-four-hour days? Two of every kind of animal went on the ark—even penguins from the South Pole and polar bears from the North? But why do we think the Bible is telling us facts when all it really wants to do is tell us the truth as it tries to understand it—God managed creation himself, according to his plan, and (compared to eternity) he did it in almost no time. Yes, factual details may well point us toward the truth, but not always the factual details as they actually happened. Our emphasis on historical accuracy and factuality as the central ingredient in the truth may well only be a new and Western, not Semitic or Middle Eastern, construct.

Third, my sense—though it is *only* a sense; I don't know—is that the planners of the war in Washington were told the basic truth about Saddam and the regime; and they were told particular "facts" that supported that truth. But they may not have been *facts* as we understand the word. Did one of the Iraqis who worked in our office actually lose twenty brothers and uncles and cousins to Saddam, or was that simply a way of impressing on all hearers the real horrors of the regime? Did the father of a translator who worked for the Americans really have his back punctured all over with an electric drill while Saddam watched and smiled? Did Saddam have stockpiles of chemical and biological weapons hidden helter-skelter across Iraq? Were there really 700,000? 800,000? a million bodies in mass graves? Was Saddam in contact with Al-Qaeda and Osama Bin Laden?

Or was there another truth, related to these supposed facts but deeper than these facts—That Saddam was a psychopathic and sadistic murderer who took pleasure in the death and disfigurement of thousands, who tortured and killed with his own hands, and who would do whatever he could, eventually, to harm his enemies, including the United States?

There's no doubt about the underlying truth. But, in a modern world that demands facts to be persuaded, the truth needed even more impressive stories, even nuclear stories, to make it effective and real.

As I say, I don't know. But now, I really wouldn't be surprised.

## Stories and Lessons

*Getting Saddam*

Before Saddam was captured, sightings of him were everywhere. He was seen dressed as a woman. He was driving a taxi. He was hidden in this house, or that house, or down the block; in Baghdad, in Tikrit, in Mosul.

But if everyone knew someone who knew someone who knew where he was, why, I would ask, did no one turn him in? The reward, after all, was $25 million dollars.

"Ah, the reward. That's the problem," a professor told me, "the reward is too big."

"Why is the reward too big?"

"Because it should only be one thousand dollars, or maybe two."

"OK, I give up; why should it only be a thousand or two thousand dollars?"

"Because of what happened to the poor man who turned in the two sons." That is, Saddam's two sons, Uday and Qusay.

"Well, from everything I know, he was paid the money—$30 million in this case—as was promised, and is now living secretly somewhere probably in Europe, enjoying himself. Do you think he was never given the money or that he's living terrorized by the thought of some friends of Saddam finding him out and killing him?

"No, Saddam has no friends; besides, the man is already dead—everyone knows the story."

Well, I didn't "know the story," so I asked.

"Yes, the Americans gave him the money, just as they said they would. They didn't even give him a check, because no one would trust that—they gave him real money, green money [which is what all Iraqis call American bills], and the American soldiers brought him to the Turkish border so he could get out of Iraq.

"But in the valley just before the Turkish border, the American soldiers killed him and took the money. They split it up. Thirty million is too much for anyone to have. The man had to be very stupid to think they'd let him keep it. Besides, the soldiers have families, too."

And that was the end of it. There were no hard feelings against the American soldiers—they did exactly what anyone might do. It's just human nature. I should not be so naïve. Besides, who would be so dumb as to travel with so much cash on him? And then the heartwarming clincher: "The soldiers have families, too."

I asked a number of Iraqis over the weeks if they had heard the story. "Yes." Did they believe it? Everyone said yes except Hasan, the translator. "No one could carry that much money in cash even if he drove it in a truck. It's just another rumor. But most people *do* believe it."

Hasan was right, it had all the ingredients of the type of story Iraqis would immediately accept: greed; Iraqi credulity and bumbling; self-interested human nature; and respect for family. Besides, it was a rumor; in Iraq, it therefore had to be true.

*From* Consigliore *to Bagman*

Every now and then the US Army would find a cache of money in its raids on one of Saddam's hiding places. Since they obviously weren't going to hold it in trust for Saddam, and since it was money that belonged to the Iraqi people, the army would give it to the various ministries or to the Senior Advisors to use beneficially. As you might imagine, much of this money went to rebuild primary schools, and a good bit went to clinics and hospitals, since these were places of enormous need and were clearly the sentimental favorites of the troops. But some of it we managed to secure for higher education.

In one case, my predecessor managed to get a little over $43,000 to give to one of the universities hurt by the looters after the war. We earmarked the funds to fix the doors, windows, and walls that the hooligans had broken down. This might not seem like much, but $43,000 right after the war, spent on local carpenters and glaziers and plasterers, could fix a lot of doors and walls.

Months went by, and the administrator we gave it to (whose name I'll keep secret) left office without anything happening. So, a few months after he had left his post, I called, and in my most irate and sententious voice I asked him what he had done with the money. We all knew that corruption was endemic to Iraqi society, as much after the war as before, but this, this was money given him by the army and the army wanted to know what had happened to the funds and the army would come and, one way or another, get it back. (Actually, the army never gave the money a second thought—*we* were the ones who were miffed. But I said it anyway.)

Quiet at the other end. Then this: "I haven't done anything with the money. I never spent it and I've been waiting for you to come and take it back."

"Where is it?"

"Under my bed."

"You have forty-three thousand American dollars sitting under your bed!?"

"Yes"

Then he added, "I've been waiting for months for you to call. My family and I are very afraid going to bed each night with all this money in the house."

So we made a date to get together the next morning at his office to take the cash back. It was a Friday, so there would be no one around, or not many. I took Jim from my office and Marv, a former Green Beret who would be our major protection, and Hasan, who knew the way and would drive. We got there and managed to get past campus security with our guns (Jim had his gun hidden in his pants, behind him, under his belt. Just as we got past the guards the gun slipped and fell down his pants leg. Why it didn't go off and blow off half his ass is still a mystery.)

We meet the good professor in a corner office, down a long hall. He's sitting behind a big desk with a large paper grocery bag in front of him. In it is all the money—over $43,000—in *twenties*. We have to count it to be certain it's all there. Do you know how long it takes for three people to count out $43,000 in twenties?

We station Marv with his weapon outside the door. We count out the bills into thousand dollar piles, then someone else recounts each pile. It's all there, almost. About $80 is missing. The professor stares at us in disbelief. He didn't take the money; he swears he didn't take the money.

We believed him; of course we believed him. If he had a larcenous heart he would have kept it all and given us some cockamamie story about how the university still had it, or how thieves robbed him on the way to the office, or something. My guess is that the army miscounted it at the beginning; it was, after all, all in twenties. Still, he was so mortified that the money wasn't exactly what we expected that he took out his wallet and made up the difference out of his own pocket.

Marv is still fidgeting in the hallway. We've been counting and re-counting money for the better part of an hour now. We manage to stuff the money into a bunch of manila envelopes we brought with us—we thought it would look like we had a few inter-office memos we were delivering; instead, we had these bulging pot-bellied-pig-shaped envelopes that looked exactly like what they were: envelopes stuffed with wads of cash.

We get to the car, with Marv still fidgeting as he walked semi-backwards behind us. We take a circuitous route to the university, deposit the money in the treasurer's office, tell the president how much he has and how we want to see new doors and windows soon. And so the morning, another ordinary morning in Baghdad, is over.

And that's how I changed from being the *consigliore* to the bagman. In Iraq, it was all in a day's work.

▲▼▲

There are no doubt a dozen lessons in this story, but I need to highlight one. This is not particularly a story of private anguish and worry, or the embarrassment of an honorable but befuddled man. It's not even a story about ordinary administrative bumbling that could have had a bad end. Rather, it's about how thirty-five years of tyranny have so frozen many good people that they still, even when they are liberated, trusted, and given serious responsibilities, are afraid to act for fear of making a mistake and being punished. Better to hide the money and keep it safe than risk misspending it and suffering the inevitable consequences. Perhaps trust, trust in one's self and in the integrity and not arbitrariness of the system, will take time. Perhaps it will never come.

*The Cabbie's Tale*

Hasan, the translator, took a taxi to work one morning. The driver was still spooked by what had happened earlier that week, but he desperately wanted to talk about it. He would have quit, but driving a cab through Baghdad's gnarled streets is the only job he knows. He would have quit because he came close to being an unwilling martyr, and he's not sure that all martyrs go to heaven, especially unwilling ones.

It seemed that a scruffy man with a package got in his cab a few days before and asked to be taken to a street in the heart of downtown Baghdad. By his accent it was clear he was not an Iraqi.

"I am going to blow up a place where the Americans are. Will you take me there and die with me?"

"What do you mean to do?"

"I have a bomb in this package, and I am willing to blow myself up to have the Americans die with me. Will you come?"

"No, I'm afraid to die. I'm not ready to die. I don't want to die."

"But those who die for Allah, those who die for just and holy causes, are given the greatest of rewards."

"Still, many innocent people will perish with you. You may not kill them. It's not right that they should die."

"It's all right; they will go to Paradise with me."

"But if they are not ready? If they have sins?"

"In martyrdom, Allah forgives all sins."

"But if you kill the fathers of children? Why should the children suffer?"

"You shouldn't worry about them. They will be the children of martyrs. You know that Allah will provide. Are you coming with me?"

When the driver again said no, he made him turn off the cab and give him the car keys. He then walked down the block and set off the bomb.

*Blowing Up the Challenger*

I once had occasion to have breakfast with the dean of a college at one of the major Iraqi universities. We had met a few times before, though we never before had gotten past the handshake and pleasantry stage. An amiable person in his own gruff way, no one would jump to call him terribly intelligent or even thoughtful. Yet, what he lacked in intelligence he made up for in cynicism—though he would be the first to call himself a realist and not a cynic.

"Tell me," he asked at one point, "you're an educated American—do you really think Arabs crashed those planes into the Twin Towers?"

"Yes," I replied, "don't you?"

"Absolutely not. Couldn't be. Arabs can't fly planes like that."

(I had heard this silliness about Arabs and their inability to do anything remotely complicated before; it's a Middle Eastern way of being self-effacing in order to make a larger point, or put the blame on others.)

"But what of the nineteen Arabs who were on the planes? What were they up to?"

"I heard they were all going to a wedding." (The fact that the planes were all scheduled to go to different American cities didn't matter. That was the rumor and therefore, as Hasan might say, it had to be true.)

"Well, then, who did fly the planes?" Of course, I thought he'd surprise me and say the Jews. (Surprised, since anti-Semitism is not part of the mentality of most professional Iraqis, though it is a strong part of the make-up of religious fanatics, as I would soon discover.)

"Americans," he answered. "You flew the planes into the buildings yourselves."

"Why would we do that?"

"In order to blame us, then come here to get our oil."

I explained that, if oil were what we wanted, we could have bought all the oil in Iraq for the next twenty years for what we were spending to get rid of Saddam. We would have cut a deal with Saddam that would have made us happy, him secure, and gas cheap.

He thought about this for a second or two, then he delivered his second, stronger, fall-back position. "From what I understand, you cannot have blacks for slaves any more in America. Your Supreme Court won't let you. But I think that you could have Arabs for slaves, and I think you flew the planes into the buildings to blame it on the Arabs so you could come here to take Arabs to be slaves in your houses."

I'm not sure what exactly I said in response, but it included the notion that Americans are neither interested in Arabs as slaves nor, especially, in killing our fellow citizens for that purpose. At this he brightened up at the thought of my naiveté.

"Of course you would kill each other to get slaves. I know you had a Civil War with each other because many of you wanted to have slaves. Of course you'd kill each other for slaves. But put that aside. Maybe you crashed the planes for the sake of learning, for the sake of science."

Now I'm sure my face was a total blank. "Science?"

"Yes, like when your great President, Reagan, blew up the Challenger in order to see what would happen scientifically. You remember, he gave that speech where he praised the astronauts for having sacrificed so much for the sake of science and for the progress of science."

Choking as I probably was on my tea at that point, my response probably sounded more indignant than rational and no doubt reconfirmed his belief that there is no motivation other than self-interest at work in human affairs. Whether it be from low motives (e.g., oil or slaves) or from higher ones (e.g., the progress of national science), all humans and all nations act from reasons of self-interest, nothing less, nothing more. Only a dumb American would think otherwise.

## Sunnis and Shi'a

It was during the week of Ashura that one of the most highly placed professors I knew, a devout Sunni, asked me if I had seen the TV pictures of Shiite pilgrims whipping themselves. No, I hadn't, though I did know that during this week devout Shi'a would do penance by flagellating themselves with chains, often tipped with blades or sharpened points. Later I would see pictures of young boys whose heads had been sliced with straight razors in order to let the blood run down their faces. Scalps do bleed rather gruesomely.

It is "horrible, disgusting" what these people, these Shiite people, do to their God-given bodies, he said. "Animals. People who do this are nothing but animals." Then he paused for a second and said, in a lower voice. "No, they're worse than animals. Not even an animal would do that to itself."

▲▼▲

I knew another Sunni who made the Hajj, the pilgrimage to Mecca. By happenstance, he there found himself thrown in with a group of Shiite pilgrims. He had never spent any time with the Shi'a before, and really didn't know any himself, but he had always thought of them as co-religionists, believing pretty much as he did. Then, he said, they began to sing a hymn. All around him were Shi'a singing a hymn that declared that the Archangel Gabriel had violated Allah's command by giving the Koran to Mohammed instead of Ali, as he was supposed to. The hymn portrayed Gabriel as, in his words, "a traitor to the will of Allah." "How could they say that?" he asked me. "These people are not real Muslims. These people are heretics, all of them. They shouldn't be allowed to sing that." Then, more quietly, in a voice just above a whisper, "They shouldn't be allowed."

▲▼▲

There were many other incidents, many other comments. The low regard, the contempt, that so many otherwise responsible Sunnis have for ordinary Shi'a was apparent even to an outsider. It's how I imagine the English once viewed the Irish, or what Americans of long-standing lineage thought of Mediterranean immigrants—superstitious, fecund, and dirty. To say that this is an arrogance that stems from those who once held power now looking down on the once powerless may be too social-science simplistic. Yes, there is now a realignment of social status, with the formerly oppressed now rising to the top. But here also were serious religious differences, coupled now not only with concern over who would rule politically, but with who might soon impose their orthodoxy on others.

Most Shi'a I knew at the time had less intense feelings towards Sunnis, whom they insisted were still Muslims, still co-religionists, but with a different view than theirs, no more. Still, as the internal conflict now underway in Iraq rages on, with Shi'a targeted by some Sunnis not as political enemies or collaborators but as infidels, the war is quickly moving from a political fight to a larger religious war—a war where Shiite brutality against their Sunni "co-religionists" now matches the depth of Sunni prejudice against them. It is a war whose final resolution no one now alive knows enough to predict.

*The Decimation*

In Erbil, in Kurdish Iraq, I had the opportunity to sit with a custodian of one of the public buildings. He was tall, frighteningly skinny, and he smoked one cigarette after another. He also seemed unable to look at you when he talked or to talk without shaking. This was right after we had captured Saddam.

He was happy we caught Saddam, though he was suspicious as to why we didn't kill him. He was worried, as were almost all Iraqis, that we'd make a deal with Saddam—just give us all your oil forever, Saddam, and we'll put you back in power. The custodian liked the Americans, and he wanted to trust us, but he really wasn't sure. "You could have killed him right there, and you didn't. Why? Why didn't you kill him? Will you have a trial and then kill him"

Now, I do have to admit that Ambassador Bremer's decision to disavow capital punishment did serve to heighten Iraqi suspicions. Why we would profess our respect for other cultures and then impose so alien and peculiarly Western a view on the people we went to support was hard to explain. Did we do it to keep Great Britain happy? Did we do it because we wanted to prove our liberal bona fides to the UN or France? Did we do it because we feared making a capital mistake while we were in charge? I don't know, though I suspect a bit of all these views combined with general State Department liberalism came into play.

Yet, to return to my new custodian friend, all this talk about Saddam was leading to something: The custodian wanted to tell me about what happened when he was in grade school. Again, I have no way to vouch for the factuality of the story, though I have no reason to doubt its truth.

It seems that part of the Ba'ath Party army was marching past his school when one of his classmates threw something out the window. A pencil, an eraser, something. It was clearly designed to annoy the soldiers, though you might be forgiven for thinking that any soldier annoyed by a passing eraser wasn't much of a soldier. Still, it was a matter of respect.

The commanding officer halted his troop and ordered all the students out of their rooms. He lined them up in the school courtyard. Then he made an announcement that the mothers of all the students would be given twenty minutes to assemble in the courtyard, facing their sons and daughters. Separating the boys from the girls and sending the girls to stand with the women, the officer lined all the boys up against a wall. He then took ten boys out from the group at random, brought them to the middle of the courtyard, and shot them dead. Six year olds, eight year olds, ten year olds. He then made the mothers and girls cheer the soldiers for having taught so valuable a lesson to hoodlums. For every mother who did not clap, one more boy would be shot. They all clapped.

I then understood what the Romans understood by "decimating" a people. It wasn't meant to punish a culprit. The officer never asked who threw the eraser, nor did he seek to punish everyone until the perpetrator was handed over. Punishing the doer wasn't the end in view. It had nothing to do with even barbaric justice. Terror was the end, no more, no less.

I then better understood the tremors in the souls of people who thought we still might make a deal with Saddam.

### Death Goes to Pick the Finest of All

Sunday, January 18, 2004. It began like any other morning. Scrambled eggs, bacon, coffee, grits ... Then came the thud that meant that a bomb had gone off or a mortar had landed someplace nearby. This was odd. Since Christmas, when the attacks against the Green Zone had begun in earnest, almost all the bombing came at night, between eight and midnight. Still, this seemed pretty far away, so we kept on eating.

Soon soldiers started running through the dining hall, since it was quicker to get outside by cutting through it. Then some soldiers ran in and said to others who were still eating to get to the north gate—"Assassins' Gate" as some Iraqis call it—

immediately. Yes, stop what you're doing, put down the coffee, and get out now. *Now!* In seconds, all the soldiers who had been having breakfast with us civilians were gone. We had no idea what was going on; though today the war became different, and worse.

Before today, things were always a little slower and more pleasant on Sundays. There was no 7:30 meeting of the Senior Advisors on Sundays. Even though Sundays are workdays in Iraq, you could still set your alarm for seven instead of six, shower, dress, and make it over to the dining hall before the doors closed at 8:30. Though we would all be at our desks or driving to our ministries by 9, Sundays were always a bit quieter, a bit tamer, a bit more peaceful. But not this Sunday, not January18.

Today, the war took a new turn, and the problems we were soon to confront became clearer. Today the fighting turned from attacks on Americans and Brits towards the Iraqis themselves. Someone had blown up his car, and himself as well, at the entrance to the north gate, the entrance where most of the Iraqis who work with the Coalition entered. Thirty-six Iraqis were killed as they were trying to get to work in the Green Zone. Among them was Hadeel.

I met Hadeel for the first time just the day before, Saturday, at lunch, though I had seen her working down the hall from me, in the Finance Ministry office, perhaps a hundred times before. She was twenty-three, with light brown hair and a flirtatious smile, and engaged to be married I was told. That Saturday I had sat with her and perhaps four or five other women, all the same age, with Suhail, one of our translators, and his newly hired wife. Like Suhail, Hadeel was a Christian and had actually taken catechism lessons from him in years past.

Today, however, she was dying. The next day she was dead. "Burned black all over," I was told by those who were, amazingly, allowed to visit her as she lay in the hospital. The other women in the car had been blown out of it when the bomb went off. Hadeel burned as the car melted around her.

In some ways, Hadeel is the lucky one. The others, I am told, no longer have faces. Blind, deaf, ears and noses ripped off, with metal and glass pieces embedded in their bodies. I don't know the truth of this first-hand, and, as I've noted, it's a mistake to believe all one hears in Iraq. But it's likely true. And, for sure, Hadeel is dead.

Hadeel's death and the maiming of the other young women cast a morbid pall over the CPA.

> As they always say, Death goes to pick the finest of all. We have lost the friend whose smile never leaves her face, always cooperative and ready to help. Till now I never heard anything bad of her. May God bless her soul in the heavens and spread peace on earth. Let's pray for her family and relatives to be given patience and condolence. Amen.
>
> Sirs, May God the Almighty keep us all in his care and safety and to give us the persistence to work it out to rebuild this country.

This was the e-mail Imad, the devout Muslim and the quietest and most serious of our three translators, sent around our office the afternoon we heard about Hadeel's death. Like most Iraqis who came to work for the Coalition, he signed on right after the fall of Baghdad. He and the two others who worked in our office—Hasan and Suhail—now knew that they, too, were marked for death. All three were at the Assassins' Gate checkpoint perhaps an hour before the bomb exploded that Sunday. They liked to get to work early, and leave by four. Had they slept a little later, or been slowed down and harassed a little more than usual by a scared or arrogant soldier at the entry, they, too, would be among the dead and maimed. And they knew it.

The forces arrayed against the Coalition had little hope of getting a bomb through the checkpoints that bottleneck entry into the Green Zone. As I said before, it's not that a bomb couldn't go off in the Zone; it's just that if it ever does, it will be constructed inside the Zone by one of the many Iraqis who still live there. But, while we Americans were waiting for something like this to happen to us, the suicide bomber was much smarter. He made it happen to them, to the Iraqis. The Americans cannot easily be terrified, but the Iraqis can.

Not all the Iraqis killed that morning were going to work for the Coalition. A van of girls going to high school was unlucky enough to be crossing the path of the bomber as he blew up his car. They, too, burned to death. Senseless? Not at all. Towards what end? Put yourself in the place of those who worked with us. For all America's might, it was now clear that there was nothing America could do to keep you as an Iraqi safe if someone wanted you dead. We can cover ourselves, more or less, but not the Iraqis. More, what seemed so promising just six months before—working for the most powerful force that history had ever seen, working for pay that made you the envy of all those who knew you, working for a new Iraq in which you would be an important part—now seemed like the admission ticket to death. Not only could the Americans not keep you safe, but associating with them, helping them in re-building your country, meant risking death.

Soon after January 18, a number of Iraqis who worked for the Coalition quit. Most stopped telling people where they worked or for whom. All seemed to have lost that mixture of pride and smugness that characterized their attitude when they thought they were on the side of History. Suhail's newly hired wife was among those who quit that week. By the end of six months, of the three translators in the office, only Imad—quiet, serious, and without wife or children—would be left.

▲▼▲

The word on the street was that it was a foreigner who blew himself up. An Afghan, most said. A Yemeni, others said. He spoke Arabic badly, at least to the Iraqi ears of those who claimed to have heard him as he talked out the window of his car before he set the bomb off.

On the next day, on January 19th, there were no public protests. No howls and cries for revenge. No headlines screaming for a massive Iraqi response to the mayhem. Thirty-six innocent fellow countrymen slaughtered, and hundreds maimed, and all the grief was quiet and private. The Iraqis who worked with us became downcast, introspective, and petrified. The Iraqis on the street said . . . nothing. It was as if, on September 12th,

New Yorkers slowly went about their business, numb. "Why don't you Americans round up all the foreigners? We know where they are. We will tell you." So paralyzed were the Iraqis we knew that there was nothing they could do, nothing other than, perhaps, turn to the Americans to do something about it. And there was nothing we could do. The dread that Iraqis had once experienced under Saddam now returned as terror.

This was the insight of the insurgency that January morning, 2004: In order to stop or hinder the liberation of Iraq, forget attacking just Americans. Terrorize the Iraqis instead. The "Lesson of Viet Nam"—namely, that over time America's determination can be worn down by casualties and that voters will grow weary of protracted foreign involvement and withdraw—might take too long to implement. But Iraqis, beaten down as they already were, hesitant and frightened as they already were, could easily be made to cower. If the Americans won't surrender, perhaps the Iraqis will.

January 18, 2004: Today the insurgency signaled that a different war had begun.

### Getting Iraqis to Fight

From the beginning of the suicide attacks it was clear that most of the attackers who blow themselves up are not Iraqis. I do not say all are not, since my sense is that some Iraqi Sunni religious extremists might well be among the killers and the killed, but the vast majority of them are not. This, at least, is the feeling of virtually every Iraqi you speak to. The bombers are always fanatics from Sudan or Yemen or Afghanistan or maybe Pakistan—never Iraqis. We Iraqis love life too much to kill ourselves, they say, with a kind of self-assured pride that makes them fully expect that you should praise them for being so considerate and level-headed.

But an unwillingness to die, I would always respond when I was feeling a bit put off by this argument of theirs, is really a double-edged sword. Sure, you may be unwilling to blow yourselves up and kill others in the process—that's good. But those afraid of dying are also incapable of dying for their country. If no one is willing to die—if they would rather desert than be shot at—then Iraq has no future: It will fall prey to those who are willing to kill and be killed. There's an ancient saying that the man who is unafraid of death is not only the master of his own life, but also the master of all others'. If a nation is unwilling to stand up and fight for itself, it will ultimately obey those who are willing to die fighting.

This was brought home to me most forcefully by Hasan, the translator. No one, simply no one, was more on the side of the Coalition, happier to see Saddam deposed, and quicker to sign up with us Americans than he. He joined with us the very first day it was apparent we had won the war. One night Jim and I were at Hasan's house for dinner. It was at the beginning of the first Battle of Fallujah, the one from which we would soon retreat so ignobly. General Kimmitt was on the television talking forcefully about our incursion into the city and how well we Americans were fighting. "Hooray for Kimmett! Hooray for the Americans!" Hasan was yelling—and he was completely sincere. "You tell 'em, general! Kill them! Kill all of them!" Hasan was quite worked up, and quite happy with the mission. Killing the Fallujans—the remnants of Saddam's forces and the religious fanatics there in the city—was, to him, exactly right. To Hasan, no one in Fallujah was innocent.

But I was annoyed. "Hasan," I said, "if you'll pick up a gun and join with our troops, I'll give you leave from the office and continue your pay. I think you should help us in this battle."

"Oh, no, sir. I couldn't do that, sir. We Iraqis are no good at fighting. You Americans are good at that, not us. I'd be useless. I'd get killed right off. No, sir, not me, please. I'd die for sure."

"You mean, Hasan, that we Americans have to continue to die so you Iraqis can be free?"

He looked at me like he had just hurt his best friend, but he didn't know what else to say. He had spoken the honest truth as he understood it. He and his compatriots really were useless in this fight.

Not too long ago, there was a picture flashed across the world that showed a bombing just outside the Green Zone that killed a number of Iraqis and Iraqi guardsmen. You can see in the foreground Iraqi guardsmen running away from the blast and towards the camera. And then I thought about American soldiers who, whenever a bomb goes off, run *towards* the explosion, hoping to protect their comrades. I hope, someday, we're able to see that happen in Iraq, for then, surely, we can start to come home.

I don't mean to make light of the plight of the Iraqis. Hundreds joined with us at great risk to themselves; thousands have joined the Iraqi police or army or the new national guard, and many of them have died. But, if I can be more bluntly honest than perhaps I should, it seems to me as a fairly careful observer that most of them have not died fighting, but have died outside restaurants, or died standing in line.

None of this applies, of course, to the Kurds, who have no trouble dying and therefore have no trouble fighting. They see themselves as a cohesive community and will always fight to protect one another. I remember the first time I visited Kurdish Iraq. I saw what I thought were homeless men sleeping on the sidewalks. But each of them had a companion or two standing up next to him, fully awake. Then I realized, these aren't street people—These are the Kurdish peshmerga guarding the streets. One will sleep on a piece of cardboard, ready to jump up with his gun at a moment's notice, while one stays awake, watching.

What this means is that the thought that we can quickly build up an Iraqi fighting force to take over from us in battle is a chimera. All Arab Iraqis I know always tell the simple truth about this—"We Iraqis don't like to die."

Jim, the person to whom this book is dedicated and who was at the dinner that night at Hasan's house, did die on the streets of Baghdad, driving back from one of the universities he was working hard to rebuild. Hasan, with my blessing and my full understanding, left the employ of the Coalition in the spring of 2004 and for a while took a job at one of the universities. Within a few months, he left. Although we still keep in touch, he will now not tell me where he is.

▲▼▲

I wrote this section in the year 2005. By 2006, with the rise of the war between Iraqi Shi'a and Sunnis—a true religious war that the media likes to call a "civil war"—things might seem to have changed. But not fully. It still appears to be foreign elements who are most eager for martyrdom, not Iraqis. While Iraqis now have less hesitation in killing, they still remain "unwilling to die." This is why it has been so difficult to stand up an Iraqi national defense force to take over from American troops. Yes, Iraqis—some Iraqis—are happy enough to kill, kill each other, kill over Allah's will. But they are not, like the martyrs and like the Kurds, willing to risk all, at least not for their neighbors and not for Iraq.

## An Assassination Attempt and a Kidnapping

Two incidents need to be recorded for posterity. They are also small openings into the minds of some ordinary Iraqis, as well as religious fanatics, the insurgents, and their common criminal allies.

*The Assassination Attempt*

Before I arrived in September of 2003, my predecessors Drew Erdmann and Steve Curda did their utmost to get the Ministry back on its feet. The Ministry building, which housed both our Ministry as well as the Ministry of Education (that is, basic education: elementary and secondary) was gutted and burned during the looting that followed the war. It was, by all accounts, the most impressive if not the most beautiful modern building in all of Baghdad. About a dozen stories high, it had two towers, one for each ministry, connected at ground level by an auditorium that was for the joint and common use of both organizations. Designed and constructed by the Japanese, it had every modern amenity, including automatic louvered windows that opened and closed with the comings and goings of the sun.

Erdmann and Curda not only had to find alternative space to house the Higher Education Ministry, but they also had to reconstitute the Ministry staff, purge it of high-level Ba'athists, and find effective leadership while they waited for the authorities to name a new Minister. Since school would soon be open, it was imperative that the work of the Ministry—getting students enrolled at the right universities, preparing the payroll, moving goods and equipment, making certain that the curriculum was shorn of Ba'athist propaganda classes, everything— get itself up and running. Someone was needed to do all this, someone respected, efficient, and trustworthy.

If I were more confident of the future, I'd not hesitate to name the person they found. Let me, for now, just call him Mahmood. Knowledgeable regarding the structure and organization of higher education (he was a professor at one of the more prominent universities), eminently good-willed, firmly anti-Ba'athist, and decently conversant in English, he became the almost obvious choice. With him, the office managed to reconstitute all 550 of the ministry's staff positions, get a strong budget put together, open the school year, and get the mechanism of higher education going once again. Nonetheless, his new connection to the Coalition made him an obvious target.

On Thursday, the 9th of October, three weeks after I arrived in Baghdad and shortly after the new Minister was named, Mahmood was severely wounded on his way to work. It was clearly a set-up. Three armed men came over to his car just after he had pulled out of his driveway, as it stopped at the corner. One man, wearing an Arabian gown, shot him three times with a pistol as he sat in the passenger seat. Both his driver and an assistant were unharmed; the assailants went directly for Mahmood. He was shot several times: in the left arm, in the face, and through his ribs, though miraculously the bullet hit no vital organ. One of the three gunmen sprayed a nearby police car with automatic fire, just to keep it from interfering. His driver sped Mahmood away to the nearest hospital. The attackers disappeared.

The timing of the attack seemed inexplicable. The attack came in October. With a new Minister in place, Mahmood was no longer the top person at the Ministry. He was now simply one of the administrators. He neither set policy nor worked directly with the Coalition, except for some administrative matters that now fell to him. Still, someone wanted him gone.

It took months for Mahmood to recover from having taken three bullets at very close range. We all expected that he'd not return, but go back to the quieter life of teaching. We totally underestimated his courage. At the beginning of December, Mahmood returned to work at the Ministry.

On Christmas morning, Mahmood went to work and found a letter on his desk. It had not been mailed, but simply placed there the night before. It began, "In the name of God, the Most Gracious, the Most Merciful." It went on "Don't elude us any more. Leave your position. Wasn't the first strike enough for you? The second will be fatal to you or to one of your family, by the will of God."

Then came a list of Mahmood's crimes and sins: His past was "filled with bad ethics against Islamic thought and values"; he once gave a set of exam questions to his sister and to one of his mistresses; he treated people despotically long ago and was doing so again. It noted that he was given his authority by the Coalition, though it exonerated us because we were no doubt unaware of his infamous, immoral past. In a footnote ostensibly addressed to the Minister, the letter went on, "This man is not honest in everything, with bad ethics and a wicked history with women." The death threat ended simply and ironically with the words, "With respect." There was no signature.

Most likely, the letter was delivered by a person or by people within the Ministry itself. The reasons he needed to die were both personal and educational: his manner was despotic and he corrupted the exam process by secretly giving exam questions to his favorites. But mostly the letter was filled with outrage over Mahmood's supposed ethical lapses and un-Islamic thoughts and values, especially as regarded women. And, while it threatened death, it seemed to promise that they would back off if Mahmood would simply resign from the Ministry.

We in the office discounted the accusations of womanizing and helping others on an exam. We had no idea if they were true or not, though Mahmood was, in all his dealings with us, one of the most honest and honorable Iraqis we had met. We relied on his honesty as well as his competence and good judgment, and were never once let down. Nor would one think, in any normal world, that helping a sister or even a mistress on an exam would be grounds for execution by anonymous gunmen. No, the core of the message was that his actions and attitudes were non-Islamic and his secularism disqualified him from any position of authority in the Ministry. Indeed, Mahmood was one of the more secular Iraqis we knew—with us, he fought hard against having the universities fall into the hand of either political factions or religious fanatics. And now he was paying the price.

There was nothing the Coalition or the American military could do to keep Mahmood safe. Putting guards around his house wouldn't work; giving him a military escort to and from work was out of the question. It would just have made him seem like a stooge of the Coalition while setting him up as a bigger target.

Mahmood moved from house to house, staying with this or that relative seemingly at random. The only one he trusted was his driver, a Christian, whom he told every night where to pick him up the next morning. Perhaps his worst worry was that he'd be killed in his office; so he kept a loaded revolver on his desk. But he came to work every day. Getting the universities back on track had cost him three bullets and the use of his left arm; he was not about to quit now.

Mahmood received a number of phone threats all winter and spring. As customary, they said that they'd be just as pleased to kill his wife as kill him. His wife, I believe, did quit her job and stay in hiding, but Mahmood kept on. Kept on, that is, until late March, just about three months after the Christmas letter. The Minister, Dr. Zeiad, had over these months whittled away virtually all of Mahmood's authority and made all administrative decisions without consulting him. Finally, in a move that he could only see as a death warrant, Zeiad took it upon himself to fire Mahmood's driver. Yes, the Minister thought it appropriate to reach down and fire a now second-level administrator's chauffeur.

When I protested the firings, Dr. Zeiad told me that the driver "drank." When I protested that a Christian taking a drink was, in any event, none of Zeiad's business, he added that the driver also kept a house of prostitution. When I noted to Zeiad that this move—firing the driver that Mahmood trusted to keep him safe since the shooting—was tantamount to helping the fanatics kill Mahmood, the Minister responded that I should know that Mahmood was "a crooked man" who sold exam questions to students. This was, of course, the same story told in the death threat letter, minus the mistress angle but now with money thrown in for good measure.

All of us could see the handwriting on the wall. The driver was not the issue—Mahmood was. The one last protection that Mahmood had from death was now removed by the Minister himself. Mahmood resigned that week. The fanatics who wanted to eliminate a stumbling block within the Ministry had won.

▲▼▲

## The Kidnapping

My staff and I became close friends with an older woman who worked fairly high up in our Ministry. She was a Christian. And, while she seemed clearly pleased that the Coalition had swept out the Ba'athists, there was always the rumor that her family prospered greatly under Saddam. But, it must be admitted, so did many Christians. Christians, being a clear and easily crushable minority, made few waves. And Saddam often relied on them, knowing that he had them, as a group, under his control. Tariq Aziz, Saddam's deputy, was a Christian, as were, I'm told, all of Saddam's barbers and cooks. Anyone who could either poison him or slit his throat had to be Christian; they were, it seems, the only ones besides his immediate family he trusted. I often have thought that part of the killing of Christians and the bombing of churches these days stems not only from fanatical religious motives but also from reasons of political retribution.

On September 29, 2003, just two weeks after I arrived in Baghdad, kidnappers took her middle-aged son. He was a dentist, and they waited for him to finish his work and grabbed him as he left his clinic. Because the family had money (the father was a well-to-do merchant and the kidnapped son was a well-regarded dentist) ransom was set at $300,000.

The son was blindfolded only when he was taken to and from the house where he was kept; in the days he spent sitting in a chair, captive, the blindfolds were off and he could take in everything. This meant he had a good look at all the kidnappers. There were around twelve of them, all about twenty to twenty-five years old. They had primitive tattoos, as criminals might have. Indeed, young as they were, they were bragging among themselves how long they had each spent in prison. In all likelihood, they were among the thousands of common criminals Saddam had released from prison and pardoned just before the Coalition arrived. But now they were criminals who had struck it rich—without anyone to stop them, they had a goldmine in terrorizing well-to-do Iraqis. And they also now had allies in the police and within the camps of religious extremists.

The only person the son was not allowed to look at was the head of the gang, a person they all referred as "Hajji"—that is, a man who has made the pilgrimage to Mecca.

The kidnappers kept him for five days, keeping in contact with the family through the son's mobile phone. But the son was no fool—he knew he was only worth money to them alive, so he refused all offers of food or drink. They'd put roasted chicken up to his mouth, and still he refused. Finally, he collapsed. Probably not wanting a worthless corpse on their hands, on the fifth day the kidnappers settled for a payment of $23,000.

The father was instructed where to drive with the ransom. He was told which of his cars to take (so they'd know when he approached) and was told to stop when he saw car lights blinking at him. Without anyone getting out, he handed them the money through the open car window. The two men who picked up the ransom were older, in their thirties, and well dressed in jacket and tie. Strangely, they both sported "Elvis Presley" hairstyles, with a big wave in the front. They drove a white BMW, without plates.

The son was returned in a convoy of three cars, with him in the middle car, blindfolded. While being returned, he could tell that they went through at least two Iraqi Police checkpoints. Even though he was sitting in the back seat blindfolded, the IP still waved them through each time. The kidnappers had told him previously that it was no use for anyone to contact the police since they "had ties to the police," and this proved them right.

He was let out on a street corner, still blindfolded, given about $1.50 in cash for a cab and told not to remove the blindfold until they honked. They had already taken his wallet, the gold cross around his neck, and a ring. One other ring, which they mistakenly thought was a wedding ring, he was allowed to keep, saying, in their charitable way, that it "belonged to his wife."

After the ransom, the mother still went to work each day at the Ministry, but the younger children were now kept home from school. The family had no one to turn to for help—the corruption of the police was manifest, and we Americans had no ability to (and, to our shame, seemingly no interest in) investigating or prosecuting the thousands of "Iraqi on Iraqi crimes," as they were called, that happened every day. We liberated Iraq only to let Iraq rot under the rule of criminals, extortionists, looters, arsonists, murders, and rapists.

The mother asked me to plead with Ambassador Bremer to do something to get them out of the country and to America—they had relatives in Arizona, Philadelphia, and Chicago—but the request went nowhere. In truth, we Americans did nothing to help those who stood by us and helped us when they were threatened or harmed in the aftermath of our arrival. And, sorry, saying that (as I was officially told) "these are the good people we need to stay in Iraq to stabilize it and lead it into the future" simply fails to move me.

What happened to the money? Some of it almost certainly went to the corrupt police, whose name in Iraq is Legion. Some might have gone to religious fanatics who now work closely with the criminal element. And some no doubt went to buy weapons for the insurgency. In the New Iraq, criminals have loads of ready clients, and few opponents.

▲▼▲

This story has a sequel. Even though we were incapable of help, my office was the only place in Iraq that it seemed the family trusted. I don't believe the mother ever even told her co-workers at the Ministry about the kidnapping, and we know they didn't go to the police. When Christmas came around, we were all invited to go to their house for a grand and festive dinner. After all, their son had been returned, and Christmas was this year like a thanksgiving. But the bombing of the Green Zone was now beginning in earnest, and we were under an unofficial lock-down that night, so we didn't go. I heard, later, that the mother was hurt by this, but I guess there was little we could do other than apologize.

To make it up to her, we did something no doubt foolish. We went to her kidnapped son's wedding. This was now early in 2004, when the dangers were somewhat greater than at Christmas. It was a gala Orthodox ceremony followed by a truly happy reception in one of the better private clubs downtown. Well, happy on the groom's side. The bride's family sat stony-faced on the other side of the hall. I was told that this is not uncommon—that while the groom's side celebrates gaining a new daughter, the bride's side sits by coldly, unhappy at having lost one. Though another Iraqi gave me an equally credible explanation of their iciness—the bride's family was nothing but a bunch of sourpusses, every one of them.

By American standards, the celebration was wild, almost lunatic—the bride and groom entered under a canopy of burning swords (whose flames were so hot that the holders of the swords kept shifting them from hand to hand, blowing on their scorched fingers and nearly dropping the swords each time); they entered to the highly jazzed-up strains of "Angels We Have Heard On High"; the band then went into discernible renditions of "Mambo Italiano" and "Hernando's Hideaway"; and not a few of the groom's relatives kept insisting that Jim, the only unmarried American in my office, dance with all the sweet young teenage girls, pick one for his wife, and take her home to the States. Everyone knew that Iraq was now Hell itself, and they danced and sang and celebrated to keep it under foot. Still, America, it seems, was forever on their minds.

The week I left for home, in June, I went to see the mother in her office at the Ministry. She was, as always, happy to see me, but sad to say good-bye. She didn't say anything about going to America anymore; she knew by now there was nothing left that I could do. But when I went in to see her that morning she was clearly not doing her work. Rather, she had been looking at an old, worn-out glossy picture brochure on Philadelphia, and she made no effort to hide it.

# FOUR

# Higher Education, Politics, and Religious Totalitarianism

In February of 2004, I went to visit Dr. Sattar Jawad, the head of the English Department at the University of Baghdad. The English Department, along with the other arts and humanities fields, is in a separate part of town, away from the main campus. The guards who greeted Suhail and me at the gates were all excited to see an American. They opened the gates with a flourish. They wanted to shake our hands, and Suhail and I obliged. They were all happy, excited, as if they had been expecting us for a long time and we had finally arrived.

Suhail quickly figured it out. It seemed that just a few days before, the guards had stopped a suicide bomber right there, there at the gates, trying to enter the campus. So now they were expecting someone from the Coalition to bring them commendations from the Coalition and, above all, a reward. When Suhail explained that we knew nothing about this, but that we'd see what could be done, they were crestfallen, but still retained hope that something good would happen soon. In any event, they were happy enough that we were there. I guess, even if we had no cash to spread around this time, maybe we would the next time we visited.

We first went to the wrong part of campus. On our right was the library of the College of Arts and Humanities, or, rather, what was left of it. During the looting, this campus had been hit hard, and the library was burned. It's now little more than a shell of a building, with its empty metal shelves still standing twisted inside. Here sixteen thousand, thirty thousand, or three hundred thousand books were torched. How many were lost depends less on the facts than on whom you ask. Suhail and I walked to the end of the campus, only to realize we had walked too far—the English Department was right next to where the guards had let us in. There were religious banners up around campus, side by side with anti-American, anti-Coalition posters. The students we met probably knew I was an American, and had that sullen, stare-from-the-corner-of-your-eyes look as we walked by; when we asked for directions, however, some put aside their insolent attitudes and tried to help. One student knew exactly where we wanted to go and took us there himself. I think he saw himself as our protector, though it could just as easily have been a trap.

The chair of the English Department is an urbane, cultured, mild-mannered academic, who could pass for a professor on any continent. The first thing I noticed was that high up on his wall, perhaps fifteen feet high, near where the wall met the ceiling, was a picture of Shakespeare. Needless to say, I had to ask what it was doing up there so high. Well, it seems that a while back members of the Ba'ath Party came to his office and told him to take the portrait of Shakespeare down and put a picture of Saddam in its place. He knew he couldn't stop them from putting up a picture of Saddam, but he could rescue Shakespeare by putting him so high up that, when Saddam's goons came back, they couldn't take him down. By the time I had arrived, Saddam was captured, his picture thrown away, but Old Will still presided over the cavernous room that Dr. Sattar called his office.

This wasn't the first time, it seemed, that Sattar had business with Saddam. Since Sattar was perhaps the finest English speaker in Iraq (he'd deny this, of course, but let's say it's true by my lights), Saddam had once wanted him to be his official translator. Word got back to him about this and he decided to wriggle out of it by feigning raucous, public intoxication. He went so far as to get himself a bottle and sit at his window, yelling who-knows-what to the passers-by. He was clearly too much trouble, so Saddam decided he no longer wanted him to be his translator. Instead, he wanted him executed. Only the coming of the war deflected that plan.

Shakespeare was Sattar's favorite author, and he tried to teach a course on him every year. He was also trying to translate Shakespeare's Sonnets into Arabic. But, beyond Shakespeare, what Sattar most wanted to teach was literary interpretation. He was able to do some of this under the old regime, but, with his limited access to the outside world, he only had small glimmers of what was going on in the field. But now there was a new problem—maybe even a worse problem. Saddam, after all, had had nothing against Shakespeare, and he had zero interest in something called "literary interpretation." But the new forces of repression on campus—the students with their religious banners, and their religious leaders—they did care, and care mightily. If a book, let's say Shakespeare's *Hamlet,* could be read in different ways, if the static words on the page might be seen from different perspectives and even contain a variety of meanings—well, this might be fine for Shakespeare, but what about the Koran? Does it, too, contain different meanings, silent meanings? Might different readers legitimately come to different, even contradictorily different, understandings of the same sacred text? And what might keep a professor armed with literary-historical tools or literary-psychological tools not from "explaining" a text but explaining it away?

Seen in this light, literary interpretation was dangerous, even subversive. It was bad enough that no two scholars might fully agree on a literal interpretation of the Koran, but to subject it to a myriad of historical, political, or psychological interpretations would be to reduce it, to bind it to a cultural or historical moment, to open it to multiple meanings or perhaps even contradictions, and to undermine its authority altogether. To a fervent Muslim, "deconstructing" the Koran must sound like blasphemy itself. It probably is. To those on the outside, religious fanatics might seem like anti-intellectual know-nothings, but dumb they are not: They know exactly what's at stake.

The universities had experienced the equivalent of a new birth of freedom with the coming of liberation. Professors knew this and, it seemed, at the beginning, so did the students. But quickly the climate on the campuses was changing. And the impetus for change, a change to a new form of repression, was coming primarily from students. Whoever has a romantic notion of students, of their idealism, their open-mindedness, and their liberality, should take a look at Iraq and think again.

▲▼▲

When the Coalition first entered Iraq, the universities were substantially on the side of our forces. By the time I left, it was one of the sectors most against us. Part of the reason for the change had to do with consistent ill-treatment, sometimes unavoidable ill-treatment, on the part of the military. Of this, more later. Part of it had to do with the psychological and ideological vacuum left by the fall of the regime. Part of it had to do with the desperate physical conditions of the universities, conditions that the coming of liberation in many ways only made worse. But most of it had to do with the unanticipated rise of religious extremism that soon took hold, not among administrators or professors but among growing numbers of newly liberated, primarily male, students.

There are twenty universities in Iraq, two graduate "commissions," and forty-six technical institutes. These last are generally two-year colleges, similar to our community and vocational colleges. As I'll discuss in greater depth in a later chapter, these various universities are far closer to European and British universities, with their high degree of specialization, than to anything we're used to in the States. This is one reason the Arts and Humanities College of Baghdad University could be miles away from the central campus. There would be no reason for a student majoring in engineering or biology on the main campus ever to have to take a literature or history or language course on the far campus. Conversely, those students studying art or geography or history on the Arts campus would almost certainly never have need of a math or science course. What we think of as "liberal education" simply has no life in Iraqi higher education. You go to university to learn one field, or one slice of a field, in depth. Or, as one professor once said to me when I tried to explain the virtues of a broader liberal education, "But why would anyone not want to be an expert?"

Saddam had more than a little respect for higher education, or, at least, for parts of it. The regime needed doctors, scientists, and engineers, and these subjects were the most highly valued of all university fields. This is true, in large measure, throughout the Middle East. Saddam himself had a Ph.D., though no Iraqi could talk about it without snickering a little, since he acquired it by force and not by study. And Saddam also started a number of universities himself, including a very new one in Tikrit, his home town, and an honors university that he carved out of the University of Baghdad, named (it will come as no surprise) "Saddam University."

These universities, commissions, and institutes are all public institutions, not private. There were, once, superb private prep schools and universities in Iraq—including the prep school I mentioned, Baghdad College, and a university, Al-Hikmat University, both run by the Jesuits. But the Ba'ath Party closed them down in the late Sixties, and they've never been allowed to reopen. At one time these were bastions of American-style liberal education in Iraq, and the most well-spoken professionals I met in any field in Iraq were often products these institutions, usually Baghdad College. But no one under fifty remembers them much any more.

Even though some fields had artificial quotas limiting the number of women to no more than 40 percent of any class, Saddam actually did much to encourage women to enter college. Thousands upon thousands of young men were lost in fighting Saddam's wars, and women were needed to take their place in the ranks of the various professions. But perhaps most importantly, Saddam dampened the role of religion and religious fervor in the universities. Women were not segregated from men, head scarves—the hijab—were never mandated, and the universities were basically secular enclaves in a society that kept sectarianism, especially Shiite sectarianism, as much in the background as possible.

To be sure, under Saddam, the universities had very little, both materially and intellectually. Academic contact with most of the non-Arab intellectual world ended long before we entered Iraq. Faculty who might once have studied in Great Britain or on the Continent or in the US now received all their training in Iraqi universities. Despite the fact that Saddam respected and admired certain publicly important fields—especially, as I've noted, science, medicine, and engineering—learning from the outside world in these intrinsically developmental and progressive fields pretty much ceased after the invasion of Kuwait and the imposition of sanctions over a dozen years before.

For example, I visited the laboratory of the Veterinary College at the University of Baghdad, perhaps the most prestigious of all Iraq's veterinary schools. There, in one room, were all the vials of medicines and bottles of chemicals needed for classroom instruction handsomely lined up on the shelves. And each was empty. I saw one bottle with, at best, a tablespoon of brown sludgy residue at the bottom. The blue label on the side read, "Expires June 1980."

Every field suffered. I was told that at the College of Law at Basra University the average number of new volumes added yearly to their library collection over the last twenty years was— eight. Academic journals had long ago ceased coming into Iraq. In some universities, periodicals from the Fifties and Sixties were the core of a faculty's research collection, kept under lock and key in glass display cases in the libraries. At the University of Tikrit, which Saddam proudly had built not long before the liberation, there is a spacious library connected to the Law College. My guess is the rooms had enough shelving for 5,000 books. My sense is it actually had fewer than eighty. And some of these "books" are merely Xeroxes of Xeroxes of old texts, hand-stitched together.

Yet, despite what little they had, after the war they all had less. There was no stomach for talking about it around the CPA, but the looting that followed the war probably did as much damage to the infrastructure of the universities as the ravages of three decades of Ba'ath Party rule. However many books the library at the Arts College in Baghdad once had, after the war they had none. I toured Mustansiriya University in September of 2003, right after I arrived in Iraq. Vandals had taken everything. Desks, air conditioners, chalkboards, chalk, doors, windows and window frames ... They pulled the wiring out of the walls and ripped out plumbing fixtures. And what they couldn't use—like books—they burned.

Much of what was taken was for use or sale. The wire stripped out of the walls had a good market in Iran, I was told. But so much of what happened was simply wanton destruction. I gather there's something in the human heart that thrills at destruction. But I guess I never understood the degree to which young men, or at least some young men, love to see things burn. Virtually every university outside of Kurdistan was torched, at least in part. From Basra to Mustansiriya and then further north, students returned to school to sit on dirt floors in charred classrooms.

None of this was because of the war. I don't know of one building that was seriously hurt in the bombing during the war by our forces on any campus. But after the war the looting began. We all saw it on TV. It hit not just the universities, but all the schools, all hospitals, virtually all public buildings, and not a few private homes. "Freedom is untidy," Secretary Rumsfeld declared, in a truly unfortunate use of words. This was not freedom; this was the ravaging of the whole country by marauders that turned a country on the skids to rubble.

The military, I am told, was under orders not to interfere. Except for the Oil Ministry, which was guarded, our soldiers stood on the sidelines as a whole country was pillaged by their own criminals.

Please do not think that I am overstating or exaggerating the damage that was done. There is hardly a way to describe what the Iraqis, at least some of them, did to their own country. I never visited Detroit or South Central LA after the riots, but from what I've seen in pictures, it was of the same magnitude, though this time over virtually a whole country. As I noted before, the building that housed the Education and Higher

Education ministries was perhaps the most elegant building in Baghdad. For all the time I was in Iraq, and now still, it is an unusable burnt-out shell.

I have no theory on why we allowed it to happen. The Iraqis, however, have many. None of them are credible, yet all of them seem believable to the victims: The Kuwaitis who entered Iraq as translators for the Americans did it in retaliation for Saddam's war on them. Or: Saddam's people did it, in order to burn records and destroy all evidence of their crimes. Or: The thirty thousand criminals that Saddam let out of Abu Ghraib prison just before the war did it in cahoots with the Americans in order for the Americans to control Iraq more effectively. Why else would all the oil facilities have been protected from the looting while everything else went under if not because the oil was what America was really there for while Iraqis were left to suffer? For whatever reason it happened—and perhaps we really did think that the marauders actually were Iraqis taking back what belonged to them or that freedom really is "untidy"—the looting turned vast swaths of the most civilized parts of Iraq to smoldering rubble. It was in this way that what began as a liberation started to be seen as an invasion.

Because of the inability, or, rather, the unwillingness, to stop the looting, many Iraqis began to think that there was something else afoot. Maybe America was there, they thought, for the oil; maybe we really were interested in occupying them to increase our wealth, or to solidify our military power. They certainly thought that our professed care for them and their futures was hollow. And then, when we in Higher Education (and in other "non-essential" sectors as well) told them that we were sent to help but that we had no money, no budgets, and no goods or services at our command, we soon lost much credibility. Young Iraqis, who at first were more than happy to use the word "liberation," now talked about the American "occupation." Their elders were more understanding, but suspicion, then antagonism, then hatred began to grow among students—not all, but many— everywhere. We were not there to help, we were there to rule.

As I noted before, something else was happening. Religious fanaticism was growing daily on campus. It was nothing at first. Then professors and staff started to report being harassed. South of Baghdad, in the southern Shiite areas, male students started to protest mixed classes with females. Even where these classes were segregated, female students were told to cover themselves completely in class, and some professors were told to segregate their classes or cancel them altogether. The secularization of past years had opened up virtually all courses to women—they had studied the same subjects and shared the same classes. Now students and teachers were being brutalized and killed amid calls for a re-segregation of the sexes at college.

In some of the universities south of Baghdad, radical students were supported by sectarian militias. At the University of Kut it was credibly reported that the university treasurer, a woman, had been a week late with paychecks and student subsidies. So students and the militia had her taken out and publicly whipped. There was nothing the local administration or the Ministry could do in such cases, nothing the professors dared to do, and nothing we Americans could do either.

While young men took the lead in these matters, the women soon followed. Even those who did not wear the hijab to cover their hair soon thought it best to do so. Some no doubt did it from growing conviction, a conviction that religion and modesty demanded a less open demeanor. Even Christian women, whose hair was often quite stylish, took to covering themselves, though they did so for prudential reasons—or, not to put too fine a point on it, out of fear.

This "re-Islamicization" of the campuses was, as I've noted, spearheaded by students, especially radicalized male students. On some campuses, students dressed in black, the garb of Sadr's Mahdi Army. Intimidating their fellow students and the university's faculty, certainly not studying, was their main concern. Of the three dozen or so professors killed in the time I was in Iraq, my guess is that almost all of them were killed by their students. Most were murdered for political reasons: they were suspected or known to be old-line Ba'athists. This happened to a former president of Baghdad University and to a dean at Mosul University. A few were actually killed for academic reasons—they gave bad grades or flunked out a particular favorite. But increasingly professors would be killed, and many more harassed, for reasons of religious purity.

In order to give students a voice in university matters, the Ministry thought it necessary to rebuild the Student Union—the official organization representing all students. On the majority of campuses, however, women were told they would be hurt if they tried to run for office or vote. Slates not approved by student religious groups were told they could not run. Students who dared to defy these warnings were threatened with death by other students. In the end, the Ministry cancelled student union elections on almost every campus—elections distorted because of force, fraud, and intimidation were no way to teach students the blessings of liberty.[1]

Only in Mosul, where the president had not been elected by the faculty but was appointed under the authority of General Petraeus and the political council he put together, was the university administration itself hard-line intolerant. The windows of the female student dorms were all boarded up except for a bit of light allowed to come through the very top, Christian women students reported being told to cover their heads by administrators, public fraternization between the sexes was forbidden, and private fraternization meant courting death. Probably because of all this, Mosul was the only university outside of the Kurdish area where the students were almost

---

[1]Predictably, the many campuses of the technical institutes—the vocational and technical colleges rather than the academic universities—were able, by and large, to conduct their elections without incident. Here were students learning to become electricians and carpenters and dental hygienists; they had no time to worry about how others should be leading their lives; they wanted to learn a trade and get ahead in this world. Which again proved that one of the best ways to undermine fanaticism is to promote work and industry, and give citizens the possibility of a better and more prosperous life. Or, as Samuel Johnson once said, rarely is a person more innocently employed than in the making of money.

Remembering that the technical institutes were among the worst hit with the looting after the war (after all, they had tools and metals and lumber: things quite worth stealing), our inability to get Congress or USAID or anyone to help these schools in any way has to count as one of the Coalition's greatest failures.

completely on the side of liberality rather than repression. If the administration were for it, they would be against it.[2]

I asked one university president about what was clearly the growing intolerance of his student body. He was himself a model of sincere religious conviction coupled with a firm belief in science and intellectual freedom.[3] I shouldn't be overly worried, he cautioned me. The situation would right itself over time: Under Saddam, everyone knew his place. Even if they hated it, all Iraqis knew what was expected of them and what they had to do. But, with the coming of freedom, the deck was not only re-shuffled, it was thrown in the air. Adults were, often, better grounded, but students no longer had all their questions answered, and they were at sea. How they should live? What they should look up to? What was right and wrong? Right now the society was not giving them solid answers. But religion would give them answers. Religion could tell them how to think, how to live, and how to act. So, in order to escape the void, they turned to Islam—and the sterner and stricter it was, the more it gave clear and unwavering guidance.

In time, even this would pass, he assured me. "Keep giving us computers. Keep giving these students knowledge of the outside world. Let them see all that is out there. Then they'll moderate their ways. Understanding brings tolerance." Perhaps, I thought, perhaps. Perhaps his analysis of the void left by

---

[2]About eight months after I left Iraq, the papers reported that about 1500 Christian students quit the University of Mosul en masse to protest the growing Islamicization of that campus, still led by the university administration. For all the loose talk in the media about how de-Ba'athification was a bad idea, a failure, it quickly became apparent that Mosul, which was exempt from Bremer's de-Ba'athification order, had become the haven for both Sunni political extremists as well as Sunni religious hard-liners.

[3]He was a Sunni Muslim as well as a local businessman with a Ph.D. His vice president was a Christian. He insisted on a mixed staff of both Christians and Muslims, not only because he was tolerant but also because it made good business sense—this way Christians could man the university on Friday and Muslims on Sunday. It was because of this kind of practical leadership that his university, the University of Technology, was the first in all Baghdad to be completely rebuilt within a few short months after the looting, even though this was a place that the looters had stripped to the ground in the space of about four hours.

freedom in the souls of students, and their longing for answers, is true. This is why people at this age actually make good students—they long to know the real truth about important matters. But I still had my doubts, for in the contest between the subtle pleasures of knowledge and the heady joys of religious ideology and slogans, knowledge rarely wins.

Soon after the CPA was dissolved and our office left Iraq, the president fled the country, one step ahead of the students he worked so hard to liberate.

▲▼▲

There was much that we were able to accomplish for a while despite the growing fanaticism on campus. Little of this was in the area of infrastructure rebuilding or satisfying the physical needs of the campuses. As I will explain later, both Congress and the United States Agency for International Development (USAID) were worse than useless in helping us fix even the most glaring problems. Still, there were ways in which we worked to advance freedom of thought, speech, and inquiry in much of Iraq.

For example, under the previous regime, the Minister of Higher Education was chosen by and reported directly to Saddam. The presidents, vice presidents, and all the deans of the various colleges were also appointed, not on the basis of their scholarly competence but because of their political usefulness. It would not be odd to see a dean without a degree in the field of the department he controlled—perhaps without a degree at all. His job wasn't to lead the faculty but to spy on it, and keep it politically in line.[4]

-------------------

[4]Suhail, our Christian translator, wanted desperately to get to America. So I asked him to put together his résumé. He was hoping for an academic position, though he had no Ph.D. He lacked a doctorate because, he said, he would have had to join the Ba'ath Party to make that move. I also noted that he had no publications to his name. He said no, though in a way he did. When I asked what he meant, he told me that he had two published articles that he wrote as an MS student (one widely known and quite important in the field of engineering, he said), but that his dean, who knew nothing about the field, took them from him and published them under his own name. I told him that, if it was true, to put it down since that made his résumé certainly more interesting. He did as I suggested, though he thought it was awkward to push it since everyone in Iraq, he said, had his work stolen by his superiors.

What the Coalition did first, under Drew Erdmann and Steve Curda before I arrived, was to dismiss all high university officials under the de-Ba'athification policy and hold elections for these offices on each campus. These may well have been the first free elections held in Iraq in decades, and it happened at the universities.

By and large, the universities chose well. The new president of Mustansiriya University, for instance, gave a talk to his faculty at the beginning of his tenure telling them that the era of intellectual repression was over, that they were now allowed to read and write and lecture freely and without constraint. They needed no permission from him or anyone else to teach their specialties as they saw fit.

In addition to this, Ambassador Bremer issued an administrative order (Order # 8), declaring that the right of professors and administrators to travel to conferences and symposia and academic meetings was no longer to be hindered. In a sense, a new birth of freedom had taken place on the universities, and the professors were its first recipients. I'm told that at the election of their own president and other officials, the professors on some campuses cried. Even if students found themselves confused by their new liberty, the academic community as a whole was overwhelmingly grateful.

This is not to say that all was about to go smoothly. Because of what I can only describe as the result of one of the most seriously misguided political moves of the occupation, who would be the minister of each sector was decided by horse trading among the members of the newly formed Iraqi Governing Council. Contrary to every measure of common sense and decent government, this Council was filled not with Iraqis from different walks of life, not with people whose interests transcended narrow partisanship or sectarianism to encompass the general good of the whole society. No, the Governing Council was made up of the leaders, and often the firebrands, of the various parties and sects into which Iraq was thought to be divided. Instead of a council that would help unify Iraq, the Coalition (with strong direction from the UN) hobbled together a Council of twenty-five partisans and gave them control over ministry appointments.[5] Since there were twenty-five ministries, each council member was given one sector in which to appoint the minister. Sadly, the Ministry of Higher Education and Scientific Research fell to the representative of the Sunni Islamic Party, Dr. Moshen Hameed.[6]

The person Dr. Hameed was given the authority by the Council to appoint was an American-educated professor of petroleum engineering, a member of the faculty of the University of Baghdad, and a fervent Sunni and party man named Zeiad Abdul Razzaq Aswad.

Dr. Zeiad was appointed minister just days before I arrived in Iraq in September of 2003. His first order of business was to dismiss all the presidents of all the universities newly elected under Coalition authority. And my first act was to countermand that order and, with Lieutenant Colonel Curda steeling me along the way, forcing the new minister to back down. All this was, of course, terra incognita; Curda and I had no idea where our authority lay. Then again, neither did Zeiad. But we were insistent that dismissing all presidents flew in the face of the will of the universities that had elected their own officers, and flew in the face of the Coalition's authority to govern Iraq until sovereignty was handed back as well. So Zeiad issued a second executive order retracting his original order, though he couldn't admit that he was doing it under American pressure but, rather, "for security reasons."

If we could claim to have won the first round in our attempts to liberate the universities from a revival of Stalinesque autocracy, we lost the second. Despite all his false promises that we would work together in helping and governing the universities, and his agreement that no action significantly affecting

---

[5]I will have a lot more to say about the Governing Council and the careless way we set up the political life of the new Iraq in the chapter entitled "Bringing Iraq to Democracy."

[6]The Sunni Islamic Party (SIP) will later more often be called the "Iraqi Islamic Party," though it is fully a Sunni organization. It is an offshoot, I'm told, of the Muslim Brotherhood out of Egypt with ties to the Wahabbis in Saudi Arabia. It was a leader in the Sunni boycott of the elections on January of 2005, though it decided not to fight against the ratification of the new constitution later that year.

the universities would happen without our consulting together, Zeiad then, on his own authority, dismissed the president of the University of Baghdad and appointed a member of his own department—and party—in his place. If he, on his own, could make and break the head of Iraq's premier university, then he could do most anything. And all the other presidents knew this and were on notice.

Dr. Zeiad did this, I'm sure, partly to regain his authority. But the word on the street was that he also did it for both party and religious reasons—that the person he dismissed wouldn't go along with establishing or re-establishing a Sunni religious center on campus. I couldn't get any of the other presidents to discuss this directly, because now, in no small way, the new birth of freedom from party autocracy seemed at an end. Talking about it would be simply imprudent.

We could have, and should have, reversed the minister's order. The person dismissed was Dr. Sami Mudhaffer, perhaps the leading academic scientist in all of Iraq. There was a rumor that he came close to getting a Nobel Prize years before. He was clearly the most prominent of all the university presidents, and had had the backing and affection of the great majority of his faculty. He would, with the demise of the Governing Council in June of 2004, himself become the next Minister of Education—that is, minister of all primary and secondary schooling in Iraq. And, in 2005, he became the Minister of Higher Education itself.

But it was clear that Ambassador Bremer had no desire for us to push the matter. While he had no use for our minister, he clearly wanted to have generally workable relations with the Iraqi Governing Council he had set up, as well as with Dr. Hameed, Zeiad's patron. Bremer was hoping that pressure within the academic community, perhaps pressure from other members of the IGC who had high regard for Dr. Mudhaffer, would lead to a reversal. But he didn't want the Coalition to be so heavy-handed as to have us reverse a duly appointed Iraqi minister a second time. Still, as I said, this was a clear mistake, since it tended to bless the re-Stalinization of the ministry and cowed the rest of the university leadership.

I don't think any of us fully anticipated the reaction—or, more specifically, the lack of any public reaction—of the other university presidents to this episode. To us Americans it seemed like cowardice. Privately, the other presidents pushed hard for us to get the minister replaced, or at least overruled. They all prized their elections and the good amount of autonomy from central control they had enjoyed before the naming of the new minister. I told them I would stand with them in confronting the new minister, if only they would stand with me. They agreed. The president who had given the speech to his faculty about independence of mind and spirit told me he would be the first to speak at the next meeting of the university presidents and to demand explanations from the minister. But, when the meeting came, somehow he missed it.

Except for the almost brazen Kurdish presidents, who had already been in power for years and were carry-overs from before the war, none of them would speak out. The Kurds simply made it clear that if the minister attempted to oust them, he would no more be obeyed than if the king of Siam had suggested they leave. And Zeiad, knowing this to be true, never challenged them. But the other presidents, all new—but all with three decades of living under of autocratic rule—were certainly intimidated. It was not cowardice as much as history, the residue of thirty-five years of tyranny, that made these leaders hesitant. And so, with our inaction and their hesitations, democracy and academic freedom lost round two.

Our office made it our mission that we would find other ways now to support the autonomy of the universities, shore up the position of the various presidents, and undermine the now growing autocracy of the ministry. For example, under Drew Erdmann, my predecessor, the presidents met every few weeks to help set policy for the universities. Now that there was an Iraqi minister in place, it was he who convened the presidents. But we made it clear that we considered the presidents and not the minister acting on his own to be the true policy-making body for the universities. I reminded them of that at every meeting, much to Zeiad's visible displeasure. With Ambassador Bremer's active support, we called the presidents together periodically, without the minister, at the Ambassador's villa within the Green Zone, to discuss their needs and policy directions for the universities. Since I was always the one who would assemble them, I was the de facto head of their organization. But two months before we as the Coalition Provisional Authority were to dissolve, I called them together to elect their own head. I did this happily, since they needed to govern themselves. They, however, still feared the power of the minister, and everyone nominated to the post immediately declined the honor. Finally, they nominated the one president who wasn't there that day, and elected him.

Perhaps the most important thing we did was effectively to remove the minister as the sole arbiter of who would be president, vice president, or dean at any of the universities. We got the minister to agree to three documents that put the election of presidents and vice presidents in the hands of selection committees on each campus, with the minister having merely the power to make the selection from a final field of candidates. With the selection of deans he no longer had even that authority, but was simply to "certify" the selection if all procedures were followed. Finally, the minister no longer had the authority to fire presidents at will; that authority was now shared with the whole board of university presidents.

Whether Zeiad agreed to these measures because he realized that our stay, and therefore our sway, would soon come to an end, or because he knew from Hameed that if he didn't agree to these procedures Ambassador Bremer would decree them as administrative orders in his own name, I do not know. But he agreed to them, and followed them, for the remainder of his tenure, which, happily, ended a few weeks before our time was up and we left Iraq for good. Later, with the coming of Allawi's government and the naming of a new minister, Zeiad, I was told, fled Iraq.

▲▼▲

It soon became apparent that the real threat to the universities was more than the autocracy of the Minister. Unless something were done to counter the growing tide of student religious fanaticism, we could have liberalized the ministry and democratized the administration of the universities all we wanted and still have lost the universities to intellectual and academic repression. Working with the CPA legal office, our office cobbled together what amounted to a Bill of Rights for the universities. I presented this Bill of Rights to the university presidents meeting in Erbil, in Kurdish Iraq, in March of 2004. It was unanimously adopted, and orders were given to print it up as three-foot-tall posters and pasted on all campus walls. I thought it was a good thing to do; most of the university presidents thought it was a *great* thing to do. Now all students could read what rights they had, and what obligations were imposed on them, and if they needed something to be passionate about, these new-found rights and freedoms could be it.

The Bill of Rights declared that the goal of higher education was to promote a broader capacity for thinking, accepting the opinion of others, and encouraging the search for the truth. It stated that there were rights to teaching, learning, writing, and publishing that could not be abridged. It secured a wide range of freedoms, from thought and belief all the way to "clothing"—i.e., the right to wear or not wear a veil. Most importantly, it stated that any act by anyone "which might threaten or coerce others to join a religion, sect, or political ideology, directly or indirectly, is prohibited and will subject the offenders to the highest university disciplinary actions including expulsion."

For a short time—a very short time—the Declaration had an immediate and salutary effect everywhere except perhaps in Mosul, with its autocratic Sunni administration. Under the Declaration, open student union elections were soon held on a number of campuses. Students who assaulted two professors in Baghdad were threatened with expulsion and quickly apologized and asked to be re-instated. Students now knew—and could point to—their rights, and administrators now felt empowered to enforce academic freedom, respect, and toleration even against the forces of religious intolerance. At least, now, there was something in writing.

But fanaticism was not to be deterred with words, and the worst elements of repression quickly rose again, especially in those universities south of Baghdad where Sadr's Mahdi Army was strongest, and in the west, where the Sunni insurgency controls all. For a short time it was true—the Declaration gave everyone in the universities an understanding of what an institution dedicated to the life of the mind is *supposed* to look like. But only for a short time.

Forgive me if I take a moment to reflect on this matter further. Although all of us in academia are great believers in the power of words and ideas, we'd be foolish not to recognize their limitations. To go back to a theme I expressed in the first chapter, the allure of fanaticism is strong, usually far stronger even than the love of life or the fear of death. Some of it's connected to the overcoming of death—the religious fanatic often assures himself of his eternal life through his contempt of earthly death. Love of life is as nothing when compared to the love of eternal life.

But some parts of fanaticism are simply connected to the desire to live life at its peak—to devote one's self, give one's self, fully and completely to something higher: God, country, tribe, friends, an idea, a principle, another person. But, just as we tend to have an idealistic view of religion, we also seem to have an idealistic view of devotion, that is, of love. We think of all love as good. But the worst crimes have always been committed by the greatest lovers—those devoted to their God, their race, their religion, their nation, their notion ... Some love is wonderful—it takes us out of ourselves, it connects us to others, and directs to us work for their welfare. Without love of one's neighbors and regard for their welfare, maintaining a democracy in Iraq will be next to impossible. But the reason one can't argue with terrorists is because their fanaticism is a species of love, a dangerous and destructive love, and love, devotion, are hardly rational things. And while we may hope to find ways of deflecting it, we have little hope of eradicating it from human affairs because it's not amenable to persuasion or argument or calculation.

▲▼▲

I discuss in a later chapter how deep the respect for specialization and for research is within the Iraqi higher education system. But the downside of this is not simply a kind of disdain for a broad, general, liberal education, but a disdain for teaching as well. Faculty lecture to large classes; rote learning and memorization are all students are used to. Engaging in a discussion, questioning what's being offered, students interacting constructively with other students in class—all these are rare to nonexistent in Iraqi classrooms. So the universities labor under a double problem. In seeing themselves as primarily research institutions, they slight teaching; yet, having been cut off for so long from the outside world, they are woefully behind in research and scholarship.

There were a number of ways out of this, but with a Minister more interested in controlling the minds of his students and faculty than in freeing them, and a faculty (as I will later discuss) more interested in privilege, pay, and position than in teaching, every progressive idea met with difficulty. For example, of the twenty public universities in Iraq, perhaps eight, including the three in Kurdistan, could qualify as reliably useful research universities. We discussed turning the remaining twelve into solid teaching institutions, with their emphasis on undergraduate instruction, and leaving the other eight to perfect themselves as comprehensive universities with quality graduate programs. We were making some progress towards this end when word came that we would be dissolved come June 30. Without us as the goads, all motion along this front stopped, and now even the smallest and most minor of the universities will insist on having its own law school and medical school and college of engineering.

Moreover, admission to university was based on a model that was perfectly rational, perfectly bureaucratic, and perfectly totalitarian. All students go to the university to specialize in something, to become a practitioner in one certain area. By and large this means that you do not choose a university that seems to offer a program that you're interested in, as one might in America. You do not find "the right college for you," one that meets your abilities and interests. Indeed, your interests have almost nothing to do with the case. Where you go to school, and what you will study, depends on what score you achieve on your qualifying exams when you leave high school. There's no saying "I want to be a doctor." If your high school grades and the results of your qualifying exams are excellent, you will be offered a place in a medical college. If they are less so, perhaps you can go to a school of engineering or study science. The lower the grades, the less "valuable" the career you will be offered to study. You pick the colleges you wish to attend, put them in order, then your grades tell you what program at these universities you will be accepted into. Yes, a truly bright student could always aim "low"—you could always turn down an admission to a medical college to study law, or agriculture, or history, or language—but the reverse is not true: No one with a low grade could aspire to a field above his rank. You can't say, "I will study and work twice as hard as the next guy and finish medical school." You will not *go* to medical school. This not only means that those who might have made good practitioners in certain fields if they had only been given the chance will be stymied, it also means that there are any number of unhappy doctors and dentists and engineers in Iraq, people who would have made fine poets and linguists and farmers and veterinarians if only they were allowed to follow their interests and aptitudes and not their grades.

There was, during our stay in Iraq, some hope for change in this regard as interest in "American-style" education—with its free choice of majors and minors and use of electives—grew. But getting any American agency or funding source—from Congress or the Defense Department or State or USAID—to see that help along these lines was a central part of Iraqi liberation was impossible. Only the Fulbright scholarship program, which was reestablished after a hiatus of over a dozen years, said to Iraqis that in American universities we prize literature, history, philosophy, and languages as well as the social sciences, and we would give scholarships to students who wished to study those subjects here.[7]

▲▼▲

Nothing in a country exists in a vacuum, unaffected by the culture that surrounds it. Despite the fact that we in the academy often think of ourselves as having a distinct mission detached from the ideas and outlooks of ordinary citizens and everyday life, no one on the outside would ever mistake our educational institutions as anything other than American. Nor would anyone mistake the nature, characteristics, and outlook of Iraqi professors and administrators as anything other than Iraqi ones, shaped, sorry to say, by thirty-five years of totalitarian rule combined with centuries of rank and status and privilege. For example, take the fact that every senior professor I met, *every* one, complained about his pay. I know, this hardly sounds different from professors anywhere. Yet, faculty pay in Iraq is actually very good by almost any internal standard. With threats to go on strike and shut down the universities, Iraqi professors had managed to get the Governing Council to place professors at the very highest three levels of the new national Iraqi pay scale.[8] This meant that a full professor was paid more than national judges, more than physicians who managed hospitals, more than anyone except high-ranking ministers and members of the Governing Council, whose salaries were supremely high by

---

[7]Thanks to the tireless efforts of one of the deputies in the office, Ambassador Joseph Ghougassian, we managed to send twenty-five Iraqis to the States in 2004–2005. However, the officials of the Iraqi universities repeatedly downplayed the significance of these grants—"a spit in the ocean," as one of them said to me, referring to the fact that twenty-five students out of over 375,000 was nothing. And one university president was enraged that it was a scholarship for "second-raters"—open to students in the humanities and social sciences but not in technology or engineering or computer science. But Iraqi students by the thousands flocked to take the exams and write the required essays, each one knowing his or her chances were slim. Such was the draw not only of studying in America, but also of leaving an increasingly dangerous situation and a stifling educational system.

[8]When I asked one university president what would really be the result of a nationwide faculty strike, he immediately answered, "Happy students."

any standard. But, then again, they were the ones who set the scale.

So, what was the complaint? Not that the pay wasn't high enough, but that there was an insufficient spread between the lower teaching ranks and the higher ones. Full professors now made easily twice what they had made under Saddam—but lecturers and assistant professors were now making three times what they made before, and the gap was now seen, from the top, as too narrow. When I asked one full professor whether he would prefer that we raise his salary or lower that of those below him, his candid answer was—"It doesn't matter; either way."

I've used the word "Stalinesque" to describe the political organization of the Ministry under Saddam, but the word applies to much of Iraqi culture in general and to the character of higher education in particular. Iraq was both a fully socialistic country under Saddam, as well as a fully hierarchical and differentiated one as well. If you can imagine a thoroughly socialist nation—a nation of food baskets for all, free education and health care for all, free electricity, subsidized housing, and virtually free fuel[9]—with hierarchy, rank, and privilege throughout, you will have a good vision of Iraqi society.

Still, as I was saying, the complaint over pay was constant. With every campus visit, I would gather faculty and staff together and ask the same question—What are the most pressing needs at this university? I don't believe I ever once heard an answer that involved students, at least not undergraduate students. Student dormitories, for example, were everywhere dilapidated, if not filthy. Never once did a professor or administrator talk about upgrading them. In some places student lavatories were more repulsive than the worst gas station bathrooms you could imagine. No one cared. No one even seemed to see that the

---

[9]Gasoline was under Saddam, under the CPA, and later under the control of the new Iraqi government, among the cheapest on earth, somewhere around 3 cents a liter while I was there. But, of course, Iraq refines very little oil itself: it exports oil and imports gasoline. With the money it makes from its exports, it then subsidizes the cost of the now imported gasoline so that it is effectively free. A more wasteful and irrational system would be hard to invent.

living conditions for female students, who after liberation were attending university in greater numbers, were so squalid that it was probably the major cause of female students leaving.[10] The answer to the question "What does this campus need?" seemed never to involve students—but it always involved the readjustment of faculty pay, and sometimes the procuring of new computers for them and laboratory and scientific equipment for their graduate students.

When the higher ranks of the professorate would complain to me that they wanted more money, I would give them the standard American answer, "Why not work for it? Publish a book, teach an extra class, tutor, consult." And the answer back was always the same: We are not to be paid on the basis of our work, but on the basis of our position. We demand higher pay on the basis of who we are, not on the strength of what we do.

All this worked to the great detriment of undergraduate education. Full professors had graduate students, they supervised Ph.D. theses, and they taught very little. Lecturers and assistant professors were the ones who more generally took care of undergraduate teaching. After all, undergraduates were just a step removed from high school students, and teaching high school was a lowly occupation.

Once, during my stay in Iraq, Anne Veneman, then US Secretary of Agriculture, was making a trip to Iraq. I had helped arrange for her to visit the College of Agriculture of Baghdad University. The college is to the west of Baghdad, near Abu Ghraib prison in fact, and on the edge of the Sunni Triangle,

---

[10]Our office fought mightily to have the Iraqi government heavily increase its budget for higher education, and we were more than somewhat successful. But the majority of the millions extra we managed to secure from the Finance ministry was earmarked to pay the salaries of professors and staff. One might think, moreover, that improving conditions for girls and women to benefit from higher education would have been a priority for US aid. But, it wasn't. We could spend a million dollars to bring twenty-five Fulbright students to the States (which was good), and have USAID give almost $25,000,000 to five American university consortia to begin a few scattered "partnerships" in Iraq, but no agency of the government could find anything at all to improve the lives of students and facilitate their education.

but the area was safer then than it is now. I went out a few days ahead to help arrange the visit. The College of Agriculture at one time had close ties to the United States. The University of Arizona had, in the Fifties, helped them get on their feet, sent them material and equipment, and even sent professors to teach. There are still two palm trees in the center of the campus called by everyone there the "Arizona Palms," the remnants of a variety of palm sent to them a half-century before. In the stairway of the main administration building are photos from the 1950s of the Arizona professors who came and helped. The college still keeps alive the memory of the kindness of Americans fifty years later.

But the College is, today, in total disarray, with piles of trash everywhere. Students would read the day's papers, and then throw them to the wind. When I suggested that the Secretary of Agriculture might be more disposed to help if she saw that the school kept its property in good condition, they complained that there was not enough money to hire janitors and custodians. When I suggested that students might be encouraged to pick up after themselves, I was told that students were there to study, not to clean up; they were students, not janitors. Then I suggested that maybe they, the deans and professors, might have an interest in keeping the place up—and I bent down and picked up some papers thrown on the lawn. You would think I had asked them to become prostitutes. I later found out that they were scandalized that a Senior Advisor would, literally, stoop so low as to make himself a janitor. I was constantly reminded of the difficulty of making any progress in a system where honor counted for more than service.

The character of higher education was Stalinesque in another way. While assured pay and hierarchy might have dampened any desire among the professional class to work harder to get ahead, the memory of the severity of punishments under thirty-five years of totalitarian rule dampened any normal initiative. During this same visit to the College of Agriculture, I had a professor come to me to sign a paper authorizing the transfer of a woman student into his class from another class. "Did the other professor approve?" "Yes." "Does the dean approve?" "Yes." "Does the student wish to transfer?" "Yes." "OK, then do it, just do it. Why do you need my signature to transfer one student out of 375,000 from one class to another?" "Please, sir," came the reply, "your signature will mean that, if a question ever arose, that you yourself had authorized it." In other words, that if anything went wrong, all blame could be shunted to the American.

All these cultural characteristics—the constant concern with rank, place, and honor, the culture of dependency that socialism engendered, the culture of fear and hesitation that despotism made—all had a serious educational effect. In the clearest possible way, it soon became apparent that higher education in Iraq existed more for professors than for students, and more for the perpetuation and improvement of certain select fields than for teaching.

In a strange way, this gave our team an audience. We preached an odd but intriguing gospel: that undergraduate education mattered, that there were effective ways of teaching that went beyond the lecture-memorize-repeat model, that students' questions should be encouraged and not suppressed . . .[11] Indeed, when I brought a delegation of university presidents, professors, and ministry officials to America in the Spring of 2004, the sight of students sitting around a seminar table, interacting with each other and with the professor in class, raising questions and working together towards common answers so intrigued the group that one president declared that he was going to go back and rip out all the desks and lecterns and put chairs and seminar tables in their place. It won't happen, and it probably shouldn't happen, at least not by fiat, but at least it was a sentiment in the right direction.

―――――――――――

[11]One American-trained professor of medicine told me, in an open meeting with all his peers present, that he was the only professor all in Iraq who taught his classes as an American would. When I asked him what he meant, he said that he was the only one he knew who allowed students to ask questions in class.

# FIVE

# Bringing Iraq to Democracy

While many Americans in Iraq talked almost daily about the coming of Iraqi democracy and its potentially grand future, the Iraqis themselves seemed far more apprehensive than we. When we spoke about the possibilities of bringing peace to Iraq, no one objected. When we spoke about making Iraq prosperous again, everyone was on our side. But when we spoke about "democracy," we didn't always have an audience. The oddest thing was that it was often the most educated, most thoughtful, and most pro-American Iraqis who seemed to be the most anxious.

Many of the Iraqi objectors to democracy actually made the same assumption that Americans made when they heard the word: Democracy means liberty, democracy means freedom. And many Iraqis of good will were, a year or more after liberation, getting nervous about freedom. With no person or institution visibly imposing order, the freedom we brought to Iraq was a freedom they saw bordering on chaos. On the streets of the cities there was little law and less order. Crime was rampant. Thefts, murders, kidnapping—all went unpunished. Old scores were settled. The looting immediately after the war, as I've noted, destroyed much of the country and demolished its most prominent and vital institutions. To have responded, as we did, with sentiments such as "freedom is messy," was to start freedom off on exactly the wrong foot. If democracy is another word for self-government, there were, on the streets of Iraq, among certain elements, precious little governing of the self.

It might be useful to understand that this was not the first time in Iraq that an autocrat was overthrown and a popular government proclaimed. On July 14, 1958, a military coup under the leadership of Brigadier Abdul-Karim Kassem overthrew the monarchy of King Faisal II. The young king and members of the royal family were killed, and their bodies were hanged by their feet outside the royal palace. The prime minister managed to escape, dressed as a woman. Soon, however, he too was captured, killed, and his body dragged behind the back of a car until all that remained of him was half a leg tied to a rope. With that, Iraq was proclaimed a republic.

Events such as these led some Iraqis I met to question whether their fellow citizens were ready for democratic rule. Or, to put it in another context: 1958 was not too long after the second election in America of Eisenhower over Adlai Stevenson. Yet who could even think it remotely possible that General Eisenhower would solidify his rule by killing Mr. Stevenson and dragging him behind a car?

Yet we must be clear. It's not that the Iraqis didn't want to be liberated from the horrors of Saddam. They most assuredly did. Nor is it that they had no interest in living their own lives by their own lights or even in governing themselves politically. While those whose minds are numbed by religious extremism might reject personal and public liberty in the name of submission to God's will, most Iraqis saw living their lives freely to be a truly desirable thing. Nonetheless, the coming of democracy seemed to imply the coming of even greater civic strife, and many good Iraqi citizens rightly pulled back from that. "We Iraqis need a leader, we need someone to punish the bad people and restore law and order." "We don't need more freedom," I'd sometimes hear Iraqis say, "we need less." A few even went so far as to say they wished for another Saddam. Not a brutal tyrant, but, still, a person who would restore some semblance of law, order, and peace to a people who now feared walking out at night.

Nevertheless, the very smartest Iraqis I met were concerned about the coming of democracy from exactly the opposite perspective. Their worries were not particularly about the breakdown of authority. They understood that no society exists for very long without authority, that chaos is always temporary. Nor was it that freedom was bad, or had bad consequences, and therefore democracy was bad for giving them freedom. No, it was those who most clearly understood that democracy doesn't always mean freedom, *those who understood that democracy in essence means majority rule and not necessarily liberty for all,* who were the most concerned about the future. And so, I must admit, was I.

▲▼▲

At this writing, Iraqis have gone to the polls three times—once to adopt the new constitution and twice to elect their national assembly and, from that, their prime ministers and presidents. These elections are touted by the Administration in America as partial proof of our "success" in Iraq. Yet, as I hope to show, the fact of elections proves nothing about what we all had hoped to gain in Iraq, namely liberty, pluralism and toleration, prosperity, and some modicum of peace. Elections may be a necessary condition for democracies to exist, but elections tell us nothing about whether the government so elected is good or bad, free or despotic, mild or furious, peaceful or warlike. There is no alchemy in either the word "elections" or "democracy" that changes the genocidal regime of Hitler or the fanatical Islamist rulers of today's Iran or the anti-Semitic and war-encouraging rants of the Palestinian Hamas from bad to good. As I remarked in the Preface, we cannot excuse murder and oppression just because murderers and oppressors are elected by the people rather than appointed, anointed, self-selected, or imposed.

Elections are a means, not an end. Even democracy is a means—a means, often the best means, of reigning in autocratic power, directing political authority towards the good of the whole, and securing the blessings of justice and liberty. But security, prosperity, equal justice, and liberty are the ends, the goals; elections and democracy are simply the means.

We Americans regularly conflate "democracy" and "liberty" together. The current administration will often talk about spreading freedom around the world; at other times it will talk about encouraging the growth of democracy. But, as we Americans once knew, liberty and democracy are not synonymous. There are democracies that are singularly unfree, and free countries that are not democracies. The trick is to get both of these goals—liberty and democracy—together. It would have done little for America's national interests, for world peace, for stability in the Middle East, or even for the interests of freedom-loving Iraqis, for the Coalition to have bled and died to overthrow a political tyranny to set the stage for a religious or ethnic tyranny to grow in its place. A democratically elected tyranny is little better than the tyranny of an unelected despot or party, and may be even more difficult to remedy.[1]

Let me approach it from another angle: I think I could be persuaded that my fellow neocons are right that, at some level, all people desire to be free.[2] We all desire to live our own lives, achieve our hopes, earn what we can through ability and luck, raise our families, and pursue our happiness as we see it. None of us believes that force imposed on us by bullies, goons, or tyrants is just. None of us wants to be a means to someone else's ends. But while I might be convinced that each of us desires to be free ourselves, I'm not certain we all want our *neighbors* to be equally free. The source of all democratic tyranny is the desire and ability of majorities to violate the rights and trample on

---

[1]"An *elective despotism* was not the government we fought for," as Jefferson commented in his *Notes on Virginia* (the emphasis is Jefferson's).

[2]We should not forget that many of those of a certain age whom we call "neoconservatives" began their political careers fighting for civil rights in the American South or working for the liberation of Eastern European countries from Soviet rule. Seeing first-hand the hardships and even death that American blacks, Hungarians, Czechs, and others suffered just to live freely helped lead to the lesson that surely the desire to be free is natural to all men. It is also a lesson that may well be false.

the interests of minorities, whether those minorities are racial, ethnic, economic, religious, or whatever. If the desire to be free is natural to mankind, so is the desire to oppress or control others. And a "bad" democracy simply changes the locus of power from one person or one group of persons to a popular majority.

"You Americans are so naïve," Suhail, our Iraqi Christian translator said to me one morning over breakfast. We were talking about the elections and about how they would almost surely result in a Shiite majority government dominated by the partisans of the Ayatollah al-Sistani. "You are so naïve. When you Americans hear the word 'democracy' you see respect and rights and liberty and toleration. When he [Sistani] hears the word 'democracy,' all he sees is power. And that's what you Americans are doing, giving power to a religious man who will put an end to all the freedoms you thought you were giving us, once he has the chance and the power."

I need to be pardoned if, like Suhail, I remain more skeptical of the Ayatollah al-Sistani and his partisans than so many of my colleagues in the Coalition. I do not believe that parties that demand that all public legislation be based on Islamic law as interpreted by Shiite imams are liberal. I do not believe that a religious leader who refused even once to meet with Ambassador Bremer, or any American, but would gladly meet with every anti-American antagonist and criminal, from Muqtada al-Sadr to Ahmed Chalabi, is a "moderate." I do not believe that the same Sistani who condemned the Interim Iraqi Constitution because it protected the rights of the Kurds and secured property rights to Jews should be thought of as terribly tolerant. Indeed, the very first time I heard, in all my months there, an anti-Semitic diatribe was from the Grand Ayatollah. One word from Sistani might prevent the killing of journalists and Western civilians in Basra, stop the frightened exodus of Christians from all of Southern Iraq, and restrain the imposition of sectarian dogmatism now rolling over Iraq's schools and universities. There is no such word.[3]

---

[3]"History," Jefferson once wrote, "furnishes no example of a priest-ridden people maintaining a free civil government." Different context today, but I'm afraid the same principle.

But there's a larger political point that Suhail understood, a point I had made to Ambassador Bremer's office when he asked us our views on the handover of all political authority to the Iraqis by June 30, 2004. Then I wrote: "If you're asking our view on the transfer of sovereignty, my answer is [exceedingly] pessimistic. Thirty years of tyranny do terrible things to a people. It breeds a culture of dependency; it breaks the spirit of civic responsibility; it forces people to fall back upon tight-knit familial, ideological or sectarian groups for safety and support.... Freedom, democracy, and rights are not magic words. They do not change a culture overnight, or in eight months. The transfer of sovereignty will bring about some form of 'democracy.' But a liberal democracy, with real notions of liberty, equality and open opportunity—without strongmen or sectarian or sectional oppression—well, I think that's doubtful."

If I hadn't been known as the most pessimistic senior advisor before I wrote this, I surely earned that title after this memo. Yet I remained less pessimistic than most of the worried Iraqis that I knew. Then again, unlike my Iraqi friends, I wouldn't have to live under the coming regime.

Those words were painful to write to the front office, since everyone knew we were under orders from the White House to hand over sovereignty to the Iraqis by June 30, 2004. It didn't matter that the Iraqis might be no more ready for the responsibilities of democratic citizenship at that point than they were ready to defend themselves without our military help. No matter, we had boxed ourselves in: We talked all the time about how we were there to give them the blessings of democracy, and the Ayatollah Sistani said that he and his people were ready for the vote—indeed, he demanded we give them the vote, and the power. So we turned over sovereignty to a caretaker Iraqi government and promised elections by January 30, 2005. Ready or not.

The reasons for worry stemmed, in part, from the fractured nature of Iraqi society. Iraq is not, as commentators always like to point out, "one" country. There is, first of all, the split between the Shiite majority and the Sunni minority. There is the further split between Arab Iraqis and Kurdish Iraqis, the Kurds being a people distinct in blood, heritage, language, and traditions from the Arabs, though still Muslim. The Kurds, moreover, are predominantly Sunni, thus giving Iraq a religious split of, roughly, 60 percent Shi'a and 35 percent Sunni.[4] But there's another division that is just as important and, in some contexts, more important than the religious or ethnic breakdown—that is, the division between more or less religious Muslims and more or less secular Muslims.

From the beginning, America's hopes for democratic and free government in Iraq depended on moderate, more secular Iraqis acting as the balance between religious fundamentalists on either side and as a counterweight to both Kurdish and Arab nationalism. If all there are in Iraq are Shiite and Sunni extremists, or Kurdish and Arab nationalists, each pursuing its agenda at the expense of the other, then Iraq cannot be one democratic country.

As I noted in the first chapter, Saddam did the world a favor by promoting secularism at the expense of sectarianism. This was changing towards the end, when Saddam thought he needed to portray himself as also a man of God. So he started a campaign of great mosque building; he put Koranic verses into the flag in his own handwriting; and he closed the local brewery, which, I had heard, he himself owned. Nonetheless, because it had always been a threat, religious fanaticism of all

---

[4]Christians and other religious sects make up only a small minority of Iraqis, perhaps somewhere around 5 percent, though intolerant Shi'a religious fundamentalism in the south is now systematically pushing many Christians into neighboring countries, especially Jordan and Syria. Oddly enough, given their interaction elsewhere in the world, I could observe absolutely no friction whatever between Orthodox and Catholic Christians. They intermarry; they worship regularly in one another's churches. For example, Suhail was born and baptized a Catholic, married in an Orthodox wedding to an Orthodox bride, goes to Orthodox services yet is a deacon in the local Catholic church and sends his children to the Catholic school, though they are technically baptized as Orthodox. There had been a very old Anglican community in Baghdad, and I had heard of some Protestant religious activity up north, though Protestants have always been few and far between in Iraq. (The ones up north must have been Baptists, since one Kurdish university official told me that he liked the Baptists he knew a lot. They were just like Muslims, he said. "How?" you might ask. "Because, they shouldn't dance, but they do. And they shouldn't drink, but they do. Just like us.")

stripes was suppressed under his reign, secular professionalism rewarded, and religious toleration generally encouraged.

It was this non-sectarian, non-ideological professional-ism—people actually seeing themselves first as architects, engi-neers, professors, or doctors rather than as Shi'a first or Sunni first, or Arab, Kurd, or Turkoman first—that we in the CPA des-perately needed to encourage if democracy with liberty for all was ever to take permanent hold in Iraq.

But, to be totally honest about it, this is not what we did. Sure, in all public statements, all public meetings, we talked about one Iraq with one democratic future. I was at meetings where university heads would say that they wanted no more of this divisive talk about hatreds between factions—they were all Iraqis now fighting for one future, one undivided Iraq—and Ambassador Bremer would thank the speaker and congratulate him for his sentiments, as did we all. Yet when it came time to put together the Iraqi Governing Council, to give the most sig-nificant example, the CPA, with UN prodding, did not put together a council of broad-minded Iraqis ready to deliberate collectively for the good of the whole. No, it put together a *party* government, with representatives of every loud and self-pro-moting interest group to be found.

Let me be more specific. I was amazed at the degree to which Iraqis at all levels distrusted the Iraqi Governing Coun-cil that we had set up in the weeks after liberation. This was a council of twenty-five people representing the various parties and factions that were thought to make up Iraqi society. Polls were taken, and, when the pollster asked the man-on-the-street whom he respected on the Council, most members of the coun-cil got approval ratings in the low single digits.

The reasons aren't too hard to find. Iraq is a country where the word "party" carries deeply negative connotations. In all my months in Iraq, I met few outside the government who pro-fessed allegiance to any party or even identified with any party. They had lived under party rule, with its ideology and programs and demands, for over three decades. Yet, in choosing Iraqis to govern Iraq, the CPA thought it should choose the heads of various parties and sects vying for control, *thus magnifying rather than muting the very divisions that so many Iraqis rejected.*

I have no way of denying that Iraq is replete with tribal, sectarian, and political differences. This is not an invention of the US media, though the media, with its constant question— Are you Sunni? Are you Shi'a? Are you Arab or Kurd? Is the government "balanced"? Is every faction "represented"?—pick at this scab with irritating constancy. Too many journalists, like too many American politicians, seem incapable of understanding something or someone unless they are able to put the person in a box, into some familiar category, which then becomes the central context for all understanding. Or, all too often, misunderstanding. Nonetheless, the best Iraqis knew that they could not form one country, one *democratic* country, unless they were somehow able to get these categories behind them and look for leaders who, one way or another, would transcend these divisions. The best Iraqis, as I said, knew this. We didn't.

This desire on the part of Iraqis to have leadership that transcended historic divisions was hardly chimerical or utopian. Iraq was, at the level of its ablest leadership, a fairly secular country, where these divisions had been partly, even largely, submerged. I knew that Zeiad, the first Minister of Higher Education, was a Sunni because he was appointed by the Sunni Islamic Party member on the Governing Council. And I knew it because he tried to Islamicize the universities as best he could along Sunni lines. But I had no idea what the religious background of virtually any of the university presidents or deans was, or of any of the best administrators in the Ministry, for the simple reason that their religion was, even to the most pious of them, *background.* Their peers did not select them on that glorious and democratic day in May 2003 on the basis of their religious affiliation but on the basis of their competence and devotion to education. And when the background was made foreground, as with Dr. Zeiad, the results were predictably disastrous.

Let me give another example. We had working in our office one Iraqi indispensable to our operations, an Iraqi who knew everyone in higher education and was respected by each of them. Was he Shi'a or Sunni? Well, he was born in Basra of Arab Muslim parents, so presumably he was Shi'a. Yet he attended Iraqi Catholic schools before going to college, became an official of Basra University, moved to Kurdistan, married a Kurd, fathered Kurdish-Arab children, and ultimately became president for a while of one of the Kurdish universities. When we visited the Kurdish region with him and wanted to attend Mass one Sunday, he remembered where the church was, brought us, and knelt throughout the service. What is he?—Muslim? Yes. Shi'a? Most likely. But if you ask him what he is, he'll just say "Iraqi."

▲▼▲

I guess what I found most amazing about the liberation, the occupation, and the repeated desire to help Iraq become "democratic" as stated by Americans at all levels—from us in the CPA all the way to the White House—was how little Americans knew about democracy. All the Americans I met in Iraq, military or civilian, would tell you either that the reason they was there, or the thing that gave them the greatest satisfaction, was knowing that they were helping to bring freedom and democracy to a people that had been suppressed for thirty years. Still, from the highest authorities to the lowest GI, we acted as if democracy was simple. At some point the Iraqis would elect their own government, they'd have themselves a "democracy," and that would be the end of it. Elections equal democracy, democracy equals liberty. That was the whole of it. Mission truly accomplished.

Perhaps we acted as if democracy is easy because we, in our own country, have ruled ourselves for over two hundred years. We established the first serious democracy in world affairs since the fall of Republican Rome almost two thousand years before. We established a democratic government back when virtually every intelligent person said it couldn't be done, that it wasn't even worth the trying. We weathered a great civil war, testing, as Lincoln said, whether a nation conceived in liberty and dedicated to the idea that all men were created equal could ever endure. We are the oldest, most stable, most established democracy on the face of the earth by magnitudes. So I thought it a shock, verging on a scandal, when I heard the President say just after I arrived in Iraq that the writing of Iraq's future constitution should be done under UN supervision because "they're good at that." Well, I'm sorry, Mr. President, they are *not* "good at that." We are good at that, or at least we used to be. Don't suppose when I say that I, along with all America, was mugged by reality in Iraq that I was mugged by the strangeness of Iraqi mores or by Iraqi culture. What most hit me behind the head was America's ignorance of what America had accomplished and what made *America* great.

In January of 2004 I wrote to two politically savvy friends in the CPA the following regarding the makeup of the Governing Council the Coalition had hobbled together:

> We're more than happy to do exactly the opposite of what [our Constitution tried to do]—we seek out the loudest and most virulent factions and empower them....[W]e gather together the representatives of the most antagonistic factions and think that's good democracy. We've done nothing to blur the lines separating people and everything to sharpen them. We will not see moderate and thoughtful people representing the wider interests of Iraq; rather we'll see ideologues chosen for the very reason that they were not mild, moderate, or thoughtful but because they were ideologues. It's the corruption that comes in the States with being comfortable with affirmative action as a way to govern—solidify factions and then proportionally empower and reward those factions.

This error—of elevating party and sect and thinking by so doing that you were "representing" Iraqis—was repeated in the election on January 30. Again under UN pressure, voting was not done in local electoral districts where candidates might have to have wide appeal to gather a plurality of votes, but by party slates, where ideology and not compromise and moderation rule. With this, we have probably not simply made gridlock and legislative bickering permanent, but also permanently imposed on Iraq our simple-minded view of how to divide the Iraqi people: Do not look at them as so many of them do (as teachers or doctors or businessmen or farmers) but rather fit them all into religious or nationalistic boxes (Shi'a, Sunni, or

Kurd). Don't encourage them, through political institutions, to moderate their divisions; rather, highlight their divisions, proclaim them, and solidify them. In this corrupt age, we can only see democracy as the representation of antagonistic groups, not, as James Madison did, as the one form of government that might help us over come our self-concern and actually moderate rather than inflame our divisions.

Today we seem to think that "real" democracy demands some variety of what's called "proportional representation." That is, we believe that real or true democracy has to mirror or represent the "interests" of the various "groups" that make up a society. Not only that, but we look to proportional representation actually to represent the strength and *intensity* of these various interest groups that make up a country. But proportional representation—the only kind of democracy the UN, the State Department, or even most academic democratic theorists seem to understand or value—leads us away from containing and moderating the passions that so often drive people and popular groups, passions and interests often antagonistic to the rights of individuals and destructive of what once we called "the common good." Proportional representation was certainly not the kind of restrained and liberal democracy the Founders of this country had hoped to give to us. It certainly isn't the kind of democracy we have prospered under for now over two centuries.

In that light consider the following: It must seem strange to the modern proponents of democracy to look at the American Founding and see, for example, people elected on the basis of geography rather than interests or sects. The Founders could have easily put together a legislative branch that proportionally represented our various and strongly held confessions, with so many seats for Anglicans, for Congregationalists, for Catholics, and so on. Or, perhaps, they could have divided the seats up on the basis of occupations—so many merchants, fishermen, bankers, farmers ... But, no; they thought best to have people vote in electoral districts where, to get elected, each candidate has to appeal to a wide variety of interests. In so doing, if the district were varied enough, the person most electable was the person who might have some "cross-factional" appeal, a person who might not be the exact exponent of your particular interest or view, but who might well be "acceptable," perhaps seem "fair" across a wide rather than narrow spectrum. And you, as the voter, would in turn have to dampen your expectations of achieving all you desired in order to have your vote succeed. In this way, American democracy tried both to moderate the passions of elected leaders, as well as the passions, over time, *of the people as well.* How different a view of democracy this is from one that underscores factionalism and emphasizes and empowers divisions.

▲▼▲

Having mentioned Jefferson, Madison, and Lincoln, I think it might be helpful to look at one further ingredient in our own conception of democracy: political leadership. Everything that was done since the end of initial hostilities and the establishment of new democratic forms in Iraq works to erode truly strong leadership. The Iraqi Governing Council set up under the CPA had a rotating presidency, a new president a month. Under the Transitional Administrative Law, there was a prime minister, two presidents, and a presidency council, all at the same time. And now, under the new constitution, there's a prime minister, a separate president with whom he shares executive power, a vice president, two deputy prime ministers, and a cabinet of ministers. Both president and prime minister are drawn separately from the parliament.

It seems to have entered modern democratic theory that truly democratic government is legislative government and legislative supremacy, with everything being done to weaken the unifying office of a chief executive. Notice how far this is from the American experience, which understood the natural tendency of democracies toward legislative supremacy, and so insisted on fracturing the legislature, not the executive! Bicameralism, different modes of election to different houses, staggered terms of office, were all meant to weaken the legislative branch, while unity in the executive was meant to strengthen it. And, in reflecting on the presidencies of Washington, Lincoln, Theodore and

Franklin Roosevelt, and others, it becomes fairly clear the degree to which we've relied on the authority of a single and unified presidency both in moving forward in peace and in staying together in times of crisis.

I'm fully aware that, after Saddam, the natural tendency of Iraqis was to shy away from strong leadership. This was surely understandable. Still, it was important to offer the Iraqis some understanding of effective and unified executive leadership, partly in order to protect liberty by balancing legislative domination, but also for the very simple reason that no democracy, indeed no nation, long exists without leadership, especially in difficult times. And a democracy that does not make way for democratic leadership will soon find itself saddled with non-democratic leadership. The easiest way to invite another Saddam is to make no provisions for moderate, checked, yet still effective and strong elected leadership. And the worse the security situation becomes in Iraq, the more naturally Iraqis will turn to someone to lead them, protect them, and destroy those who harm them—no matter what's said on paper in their constitution. But by then it will not be democratic leadership but anti-democratic leadership.[5]

▲▼▲

One thing about democracy the CPA *did* understand, though it was dissolved too soon to follow through on it properly, was that at the heart of all decent democracies lie smaller democratic institutions, the pieces and building blocks of what we today call "civil society." Democracy, it seems, is not first learned nationally, but locally. We learn to be democratic citizens by being thrown together with others in some common endeavor. So we band together to build a hospital, or be part of the local

---

[5]See Lincoln's Speech to the Young Men's Lyceum on January 27, 1838, for perhaps the clearest insight into why it is that times of crisis without sufficient leadership are the times of the greatest dangers to democratic life. Imposing democracy on a country, as we have done in Iraq, might well result in chaos—but only for a while. Chaos is always temporary, despotism far more permanent.

PTA, or set up the farmers' cooperative, or join the Boy Scouts. What do we learn from such private associations? Well, we learn to talk with and understand people whose views might be different from ours, to listen to others, to moderate our own desires in order to accomplish a common objective. We learn, in other words, how to be citizens.

Despotism, of course, hates civil societies and private associations. There are no Rotary Clubs in North Korea, no Knights of Columbus in Cuba. When some physicians connected to the CPA helped Iraqi doctors establish something akin to a national medical society, no one there could remember such a thing since before the coming of the Ba'ath Party to power. Yet, nothing serves better as a check on power, and as a nursery for the growth of civic sentiment, than such associations.

In some ways this means that the best and most long-lasting democracies do not begin with electing a democratic government, they rest on the foundation of an already existing democratic *people*. We Americans were a democratic people long before we wrote our Constitution. We governed ourselves in our localities, we worked together and compromised with one another to accomplish common civic tasks, and we banded together in private associations to achieve common goals. The more these associations were inclusive, the more they cut across ethnic and religious lines, the more valuable they were in cultivating the habits necessary for democratic citizenship. Yet these associations are exactly what tyranny in Iraq eliminated. Without them, all organization will be on the basis of sectarianism and ethnicity and tribe—exactly the lines that make common citizenship together in one democratic country so difficult.

Another way to view this same issue is that what is needed in Iraq for it to be fully democratic is a kind of patriotism that transcends petty factionalism. There was, as I've said, some of this belief in Iraq as one country with a common future on the part of many secular and professional Iraqis. But we, as the promoters of democracy, had to promote this grander vision, and this we did not do. Instead, as I've noted, we established governing structures that underscored fractures and divisions, sect and tribe and party. Sad to say, in our attempt not to "impose" our own way of life on the Iraqis, we wound up acting as if the true model of democratic governance was not America but Lebanon.

▲▼▲

It isn't simply their history of autocracy that dampens the life of freedom in Iraq; we also have to look at what decades of socialism have done to their character. In Iraq, there are virtually no taxes. During my time in Iraq, 97 to 98 percent of national income came from the sale of oil. This sale of oil, in turn, subsidized everything. But "oil spoils," as Suhail would always say. And what it spoils most is the character of a people.

The sale of oil, and the various state subsidies it made possible, dampened the spark of independence and created a culture of dependency that hardly bodes well for the establishment of free government. Gasoline, as I mention elsewhere, was about three cents a liter in Iraq, probably the cheapest gas in the world. But Iraq refines very little gasoline itself. It has no private companies doing that work. Oil is refined elsewhere, in other countries, and the government imports and subsidizes it completely. Iraqis are willing to wait in line for hours, sometimes days, to get this virtually free gas from dilapidated public stations rather than have better, more efficient, securer supplies for which they would pay market price.

The culture of dependency bred by socialism touches every aspect of life. Publicly subsidized housing dampens the desire for home ownership and improved living conditions. Food baskets, which go to everyone, high or low, simply mean that the poor are dependent on handouts and the rich make a quick dinar by reselling their subsidized food to the needy. And agriculture is depressed in Iraq because farmers find it more profitable to sell the heavily subsidized fertilizer they get annually from the government to Jordanians rather than to use it to grow crops. Farmers in Iraq, I was repeatedly told, were not really farmers, which would take hard work over the year, but rather urea resellers, which took only a week, or less, and a truck.

All this has, of course, a political effect. People who are children of the state will find it hard to be thoughtful rulers of their state. Accustomed to being fed and clothed, housed and subsidized at all levels, people will find that their initiative and independence will come harder. At a meeting in Hillah I mentioned to local leaders that if they wanted to have greater control over their local affairs, their schools and roads and hospitals, they would have to tax themselves locally. This, they replied, they would never do; Baghdad would supply their needs. They would not think of adding to whatever fees the central government might charge taxes of their own. They were used to getting, not giving. And I could only tell them that, then, they would always be controlled.

▲▼▲

Let me try to summarize my worries about the future of Iraq as a democratic nation. We Americans love democracy. And we love it for very good reasons. We have lived under a form of democracy for well over two hundred years, and we all understand that, somehow, this way of life is at the heart of our freedoms, our national security, and even our prosperity and our personal happiness.

Yet ours is no ordinary democracy—and we should try to understand what was done in America to make our democracy the fine thing it is before the next time we try to export it. I don't say all this out of a kind of reflexive patriotism or chauvinistic pride. I say it because it's the simple truth—before America, to refer to a country as a "democracy" was, more often than not, not a term of praise but a reproach. If America has done nothing else for the world, however, it has done this: It has tamed democracy, and made democratic government safe for the world.

Indeed, we have been so successful in calming the repressive and illiberal character of historical democracy that we now run into the opposite problem: we now see democracy simply as good; we see it as a cure-all for the ills of the world and all nations; we see it as simple, and we see it as infinitely exportable. What we have lost sight of is the fact that democracy may not be simple at all—that our own democracy had to be constructed out of any number of arrangements and institutions that tempered democracy's tendencies to be chaotic and unjust. And we have also lost sight of the fact that even the best democracies aren't simply "exportable" the way a country might ship off toys or new fashions. In fact, free democracies may only work in certain times and places, with people of a certain character. It may be false to think that any nation can become democratic any time it wants simply by throwing off its current rulers and giving people the vote. Or, more precisely, it might, by doing that, become "a democracy," but not a good one.

▲▼▲

Think, for a moment, of all we in this country had to do to make democracy begin to work for the benefit of all and not just the majority: At the national level, we separated political power between three branches; we further subdivided the legislative power between two houses; we gave each branch of the national government a check on the other; we established different terms of office—some two years, some four, some six, some lifetime; we set age and residency requirements; we set up staggered elections; we established calendared elections uncontrolled by any party in power; we divided the objects of political power among local, state and federal governments; we decreed some things beyond the control of any majorities, no matter how large. In sum, we made democracy as cumbersome and complex as we could in hopes of moderating and restraining majoritarian demands. Legislation now needed the consent of representatives elected by the direct vote of the people in local districts, the assent of a smaller and more select body of senators selected state-wide and for longer terms, and, almost always, the consent of the president, elected nationally. Plus, of course, a national Supreme Court with ultimate say over the constitutionality of all legislation.

These various mechanisms did more, however, than work to moderate the demands of any temporary majority bent on exploiting minorities. They also worked to solve the problem of democratic instability and lack of democratic thoughtfulness. It is with good reason that those among us who want to see quick and decisive legislative action are so often disappointed in the cumbersome, slow process which retards all legislative activity while it promotes discussion, debate, and, one hopes, deliberation.

Still, why do I raise what probably seems to most of the world as merely historical or academic concerns? The reason is not that I doubt that we can bring democracy to other nations. We obviously can. But if all we give them is democracy, and not liberal or moderated democracy, we will be doing neither them nor ourselves nor the world any favors. Let me lay out my concerns up front, and examine them as we move along: If we, as the Coalition, fought and died to eliminate the political tyranny of Saddam Hussein only to hand Iraq over to a religious autocracy in democratic form, what have we accomplished? If religious sectarianism in Iraq allies itself with the forces of religious oppression in Iran, what good have we done for the future of freedom and the hopes of the liberationist elements in Iran—or for safety of the rest of the world? If we leave the ordinary Iraqi less free in his ordinary, everyday life than he—or, especially, she—was even under Saddam, what happened to the "noble cause" all of us went to support? Finally, if we promote the form of democracy, but allow it in substance to become nothing more than a vehicle for the promotion of terror and religious fanaticism, then we have done all the world a monumental disservice. How much of this could have been avoided if only the Administration had a better understanding of what it really took to bring freedom and political moderation, and not merely simplistic "democracy," to Iraq?

I argued in the first chapter that the cultivation of liberal democracies was in America's national interest. There I noted that liberal democratic states rarely, indeed I believe never, fight one another. If universal peace is a proper goal, then the spread of liberal democracies is a proper means to that worthy end. But the operative word is "liberal." Majoritarian democracies that lack institutional checks and balances, that fail to promote equal liberty, that impose sectarian strictures on non-communicants, or that are blind to the principles of limited government and the health and independence of the private sector are no less a threat to both world peace and our own national interests than tyrannies of any other stripe, even if they do style themselves "democracies."

My worry goes far beyond Iraq. As I wrote in the Preface, I'm concerned that we see the spread of democracy of any type, liberal or not, simply as a good in itself. But what would we say to a democratic Pakistan if the government freely elected by the citizens of that country were loyal to Al-Qaeda and the religious principles of the Taliban? This is hardly an idle question, since what may well stand between us and a "democratic" Islamic terror state armed with nuclear weapons is the singularly non-democratic person of President Musharraf. Left to themselves in open and fair elections, that might well be the kind of state Pakistanis would choose. This is, of course, exactly the kind of extremist state Algeria voted for itself in the early 1990s. Or consider Saudi Arabia with an elected but thorough-going Wahabbi government in place of its non-democratic ruling family, a Wahabbi government fully in support of terror worldwide. And, of course, we have the more recent example of a democratically elected, popularly supported, Islamist Hamas regime now in power in Palestine, dedicated to both Islamic fundamentalism and the destruction of Israel. No, there's no magic in the word "democracy" that turns a nation from bad to good—good either for all its own citizens or good for the rest of the world.

▲▼▲

Let me add a postscript to this chapter: In July of 2005, I returned to Iraq with six academic colleagues. Without the sanction of either Defense or State, we went as private citizens to meet with a few of the drafters of the new Iraqi constitution. For obvious reasons of security, we stayed in Erbil, in the Kurdish region of Iraq. Kurdistan is safe—people in town knew we were there, the local papers and TV freely covered our proceedings, and lawyers and scholars and politicians came and went without worry. But, unlike a year before, there was no chance whatever that we could have held these meetings in Baghdad or Basra.

Were we safe? Yes. Were we effective? I'm afraid we were not. The Administration touted this new constitution we helped work on as proof of Iraq's advance into a rebirth of freedom, into a new liberal and democratic way of life. Sorry to say, this again may be a case of hope ascendant over reality.

Among the most obvious things about the new constitution are the repeated references to the place and role of Islam and Islamic law. To be sure, no one should be much surprised that the new constitution declared Islam to be "the official religion of the State." While the world could have hoped for a more inclusive statement, any number of decent democracies manage to combine a state religion with true religious liberty and diversity, or even with pervasive secularism: One need look no further than Great Britain.

Nor can anyone predict how the tension between certain statements—"No law that contradicts the rights and basic freedoms stipulated in this constitution may be established," "No law that contradicts the principles of democracy may be established," and "No law that contradicts the established provisions of Islam may be established"—will wind up being resolved. But I remain highly pessimistic. We know that there are similar statements in the new Afghan constitution. But we also witnessed recently the case of a poor Afghan who declared himself a convert from Islam to Christianity and who needed to be secreted out of Afghanistan to Europe since his death was decreed by all those who could speak for "the established provisions of Islam." [6]

Nonetheless, if I may hazard an educated guess, the real way theocratic rule will grab hold of the new Iraq may well be less through its legal/constitutional framework or the pronounce-

---

[6]In addition to professing a belief in "the fundamental rights and freedoms of the people" and its respect for "the Universal Declaration of Human Rights," the Afghan constitution (like the Iraqi constitution) states that "no law can be contrary to the beliefs and provisions of the sacred religion of Islam" (Preamble and Article 2). How could it be possible to square the killing of a convert with a formal profession of individual rights? Easy— there is no "right" to forsake Islam for false gods. Apostasy is no more a human or religious "right" than insulting Mohammed is a free press "right." No amount of what seems like Western casuistry can convince a good Muslim, or a good Muslim country, that sins are "rights."

If this kind of analysis ever takes hold, the tension between Islam and modern natural right will be resolved, and resolved to the detriment of all liberty.

ments of its religious authorities or through its legislature and laws than through its courts.

Unlike in America, where the courts have the authority to strike down legislation contrary to the national Constitution, under the new Iraqi constitution the Supreme Federal Court of Iraq has the power to declare a law unconstitutional not only if it violates the words of the constitution but also if it violates "the established provisions of Islam." Moreover, the court need not wait until a case arises challenging the law, as in America; rather the Court can (as in neighboring Iran) simply strike down the law without challenge and before it takes effect. Additionally, in order help to make this rule of religion paramount, a number of clerics well-versed in religious requirements—"experts in Islamic jurisprudence" but who are not themselves jurists— will sit on the Court alongside the appointed judges to make sure the various theological strictures are applied.

To think of this supreme legislative-judicial body as in any way modeled on our own Supreme Court is misleading: It is more clearly an imitation of the twelve-member "Guardians Council" that dominates Iran. That body, too, has complete revisionary power over all legislation; it too is divided between jurists and clerics; and it, as we all now know, has imposed the strictest of Islamic control over the daily lives of its citizens— exactly as I fear will happen in Iraq.

Allow me one final comment on the imposition of Islamic rule over Iraq. The fairly extreme form of federalism the new constitution promoted—a federalism where regional legislation virtually completely preempts federal law—was a shrewd way for extremist religious Shiites to keep full control of daily life in their own southern half of the country.[7] That is, even if

---

[7]Article 111: "All powers not stipulated in the exclusive authorities of the federal government shall be the powers of the regions and governorates that are not organized in a region. The priority goes to the regional law in case of conflict between other powers shared between the federal government and regional governments." Also, Article 122 (4): "Articles of the constitution may not be amended if such amendment takes away from the powers of the regions that are not within the exclusive powers of the federal authorities except by the consent of the legislative authority of the concerned region and the approval of the majority of its citizens in a general referendum."

more moderate or secular representatives ever manage to pass progressive and liberating legislation nationally, and the Supreme Federal Court allowed such laws to stand, they would still be of no effect if they conflicted with more restrictive religious laws or practices in the Shiite dominated areas.

Given all this, one possible scenario that will play itself out is that Iraq will harden into exactly what I suspect the Grand Ayatollah Sistani wanted all along—a sectarian Shiite theocracy under the *forms* of democracy and constitutionalism. It is, to Shiite sectarians, preferable for this religious rule to be pervasive throughout all of Arab Iraq; it is sufficient for it to be dominant in the majority of Iraq that has a strong Shiite presence.

Predictions are hard, and surprises always possible. Nevertheless, with a constitution that pays lip service to individual rights but forbids contravention of Islamic tenets, that empowers rather than moderates factionalism in its legislature, that gives the courts power to overturn all legislation in the name of religion, that prevents the general government from intervening in local or regional repression, and that works against strong executive authority, the deck is surely stacked against much hope for moderate, mild, and liberal democratic rule.

# SIX

# Education and Democracy

Two and a half months after I arrived in Iraq, I returned to Washington to give a few talks at the various think tanks in the area in hopes of drumming up some interest in Iraqi higher education. While there, word got to me that some officials at the World Bank wanted to talk about support. So I made my way over to the Bank and met with a charming Iraqi-American, an economist who also had gone to the Jesuit prep school in Baghdad before it was closed down by the Ba'ath Party in 1969. I also met with an enormously unpleasant European who made it quite clear that she preferred to talk only with Iraqis in higher education and not with any American. She had tried, repeatedly she said, to contact the Minister himself but he never managed to return her phone calls. So, sadly, she was stuck talking to me.

Other than the fact that he was generally incompetent (which I kept to myself), I did not know why Dr. Zeiad refused her calls, though I found out later that he had no idea what the World Bank was. I could only envision his face when his assistant would tell him the World Bank was on the line—he probably had the same reaction most of us do when our bank calls: Does any bank ever call with good news? So he kept refusing her calls.

But I'm avoiding the important point. When she asked me what projects were underway for educational rebuilding and reform in Iraq, I mentioned the physical and intellectual needs that were there—everything from desks and chairs and chalk through rebuilding whole libraries to establishing modern internet connections to money for travel to conferences and professional meetings. The unspoken response, especially from the European, looked like little more than boredom over so pedestrian a list. Then I mentioned that at least three of the universities were toying with the idea of strengthening their liberal arts offerings, even to the point of creating new liberal arts colleges. With that the woman's attitude changed from bored to contemptuous. "Just what the world needs, more unemployed Iraqis."

▲▼▲

In truth, her contempt would have been shared by most educated Iraqis. The system of secondary and post-secondary education in Iraq follows far more closely the European model than any American model. Specialization, not breadth, is the hallmark of the system. Students are, in a sense, trained more than educated. One enters into higher education hoping to become a good computer scientist, or electrician, or scientist, or schoolteacher. One leaves school or the university good *at something*.

In Iraq, this specialization, this expertise, begins early. Already in secondary schools students are divided into tracks— the science and engineering area; cultural studies, or what we would generally call the arts, humanities and social sciences; and vocational studies and industrial trades. Yet, as we've already touched on, students do not concentrate in these areas on the basis of their abilities or interests but, rather, on their intelligence. The smartest students will be herded towards the sciences and engineering and will be expected to go to the university to study medicine or to become a scientist or engineer. The less intellectually gifted students will go to university and study law or literature or politics or history. The poorer students will become teachers or technicians or tradesmen of various sorts, if they enter post-secondary education at all. For a very bright student to decide to study the arts rather than medicine, or history rather than engineering would be considered a foolish waste of one's talents. And, again, students will concentrate in a field not based on interest or aptitude but because their intelligence slots them into higher or lower, more respectable and less respectable, fields.

I had no interest, I would tell the university presidents again and again, in having them diminish their respect for the sciences, computer science, medicine, or engineering. I only wished for them to try to have greater respect for the humanities and social sciences, for political science, history, philosophy, and languages. I knew there was good reason for autocratic regimes, bent as they are on control and even conquest, to prize engineering and the sciences, but I also knew that democracy needed history and philosophy and economics and foreign languages. Not that democracy could "afford" such studies, as if they were frills or tastes that now could finally be indulged in; rather, that such studies were as important and central to their future new political life as engineering was to the old. But more on the liberal arts and politics in a few pages.

Because the aim of higher education in Iraq is the imparting of specialized knowledge, large lecture classes are universal. The professor lectures; you sit in your seat and write down what he says. The more liberal idea of a seminar—of a few students sitting around a table, discussing a book or an idea, asking questions of themselves and the teacher, explaining and defending their insights—is simply inconceivable. The universities hired the expert, he lectured, you listened, studied, memorized, repeated what you heard, and you passed. Learning was not a common journey of discovery but the passing on of specialized and expert information.

One predictable result of this love of expertise and specialization is the preference among virtually all the professors I met for graduate over undergraduate education. In fact, the pay scale was such that you got extra money based on the number of graduate students you had under your supervision. In the end, the higher your degree and length of service, the fewer students you had; and the fewer students you taught, the higher your pay.

Now, I'm the last person in education to praise the practice of liberal education in America. While Americans talk about the liberal arts and liberal education all the time, it often seems we barely remember what it means anymore. Sure, we know it has something to do with becoming "well-rounded" (whatever that might entail); that it has something to do with breadth as well as depth; that it's different from a technical or vocational education—but what exactly it might look like, or what might make it up, we're no longer so sure. We encourage our students to go to liberal arts colleges, then we immediately start hounding them to pick a "major." So we almost naturally think of some kind of specialization as soon as we think of college. Moreover, if our student tells us he or she is going to major in philosophy or literature or history or one of the arts, we quickly ask about career options: "But, dear, what will you *do* with a major in classical literature?" Utility and expertise are barely further from us than they are from the Iraqis. And, like the Iraqis, we all know professors who think teaching college students superior to teaching high school students, teaching graduate students more professional than teaching undergraduates, and spending out your days at a research center or think tank— where you don't have to be in contact with students at all— the very pinnacle of professorial life.

Still, having said that, I have to recognize the fact that we do praise the idea of the liberal arts even if we're unsure of its content or activity, and that praise means something. And we also praise the great undergraduate professor who excites students in a freshman survey course. By and large, this praise means that we think it's good to have some breadth in the world of knowledge— that no one should graduate from a great university without having read some fine books or studied some serious thinkers or gotten some knowledge of science and history. On the surface this should strike us as odd, for while it might be easy to see the personal good that one might derive from a liberal arts education, it's harder to see the *societal* good. I know what good a farmer or an electrician is to society, but it's harder to discern what good a "poetry major with a minor in philosophy" might be. But, still, we accept it and, often, even encourage it.

But there was nothing like any of this in Iraq—at least nothing before we started talking together about it.

▲▼▲

Now, circuitously, to politics. It wasn't long after my unpleasant experience with the woman at the World Bank that I had occasion to go up north, into Kurdish Iraq. It was winter, and snow was on the highest peaks of the mountains in Kurdistan. I asked Suhail to drive and to be security, and Omar, an Iraqi-American who worked in the office of basic, not higher, education to come along and help. We were driving to Dohuk, through Mosul. Omar was born in Mosul, and left it when he was very young, his family escaping to America. And Suhail's family had originally come from Mosul, from what was once a large Christian community in the area. The area has impressive Biblical roots; the province that Mosul is in is called the governorate of Nineveh, the place where Jonah was sent.

Mosul is a bustling city, smaller but no less hectic than Baghdad. General Petraeus and the 101st Airborne had control of the city right after the war, and he ran it in radically different ways than the rest of Iraq was run. For example, under General Petraeus there was virtually no de-Ba'athification of public officials. In the General's view, rather than humiliate and ultimate pauperize the now surrendered enemy, driving them into future acts of desperation against the Coalition, he allowed them their jobs and their pensions. In doing this he was acting far afield from the policy of Ambassador Bremer and the provisional authority in the rest of Iraq. Whether or not he had gotten this dispensation willingly or not, I don't know. But the theory was that employed, well-off people are not revolutionaries; that economic self-interest is the prime factor in human activity. Odd how both the right and left converge on this point: the capitalist right understands man to be an economic animal, rationally calculating his economic costs and benefits in deciding on his activities; the Marxist left sees poverty coupled with capitalist excess and competition as the cause of despair and revolution. Both capitalists and Marxists, in their different ways, see economics as the prime cause of our political troubles, and, also, as the cure.

Mosul was still calm in the winter between 2003 and 2004. Soon, however, Petraeus would be gone, and Mosul began to rival the worst sections of Baghdad for attacks on Coalition forces and violence against Iraqis. Perhaps it got worse because he and the 101st Airborne left. Perhaps it got worse because foreign elements moved in. Or perhaps it got worse because neither Marxism nor capitalism fully understands the nature of religious fervor, blind attachment to revered leaders, or the strength of political ideology. We have to hope that economic motivation can do *something* to rescue humanity from the degraded and destructive depths the human heart can reach, that economic liberty and a modicum of comfort and even prosperity can soften the tyrannical and abusive side of man's nature. But, from all I have seen, we delude ourselves when we think that either eliminating poverty or increasing the attachment to production and prosperity will, *of itself,* solve the problem of war or tyranny or terrorism. Often, to be sure, those who decapitate strangers and shoot children in the back are poor and uneducated. Other times they are wealthy and have Ph.D.s.

Suhail, as I said, was our security on this trip. He had his AK-47 loaded, next to him on the driver's seat, covered with a blanket. Our Coalition identification got us through all the checkpoints without trouble and without being searched.

We were met at the border of Kurdish Iraq by a security contingent from the University of Dohuk, sent down by the president. In part because they take security with consummate seriousness, and in part because they form a cohesive community devoted to each other—and Americans as well—the Kurds live in more than relative safety and peace. Having left Nineveh and entered the region of Dohuk, all anxiety over security simply was over. I do not believe one American, soldier or civilian, has been killed or even hurt in Kurdish Iraq since the war began—or maybe ever.

Dohuk is a sweet town, set high among the mountains of northwestern Iraq, with clean, wide streets, fully functioning electricity, visible economic activity, and a high degree of secularization. There's a shopping mall, with a supermarket/department store near the university with women wearing the hijab, wearing crosses, or simply dressed as you'd find them in any cosmopolitan city. In fact, the place looks like a small European city, complete with the Catholic cathedral on top of the hill in the center of town. If one had to pick the mirror opposite of, say, Fallujah, one would pick Dohuk. I always wondered why CNN never made it there for interviews.

The president of the university is Dr. Asmat Khalid. A less prototypical university president would be hard to envision. Short, stocky, gruff, he seems more the head of a New Jersey truckers local than the founder and president of a major university. Yet he began the university in the early Nineties, under the protection of the No-Fly Zone. He started with a medical college attached to the local hospital. The college overlooks the parade grounds and the killing fields of the Ba'ath Party and their armed forces. The university then added a law college, which it built directly above the Ba'ath Party's semi-underground prison. You can still go into the prison—dark and drear, with two rooms, one for men and a smaller one for women, and a little window that peered in from a higher area where officials could watch the prisoners being tortured in the space directly below. With exquisite regard for symbolism, this is where, as I said, the university built the law college. They then added an engineering college, science facilities, an agriculture school, a college of education, and a college of arts. In the college of arts the only subjects are Kurdish and English language studies and history. A minimum grade of 91 on the secondary school exam is a prerequisite even to apply to the medical college, an 88 for the engineering college, 86 for science, but only 80 for history and a mere 65 for the college of education.

Dr. Asmat was the first of the three Kurdish presidents to approach me about starting something different. He wanted his to be the first institution in all Iraq to connect higher education to the coming new age of freedom and democracy. He wanted to begin what he termed the "College of Humanity." It would be a college that understood the interaction between the humanities and the promotion of "humanity," of a way of life that was civilized and humane. The college would contain all the usual humanities fields, but with a tilt towards the building of permanent democratic systems. Thus there would be courses in political philosophy, democratic theory, western civilization, the history of liberty, human rights. No one, he told us, would be allowed to graduate without having taken and passed the human rights course. There would be more (sociology, journalism, and mass communication) to train objective journalists to counter the constant Al-Jazeera propaganda that was everywhere, even up in Kurdistan—and, significantly, a course in Comparative Religion. Would he really introduce students to the Old and New Testaments in such a course? "Yes, of course," he answered. And would he, I asked, ever hire a Jew to teach the Old Testament course? A pained and puzzled look at my ignorance—"Of course; why not?"

The language of instruction would be English, not Kurdish or Arabic, in order to have an international, multi-ethnic, multi-cultural faculty and student body. English, he explained, was the only international language; it was the new Latin of the civilized world. If there was any hope of drawing the best teachers and the best students from Arab Iraq and from all neighboring countries as well as America and Europe, English would be the language spoken.

So, this is where our conversations connecting higher education and the growth of democratic institutions began. There would be no viable democracy in Iraq without either educated democratic leaders or an educated citizenry. But it was hard to imagine any kind of democratic statesmanship emerging from leaders who had no knowledge of the history of the world or other countries; who spoke no other language; who had never studied any great literature and thus had no idea, beyond their experiences, of the possibilities, for good or ill, inherent in our human souls; who had never studied political science or political philosophy or been exposed to the ways of other religions. A well-constructed liberal education, an education that took seriously exposing students to knowledge of the world writ large, would be an education that took seriously the education of leaders and statesmen. And I know of no democratic nation either founded or sustained without democratic leadership.

But more. While democracies surely need the wisest and most perceptive leaders they can find, democracies are still places where the people rule. And if the citizens of a democracy are foolish, so finally will be their government. No amount of wisdom in its elected officials will in the long run save a nation if the ultimate rulers, the people, are ignorant—and I don't mean simply ignorant of their rights and responsibilities but ignorant of the world and of human possibilities that history and literature and philosophy might help teach.

In the previous chapter, I spoke about the crafting of democratic institutions and the civic character of democratic people. It takes nothing away from what I mention there to say that no institutions, no constitution, no set of decent civic values will long protect a people swayed by every insane rumor, or insensitive to the designs of tyrants and foreign foes, or unable to understand their own national strengths and weaknesses. It should be remembered that one reason that stable and long-lasting democracies were so rare in the world before the successful establishment of the American experiment was that democracies were not only hotbeds of injustice, of majorities riding rough over the rights of minorities, but that they also consisted of the chaotic rule of the ignorant and unaware. It would be the diffusion of knowledge generally among the people, Jefferson taught, that would preserve the freedom and happiness of a democratic people. It was Jefferson who on his tombstone had listed his founding of the University of Virginia as equal in importance to his writing of the Declaration of Independence and his responsibility for Virginia's Statute of Religious Freedom. Jefferson left out any mention of his presidency. To Jefferson, starting a liberal arts university was of greater importance for democracy and America's freedom than being President of the United States.

Nor was the link between education and democracy limited to romantic democrats like Jefferson; even as great a realist as James Madison knew of nothing "more edifying or more seasonable than that of liberty and learning, each leaning on the other for their mutual and surest support." To cultivate wisdom in its leadership and wisdom in the people, a new and liberal form of education was now called for.

But in going this far we have barely scratched the surface of the relationship of liberal education to democratic health.

Later that evening there was an episode that led me to understand how deeply Dr. Asmat understood what he was up against and how radically education in Iraq would have to change. Over dinner, Suhail and Dr. Asmat got into a heated discussion. As best I can reconstruct it, it had to do with how far a university could go in revering past political leaders without crossing the line that separates scholarship and objectivity from partisanship. Omar leaned over to me and whispered that I should stop them—they were fighting.

But it was clear to me they weren't fighting but arguing: laying out their positions, marshaling evidence, debating the consequences. They were doing something I had not seen in my then nearly six months in Iraq—they were having a rational argument. Before this, I had seen many Iraqis fight but never make an argument—a real argument. It had seemed that to Iraqis, deliberation simply meant stating a position and declaring your belief in it. If more people applauded you than applauded the other guy, you won the argument. But it never had anything really to do with argument or reason or persuasion truly, but simply *assertion.*

When I asked President Asmat why this was the first rational political discussion I had heard in six months in Iraq, he gave me these reasons:

> First, their religion: the truth was written, and was not to be questioned.
>
> Second, their fathers: if their fathers said it, and if their fathers' fathers said it as well, then it was true. To question what your father has said is tantamount to saying he hasn't told you the truth: so no questioning there either.
>
> And third, their education: the professors and the textbook are there to tell you the truth—you are not there to question it, you are to learn it and repeat it. And if you memorize and repeat it exactly as it was said, you will get a good grade. To question your professor is to say he may have been wrong, or not explained it well. This way of teaching and learning, Khalid said, had so "infected" the Iraqi mind that he wondered if Iraqis could ever be free, since they were incapable of thinking for themselves.

Now they would always wait to be told what to do, wait to be told the truth.

But this, he said, might change. If I would help him, he and a few other university presidents would begin universities, or reform their current universities, so that thinking, questioning and deliberation could take place: We can't change the nature of Iraqi religion; we can't change the character of the Iraqi family—but we can change Iraq's educational experience. We can let students *think* about their course of study, choose their majors freely, see more than just their specialties and give them breadth and not just narrow, expert depth. Give them, in summary, the ability to reflect and choose. Give them the tools for rational deliberation. Then, maybe, democracy might grow. But only then.

With this, the true and complete benefit of liberal education to Iraq's future became crystalline: It would not simply be the *courses* common to a liberal arts curriculum—history, philosophy, literature, languages—that would be of value to the new Iraq, but the *method inherent* in the way the liberal arts are regularly taught: discussion, questioning, piecing out answers together by deliberation, weighing differing interpretations of the same event or text, reasoned argument.

Although I was once the president of an American liberal arts college and, prior to that, a senior official in the National Endowment for the Humanities, I have not hesitated to be critical of the liberal arts in general and the humanities in particular when I thought appropriate. Part of my dismay with the liberal arts often was that it always seemed to prize "critical thinking" over just plain thinking, that it gloried in the relativism of differing views and perspectives rather than do its best to get to the heart of the matter, and that it always seemed happiest when debunking history, deconstructing literature, or dethroning old orthodoxies. I think my criticism of the liberal arts is right, for America. But I recognize that the battle is all uphill—that questioning, criticism, and maybe even a touch of cynicism are endemic to these arts and subjects we call "liberal." But while I might fight against the tendency in America, I relish the thought of any and all critical approaches in authoritarian states. There the disbelieving stance of the liberal arts is an invaluably ally in the fight for personal and national liberation.

Beyond subject matter and method, the American academic notion of majors *plus* minors and free electives, of choosing and fashioning one's own course of study, of understanding then combining one's own aptitude, interests, and intelligence to fashion a future for one's self, would cement the making of free men and women with free minds. In the end, President Asmat might have even understated the matter: this kind of liberal and (let's be candid about it) *American* education might be the atom which, once cracked, might lead to religious and familial reform also, not just educational reform with a political effect.

Sorry to say, I could find no financial support for this endeavor of the president of Dohuk University from the CPA whatsoever. Despite hundreds of millions allocated to "democracy projects" and "democracy building," nothing would be forthcoming from the CPA to help Dr. Asmat. Hundreds of millions were spent on far less worthy, far less important projects than this—in fact, nothing was spent on this. In the end, I requested the grand total of three million dollars to begin this project, and even that very minor sum was rejected—partly because it was deemed too much and partly, perhaps mostly, because this and the other two "American university" projects were all in Kurdish Iraq. But, as we'll see, it's hardly strange that this new leap into freedom came from the Kurds and the Kurds alone.

Nor is the fault all the CPA's. No American university seemed interested in helping this or either of the other two projects I'll describe shortly, at least not with any help that could be called noteworthy. Some universities said they couldn't help unless there was some money in it for them—which there wasn't. Others were worried about the security situation and the dangers involved in sending faculty to anywhere in Iraq. Some, like the president of my own alma mater, simply wouldn't answer my letters. I even heard that it was said by a professor at LeMoyne that American universities would have been more likely to help their Iraqi colleagues if the senior advisor (namely me) were someone other than a conservative Republican. So the problem ran the gamut from fear to finances to fatuous silliness spouted by self-serving academics.

Nor was any help forthcoming from any federal agencies. For example, when I mentioned this endeavor at Dohuk to the woman high in the administration of USAID projects in Baghdad, her first response was sympathetic. But the best she could imagine had nothing to do with financial support; rather, she suggested that her office might be able to put together a course describing all the valuable projects USAID had supported around the world and teach it as part of the curriculum! It would be hard to find this combination of uselessness and self-importance imitated in any other federal agency.

▲▼▲

Let me break the narrative for a short while and try to explain why it is that the initiative to experiment with novel and liberating educational models captured the imagination of Kurdish and not Arab Iraq. Perhaps I can explain it in a word: *"Inshalla."* "Inshalla" means "God Willing," and, while I heard it once in a while in Kurdistan, I heard it repeatedly in the rest of Iraq. "Tomorrow we'll meet at twelve for lunch, OK?" "Inshalla." "Will I see you at the faculty meeting next week?" "Inshalla." "If you click this icon twice, you can get connected to the internet." "Inshalla." Even things that might happen simply given the ordinary course of cause and effect were ascribed, or blamed, on God's will. More to the point, actions that were, or should have been, fully in Iraqis' own control were seen as more generally done or not done because of God.

At first, I thought of this as little more than a small bit of pietism and self-effacing modesty. But perhaps it was not so. If all were in God's hands then not only should Iraqis not be praised for good results, they should not be faulted for bad. God was the primary agent of causation in this world, and we shouldn't hold Iraqis responsible for what happens in it. "Inshalla" was a way of both saying yes, and shrugging at the same time.

The Kurds rarely used the word, or any Kurdish equiva-lent. Their character led them always to say something like "I'll see what I can do" or, more simply, "yes." The attitude of can do and will do had some time ago replaced the fatalism of the rest of Iraq.

For example: Saddam cut off all electricity to Kurdistan after their revolt, while they were under the protection of the No-Fly Zone. It took them around two years or more, I heard, to build their own dams and generate their own electricity. When I asked a doctor in Dohuk how it was possible to per-form surgery without electricity or lights he said they had to do it with flashlights. When I asked where they got the batter-ies, suffering as they were under Saddam's embargo and the UN embargo as well, he answered forthrightly, "We had to smug-gle them in from Turkey."

No fatalism, no shrug, no waiting for God. It is this spirit that led the Kurds not only to admire freedom but also to embrace it. It was no wonder that they, and they alone, were looking ahead to the independence of spirit and of mind that is the promise of a liberal—a liberating—education.

▲▼▲

One last characteristic of the Kurds that I mentioned above bears repeating and underscoring. It's easy to talk about Islam as a creed so rooted in justice and what all humanity owes to the one God that toleration and respect for others develops only with difficulty. And surely nothing that is said or done these days by the most virulent anti-Western Islamists would lead anyone to believe Islam to be a religion of tolerance, much less peace.

But it has to be said that I found inter-faith and inter-national toleration and friendliness everywhere among the Kurds. President Asmat not only has photos of him with the great champions of Kurdish liberation, he has one of him with Nelson Mandela, his great hero. I've already alluded to the secure place of Christianity in Kurdistan, even though Christians com-prise only a small fraction of the population. But perhaps the sweetest eye-opener came on my first visit to Sulaimani, in Eastern Kurdistan. I was sitting at dinner next to a more than moderately religious Kurd, a Sunni, as most of them are. Nazar drank no wine; he was going to make the hajj, the pilgrimage to Mecca in a few months. During dinner, his cell phone rang. "Da, da, di, da, da, da, di, di...." "Nazar," I asked, "do you know what melody your phone is ringing?" "Yes, of course I do. It's 'We wish you a merry Christmas.' It's one of my favorite tunes."

▲▼▲

A few final words on liberty and liberal education. As head of the Coalition, Ambassador Bremer was contacted in the fall of 2003 by both Jalal Talabani, the leader of the Popular Union of Kurdistan, and Nechirvan Barzani, Prime Minister of the Kurdish region and head of the Kurdish Democratic Party, for support for an "American University" in each of their regions (Talabani in the eastern part of Kurdistan, Barzani in the center and west). Bremer wrote letters to both of them supporting their ideas.

Of course, the problem was that two full-fledged, comprehensive "American Universities" in Kurdish Iraq was more than the market would bear. Two would mean neither might succeed. Getting this mess resolved amicably, without getting either Barzani or Talabani mad at Bremer, was now my job. So on the same trip when I went to Dohuk, I asked the presidents of the universities of Sulaimani, in Talabani's territory, and Erbil, in Barzani's, to meet me in Erbil to hammer out a solution.

The presidents of both Sulaimani University and of the university in Erbil—known as Salahaddin University, the same Salahaddin who fought against the Crusaders—are gentle and urbane men of the first rank. The late President Kamal Khoshnaw of Sulaimani was an agricultural scientist and President Saedi Barzinji of Salahaddin a human rights lawyer. Soon, President Barzinji stepped down and was replaced by Mohammad Sadik in that office. (A returning exile educated in Great Britain, Mohammad spoke English so beautifully that this Brooklyn boy—whom he sometimes called "Old Chap"—was just out-classed.)

We finally decided, together, on the following course of action: Dohuk would begin its College of Democratic Studies as soon as it could. Dr. Sadik's university in Erbil would begin a full-fledged liberal arts university with a complete range of subjects, from mathematics and science to literature, history, philosophy, and art. It would be a five-year course of study, with English taking up the first year so as to prepare everyone for the courses that would follow. Just as in American universities, students would major and minor, based on their interests and ability and not simply on the basis of where their IQ would slot them. And even though the local government would contribute the land and perhaps some seed money, the university would be established as a private, independent entity, with an independent Board and an administration and faculty distinct from the current public university. Tuition would be charged, since all people respect what they work for and pay for far more than what's given to them gratis. Again, it speaks volumes about the Kurdish mind that they would establish an institution whose purpose was to challenge the current university, and, by competing with it in its own city, force both universities to be the best they could be.

The new university in Sulaimani would not be a comprehensive liberal arts university as they originally wanted but would concentrate in the other great areas of modernization—computing and information science, business administration, public administration, and free market economics. It would be called The American University of Iraq in Sulaimani—on this there was no hesitation and no compromise. Here, too, instruction would be in English; here, too, the first year would be English language training to prepare everyone for the work to follow. And here, too, instruction in business or computing would be leavened by courses taken directly from the liberal arts. As Barham Salih, the driving force behind this new university who later became the Iraqi Minister of Planning and who is currently Iraq's deputy prime minister, wrote when the idea of an American University in Sulaimani was first conceived, "Education will be the linchpin in developing a new, secular, democratic Iraq. [It] will be essential in eradicating the vestiges of the Ba'ath mentality that privileged obedience over innovation, deference to authority over critical thinking and violence over conflict resolution."

It takes nothing away from the importance of security in Iraq, or its progress in economic improvement, or in developing its oil fields to say that changes in higher education are central, vital, to bringing Iraq into the family of civilized and free nations. Today, the willful submersion of reason and the excitement of the most bloodthirsty passions grow daily. I hope I'm not so lost in airy speculation as to think that education alone, divorced from law, order, personal safety, and economic growth, can solve the problems of political repression and religious fanaticism. But I do know, as Dr. Asmat said, that the liberation of a people's minds and the liberation of a country grow together. I was honored to be part of the birth and growth of these three projects in Iraq and dismayed beyond words at the inability of America or the Coalition to find any avenues of support. My only solace is in knowing that the actors in this unfolding endeavor may be slowed by our failures, but they will not give up.[1]

---

[1]As of this writing, the US State Department is considering offering up to $10 million to help establish one of these projects, an American University of Iraq to be located in Sulaimani. If and when this happens, it will be one small but important way of helping all of Iraq move in the right direction.

# SEVEN

# "All Assistance Short of Actual Help"

When I arrived in Iraq in September of 2003 I learned of the Administration's decision that certain sectors, primarily sectors that looked like they might have international appeal, would not be supported in any serious measure by American funds. Rather, we and others with supposedly similar cachet—education, youth and sport, health, culture—would largely rely on the generosity of the "international donor community," that is, the generosity of good-willed nations other than the United States. This decision had a certain logic to it: America would concentrate its money in those areas that other nations might find politically difficult to fund, and leave to other countries the role of rebuilding schools and hospitals and museums, activities they might find more agreeable. And why not? A nation that hesitated to support the liberation of Iraq militarily might still wish to assist in rebuilding that country's schools or clinics or libraries.

Pretty much the whole month of October was spent trying to figure out how best to present our case to the donor community, which would meet at the end of the month in Madrid. I received hundreds of pages from the universities listing all the equipment and material that they never had to begin with, or that they needed to be current, or that they had lost in the looting. In putting this proposal together, I was aided enormously by a needs assessment done by three US university presidents who flew to Iraq earlier that summer.[1]

For whatever reason, the Minister, Dr. Zeiad, couldn't make up his mind whether or not to attend the conference of donor nations. So I made arrangements to go with one of his assistants, a smart Iraqi professor who now worked at the ministry. So, on Wednesday, October 22, Dr. Abdul-Rahman Hussaini and I flew out of Baghdad International Airport in a C-130 specially fitted with actual airline seats rather than the horrendous strap seats strung along the sides. It was upgraded because most of the Iraqi Governing Council decided they needed a trip to Europe, so they came along for the ride.[2]

Colin Powell flew out from Washington for the meeting and gave a pleasant speech on how sorely Iraq needed international reconstruction funds if it had any hope of being rebuilt. One after another the various international representatives rose up and pledged millions for this and billions for that. Japan was especially generous, singling out education as an area in which they were particularly interested in helping. Some poorer nations pledged little more than good will. I remember Sri Lanka saying they had no money to give, though they would try to send tea. Kuwait, Spain, and South Korea pledged hundreds of millions. But Germany, France, and Russia themselves promised nothing, boldly saying that they would offer no further financial contributions beyond their "present

---

[1]The three were Ray Bowen (President Emeritus of Texas A&M University), Lattie Coor (President Emeritus of Arizona State University), and Gregory O'Brien (Chancellor of the University of New Orleans).

[2]With a few exceptions, members of the Council treated this as a junket and not as the first serious step in rebuilding their country. Some thought shopping, not negotiating with delegates, to be at the top of their list of priorities. Indeed, our departure from Madrid back to Baghdad was postponed a day in order for them to revisit some department stores and make more purchases. Nevertheless, I was told this was the first time some of them had seen this kind of European abundance, and they were amazed by it. I guess I should be more understanding.

engagement"—that is, beyond their outstanding loans to Saddam, which they now wanted paid back.[3]

Except for the American contribution, which took up virtually all of the $18.4 billion "supplemental" the Congress was slated to approve, and $1.5 billion from Japan, almost all the money would be given in the form of loans or trade credits rather than grants. So, in addition to the billions left in unpaid debt from the Saddam era, now more would be added. What was intended as a conference of donors devolved into a conference of moneylenders.

Still, the Iraqis were not unhappy. In our ministry, we went with a list of needs that totaled over $1 billion, and which, if completely funded, would have made Iraqi higher education the most up-to-date in all the Middle East. And, by my rough estimate, we counted somewhere between $400 to $600 million dollars pledged in either grants or loans. If this wasn't everything we had hoped for, it was still far beyond anything we had at present. Don't forget, the $18 billion supplemental that the Administration asked Congress to fund included *nothing* for higher education, so virtually all the money needed to rebuild Iraqi higher education had to come from the international community.

Nonetheless, in the end, the promises made in Madrid amounted to very little. The insurgency, of course, made spending new money in Iraq in any sector extraordinarily difficult. In some cases, nations simply refused to follow through on their pledges, insurgency or not. And, hard as it is to admit, in other cases the fault lay squarely on the shoulders of individual Iraqis. For instance, except for the Japanese and American offerings and a very few others, almost all donations were to be funneled through the IMF or the World Bank. But these institutions have

---

[3]For example, on October 18, just before the meeting began, the German finance minister told reporters, "We do not only expect to get our money back; we will get our money back." So ordinary Iraqis, who never saw a cent of these old loans, would now have to pay for the pleasures of the tyrant and the cost of the armaments that killed their relatives. No wonder ordinary Iraqis spat on the ground when speaking of the French, the Germans, or the Russians.

rather complex and difficult procedures and our Minister simply wouldn't play along. First, you'll remember, he wouldn't answer the World Bank's phone calls. Then, when we finally got him to attend a meeting in Amman with World Bank officials, he turned petulant when told he wouldn't be *given* money but that he had to *apply* for it. Declaring that the World Bank representatives were, in his best English, "losers and cheaters," he left the meeting, put an assistant in charge of any negotiations, and stuck the Bank with an outrageous hotel bill. So the many millions that were, we hoped, soon to be donated to the World Bank, would now sit there. Months of constant and difficult work by my office, by the three visiting university presidents, and by the Iraqi university officials who helped with the facts and figures—all gone in little more than a fit of ministerial pique.

Sorry to say, even in those areas where we could go around the Minister and help the universities directly, the strength of the growing insurgency made any success evanescent. For instance, Curda managed to get the South Korean government to donate $5 million in computers, satellite connectivity, and training to all the universities. We spent the better part of the end of 2003 negotiating the details of the contract, visiting the universities to secure the appropriate rooms for the equipment, and putting together the teams on each campus that would be involved in the training. Yet, by early 2004, when the equipment was slated to arrive, conditions at the universities had turned so unpredictable that Korea decided to delay implementation.[4]

By early 2004 it was clear that we in higher education would be getting next to nothing from the donor community,

---

[4]Asians had a particularly difficult time working in Iraq because there was virtually nothing they could do to disguise their national origins. Still, the insurgents made putting computers in some universities difficult for everyone. The University of Oklahoma managed to get a good number of them selectively placed, but in one, Al-Anbar University, the insurgents kidnapped the president of the university claiming that he was a tool of the Jews since he allowed "Israeli" computers to be put in the university to spy on them. In fact, not only will insurgents say whatever they want, no matter how untrue, but they soon give the lie to their own statements. This group released the president after they were paid a ransom, which is what they were after all along.

nothing from the World Bank, nothing anytime soon even from responsive nations such as South Korea, and, of course, nothing from the USA.

In addition to the fact that no money was flowing into Iraqi higher education from any source, no money was available to my office for anything. We had no budget. Nothing. Zero. If any of us in the office took a dean out to lunch or a professor out for coffee, we had to pay for it from our own pockets, or rely on the charity of our guests. Sometimes we hesitated to spend a few days on any university campus helping advise the faculty or staff since it was the university we were hoping to help that had to put us up in hotels and feed us out of their own meager budgets. We had cars and gas at our disposal; and the military sometimes could help with long-distance transport, flying us here and there by helicopter. Beyond that, we were on our own.

To make matters even worse, on top of all this we were forbidden to request any money from private sources. To do so, we were told, would put us in violation of federal law that forbade US government officials from soliciting assistance from private companies. It's not an unreasonable law; the government should hardly be in the position of looking like it's shaking down private industry or setting itself up for some quid pro quo. Still, the unhappy result of all this was that, after liberating a country from dictatorship, we failed in our obligations as an occupying and administrative power to protect the country from looting and vandalism, failed to help rebuild the infrastructure of higher education—or even find them chairs and desks—and failed to spend the kind of money necessary to connect the universities to the outside world, restore their labs, or even buy them new books.[5]

I will, before this chapter is done, outline all the many good things we were able to accomplish in Iraq in the year we

---

[5]Hard as it is to say, the CPA managed to get more supplies and hard goods into the universities from the remnants of the Oil for Food Program than from our government or from foreign donations. That the hated and corrupt Oil for Food Program was more profitable to our sector than the whole of the US Government was a sad story not lost on the average Iraqi.

all were there. But most of the good we did depended on private donations and charity, and on the encouragement and ideas we could give them for free, not on money.[6]

▲▼▲

There was, however, one pot of good American dollars that was earmarked for higher education, and that was in USAID—the United States Agency for International Development. There, in USAID, was over $20 million dollars to help get Iraqi universities back again on their feet.

Actually, "getting back on their feet" is an exaggeration. Rather than working with our office to get at the true needs of Iraqi universities, USAID decided that "partnerships" between certain select American universities and a few Iraqi university departments would be a nice idea. And, in the abstract—but only in the abstract—it *was* a nice idea. Sorry to say, there were many far better ideas, and far more pressing needs, than giving over $20 million dollars to American universities so that particular departments at a few universities could work with a few others in Iraq to improve their programs. Nonetheless, this is what USAID decided was needed in Iraq and the HEAD Program (which stood for "Higher Education and Development") was launched. Soon, out of approximately forty-five applications, five American universities or consortia of universities were selected to receive between $3.77 million and $4.99 million apiece.

Despite the fact that at every turn the agency attempted to portray these grants as a mutually agreed upon endeavor between our office and theirs, we were from the start deeply troubled by the expenditure of these kinds of funds for so limited a set of objectives.[7] USAID had no understanding of the conditions we

---

[6]I once wrote that I felt not unlike a contestant on a bad TV reality show: "Go to Baghdad for about a year in the middle of a war and fix their educational system. But you must do this without any money, nor can you ask for any money. If you ask the government for money, you will not get it; and if you ask private sources for money, you will be breaking the law. Good luck on your assignment."

[7]Before setting off for Baghdad, Ambassador Ghougassian and I endeavored to meet with the woman we were told had written the request for proposals.

were facing at the universities, scant understanding of the needs, and no understanding of what was at stake. And, because it is an agency that, while housed in the State Department, prizes its independence, working with them in a collaborative way, except on their terms, was immensely difficult.[8]

Working with the Fulbright Program was the exact opposite to this. Thanks to the efforts of one of the office deputies and the openness and support of the Fulbright people in Washington, the Fulbright Program was re-established between the US and Iraq after a hiatus of over fourteen years. For a fraction of what the HEAD grants were costing, twenty-five of the best Iraqi students came to study in the States, and the program is probably sound enough to continue into the foreseeable future.

Getting sufficient funds even to begin the rebuilding of the destroyed infrastructure of Iraqi universities, much less to make any progress in advancing the intellectual life of professors and students, was a series of constant frustrations. When I arrived in September the office was all abuzz with a promise that OTI—the Office of Transition Initiatives (itself connected to USAID)—was going to supply the universities, through one of its contractors, with desks, chairs, doors, blackboards, lecterns … whatever was needed to get the universities back up to some semblance of normality. A "University in a Box," as it was called, would be delivered to each damaged institution. So Steve Curda

---

We needed an explanation as to why this narrowly focused program and not something of more general use was decided on. But her office claimed she was too busy to see us on any day before we were to leave, so we never could find out her answer. Knowing we were stuck with the project, we worked conscientiously to make the grants as productive as possible. Sorry to say, USAID took every occasion to tout our assistance as agreement with the project, which most assuredly it was not.

[8]Since my office was expected to work with the grant winners and support their missions as best we could, I asked to see the proposals submitted by the grantees. I was told that they were "proprietary." So I told USAID that I would sue to get them under the Freedom of Information Act if they did not turn them over voluntarily, and I went to the lawyers in the Justice Ministry of the CPA to begin the action. USAID relented and sent us the winning proposals, but with all dollar amounts blackened out, since, I suppose, no one should know exactly what a public agency is spending public money on. All this while we were fighting for complete transparency in the workings of the government of Iraq.

had our office get each university president to make a comprehensive list of classroom needs. Our office then spent days working and re-working the list so that it made sense and was fair
to each university. But, when we submitted it, we were told by
the contracting company working for OTI that, despite what
we might have thought, they didn't actually have a *contract*
with OTI but needed us to do all this work so that they could
then submit it as a *proposal!* We were outraged, and the university presidents, who had spent so long preparing the plan, fluc-
tuated between feelings that ranged from disappointment to
betrayal. Again, America made promises and failed to keep them.
How much better had we just kept our mouths shut and said
nothing.[9]

Yet even this is not the worst. Towards the very end of
2003, we in Higher Education and the Ministry of Education
(that is, the ministry in CPA working with elementary and secondary schools) learned that, through the good offices of Representative Lowry of New York, over $90 million would be
earmarked in the supplemental appropriations bill for "education." Finally, it seemed, we would not be left hanging. Not
knowing how much of this was to be allocated to higher and
how much to basic education, the two senior advisors from
basic education and I got together and hammered out a reasonable division of the funds. Basic education had needs even
greater than ours, so we decided that 60 percent of the money
should go to basic education, and the rest, $36 million in all,
to us. The senior advisor in Finance then had us lay out in detail
how each of us would allocate the funds.

In our sector, the allocation was easy: some would go
toward rebuilding basic science labs at the universities, somewhat more to restore libraries, and a larger amount to the various technical institutes and colleges to rebuild their vocational
education programs. If Iraq was ever to be rebuilt, it would be

---

[9]In the end, OTI found money to purchase about 8,000 desks, or about 10
percent of what was needed, and no money for anything else. We decided to
send all the desks to Basra, to be divided between the university and the two
technical institutes there. "A spit in the ocean," as the Iraqis might say, but
we were grateful even for this little bit.

with the skills and labor of electricians and machinists and carpenters from these schools.

Sorry to say, the $36 million we had anticipated was reduced to $8 million, with the rest all given to basic education. Moreover, the allocation was not being given to us directly, but, rather, to USAID! Soon, one of the women from the HEAD office came to see if I would consider allocating the money not to the technical institutes or for labs or libraries but to help continue the HEAD grants! I'm sure I said some rather unpleasant words not only about my continued poor impression of the current grants but also about the arrogance of her agency which, despite all its fine talk about how supportive they were of our office, was now attempting to take away the only reconstruction money our sector had received in a year. She left not a little unhappy.[10]

Eight million dollars were not enough to reconstruct and refurbish the libraries, nor anywhere near enough to rebuild and restock the technical institutes. So, after talking with a number of ministry officials and university presidents, we decided the money might best be spent covering the reconstruction of the universities' basic laboratories. The Project Management Office of the Department of Defense, set up under Admiral Nash, told us they would oversee the project. By the time the Coalition Provisional Authority was dissolved in June, the Project Management Office had still not managed to issue any contracts for something as simple as buying test tubes and Bunsen burners for the universities. The project languished until the rise in insurgent activity made it undoable. So again, in the end, there was nothing.

▲▼▲

Nothing, that is, of a material sort in any substantive way from the Federal Government, other than the Fulbright grants. But

---

[10]Why it was that our portion of the $90 million was reduced in the final congressional allocation from $36 million to $8 million was never made clear. Calls to Representative Lowry's office were not returned. To say that it wound up being $8 million because that's what USAID needed for it to continue the HEAD project would be merely speculation on my part.

here's where the American private sector and others stepped in. The UK, the Czech Republic, and Italy all stepped up to the plate with a number of scholarship programs. Despite the fact that we had no money allocated to us to help replenish university libraries, a few American universities helped, as did the British Council, which by the time I left had probably sent to Iraq over ten tons of books.

Why some American universities helped and others would not is something of a mystery. Few of the more "conservative" colleges responded to any request for aid. As I've said, the president of my own alma mater wouldn't even respond to three personal letters from me to him. Yet Duke University, surely on anyone's top-ten list of "liberal" universities, responded magnificently. At the urging of an emeritus history professor and with what I learned was the "enthusiastic" support of the president, Duke sent thousands of books to Iraq at its own expense.[11] And, of course, it was Duke that offered safe harbor to Sattar Jawad— just as it was liberal Harvard that gave shelter to Tahir Bakaa, the liberal and secular Minister who succeeded Dr. Zeiad, and found ways of bringing a good number of Iraqi scholars and university administrators over for scholarly conferences and symposia. I'd be surprised if the leaders of those universities were supporters of either the Bush administration or the war in Iraq. But they clearly had no trouble in seeing that there was more at stake for education internationally than playing partisan politics.

In the for-profit sector, IBM sent representatives to work out training and travel agreements with the University of Technology in Baghdad, and the Burpee Seed Company found the

---

[11]Of course, it had to be at its own expense since there was no government program that could reimburse anyone even for postage. We had any number of institutions willing to make contributions not only of books but also of computers, excess scientific equipment, older machines for the medical schools, you name it. Every bit of it would have been of value to Iraq. But the institution not only had to give us the goods, they also had to package it all and ship it at their own expense. Duke and a few other places were willing to do this, though it's understandable that most places would be unwilling to pay for the opportunity to be charitable. Unfortunately, the "Denton Program," under which material could be shipped on US vessels for free if there were room, turned out to be of no value to us in these efforts.

means and money to deliver almost four tons of vegetable seed to the various agricultural colleges in Iraq. All our office had to do was have a central collection point for anything sent, and figure out a means of distribution, which we did. Of course, I had to convince people at the Pentagon that these were free gifts, unsolicited in any way by me. But that was easy, since they were. Had we been able to solicit, and, above all, had we been able to reimburse donors for something as simple as postage, we might have been able to make up for many things the government didn't supply.[12]

▲▼▲

Despite all our efforts, honesty demands that we admit that the first goal of my office—rebuilding the physical infrastructure of Iraq's burned, damaged, and decayed universities—was a failure at least insofar as direct help from the US government was concerned. Nonetheless, just after liberation, before the bombing of the UN headquarters and when military movements were more or less unimpeded, our office did manage to help close out the school year by coordinating over three million exam books, twelve thousand reams of paper, and over $92 thousand worth of fans and other supplies for the final exams with UNESCO. The army was also able to deliver dozens of industrial-sized air conditioners to the various universities in central Baghdad for their summer sessions. More than a little success came from enlisting the assistance of the military in rebuilding damaged structures or in giving some of the found money that Saddam had left behind to projects in our sector. This was how a new

---

[12]Not only did USAID give, in my view, unconscionable amounts of money to a few select American universities for so little gain, they also made it next to impossible to ask the university community to help in any significant way with rebuilding without promising millions that none of us had. The more than three dozen universities that were rejected in the competition had no interest in turning around and offering their services gratis. And universities that were not in the competition also were quick to say no. When I spoke to one university that had a pre-eminent program in a field desperately needed by Iraqis—petroleum engineering—the dean, whom I knew, said he'd not do anything unless we paid him as handsomely as USAID had paid the others.

dorm was built to take the place of the one that other parts of the military had seized from Mustansiriya University, how a dormitory for female students was set up for Baghdad University, how the only Museum of Natural History in Iraq was put back together again, and how doors, walls, and windows were finally rebuilt at Baghdad University, once we got the money out from under the bed. The army also found ways of setting up internet cafes on different campuses and even getting television sets into girls' dorms. Still, while these projects were helpful, in all candor they relied not on any strategic plan but on the helter-skelter interests of this commander or that.

One area where Jim Mollen was particularly adept was in showing our Ministry how to get every possible dinar it could out of the bumbling Iraqi Ministry of Finance. We even managed to have them turn a blind eye to the money each university made from such things as book sales and parking fees and evening school tuitions, all of which was supposed to be turned into the national treasury. None of this came anywhere close to supporting the projects we so optimistically went to Madrid to have funded, but at least we were starting.

▲▼▲

Given the narrative above, it should be clear that most of our achievements, such as they were, were generally unaccompanied by high dollar totals or tangible material objects. Some things that sound minor to us here in America—like the joining of the three Kurdish universities with the others in Iraq into one Ministry, or beginning the integration of Kurdish and Arab students in the universities—were of major importance to Iraqis and the future of any unified Iraq. Some policies were recognized as significant from the start. The previously required indoctrination classes in Ba'athist ideology and in the achievements of Saddam, all the special allowances given to Ba'ath Party members in university entrance exams, the infamous "friend of Saddam" entrance bonus points, or the limitation placed on the percentage of females entering certain fields—all these were, and to this day remain, eliminated. The faculty at each university was empowered to select its own leadership—its own deans, presidents, and other high-ranking officials. Travel for academic purposes was protected by an order from the Administrator and widely taken advantage of. University professors, presidents, and ministry officials traveled to the States to get a better understanding of a different and more open style of education. At least one American University in Iraq should soon be opening. Both undergraduate and graduate scholarships were begun, in America and Europe, with every scholarship awarded in an open and transparent competition.[13] The universities were given significant latitude to plot their own curricular future, to hire their own staffs and professors, and to improve their offerings without central domination. The university presidents were empowered to meet and deliberate together in policy formulation. All this culminated in the Declaration in Erbil which condemned political and religious intimidation and defined the rights, freedoms, and responsibilities of all university members.

Clearly, there was a tendency in all that we did towards academic openness and dialogue, freedom of inquiry, democratization, and individual liberty. As I mentioned earlier, the election by the faculty of its own leadership was probably the first set of democratic elections in the new Iraq. Nonetheless, since universities are easily intimidated, especially by well-armed fanatics, not all these reforms continue in practice.[14] But they

---

[13]It might seem obvious to us that scholarships should be awarded impartially and through fair competition, but corruption is so endemic in Iraq that often fairness itself seems corrupt. It was understood to be an embarrassment to many in high places if they couldn't use their position to advance the welfare of their family and friends. If unchecked, many would naturally choose nephews and nieces for awards; to do less might be seen as an immoral betrayal of one's family obligations. Minister Zeiad went so far as to declare that Iraq would not recognize any graduate degree awarded to any student who was chosen by a process in which he had no hand, and told us that he firmly believed that those who received Fulbright grants got them because they paid bribes to our office.

[14]One sad example: Our office worked diligently to rescind the Ba'ath Party's expulsion of the American Jesuits from Iraq and restore to them the property of Al-Hikmat University and Baghdad College. Obligingly, indeed happily, the Iraqi Governing Council restored all expropriated buildings and property in December of 2003. My office was in contact with the Jesuit Provincial offices back in America, and I met with two Jesuits who came to Baghdad to review the situation. But I'm morally certain that the restoration of the

remain there, "on the books" in a sense, the result of the joint efforts of the Coalition and the academic community of Iraq, and will no doubt surface again when—if—Iraq ever emerges from this new wave of violence and fanaticism.

▲▼▲

To paint this picture of minimal material assistance with fragile intellectual and spiritual help is, I believe, to paint truly. If one understands aid only in material terms, then indeed it was "all assistance short of actual help"—to use a phrase thrown out by one of the more urbane and insouciant British generals stationed with us in Baghdad. But, if we're willing to count the opening of new intellectual vistas, new insights into teaching and learning, and the various cross-cultural connections we were able to forge as actual and true help, then perhaps a good deal was accomplished. And even though I've labeled these as "fragile" given the ease with which any violence can stifle their execution, it's because of their immaterial nature that they might survive even when desks and chairs will be gone. Ideas often have a permanency that objects cannot hope for.

Still, I have tried to be clear-sighted throughout this narrative both about our expectations and also about the reality "on the ground." If we will the ends, we should also will the means. To think that we could prosecute a war unpopular in foreign capitals and expect that those nations might help either us or Iraq from some new-found charity or respect for humanity is silly. Even if they had been for the war, they still would refer to their own interests and not the interests of Iraqis or the desires of America.

More often than not, America talks about self-interest, and acts from beneficence; other nations prattle on and on about humanity, and act from self-interest. To use a metaphor I heard from Dr. Zeiad, to be thrown into the arms of the international

---

college and university will not happen, if for no other reason than that it's now impossible to secure the safety of anyone involved in such a venture given the control Islamic religious fanatics now have over virtually all public life.

community is no different than to be thrown to the wolves. Recall that only we and, to an extent, Japan, were willing to give money in Madrid without expectation of repayment. What is it about the natural self-interested calculations of other nations that we do not understand? To have expected either assistance on one hand or gratitude on the other was to play the fool.

Again, in willing the end, we must will the means. To have spent billions on defense and reconstruction and little to nothing in those areas on which the foundations of a reconstructed and democratic society will depend—schools, higher education, exchange programs, culture—is shortsighted and worse than counterproductive.

But, above all, we needed to be candid. If nothing was to be forthcoming by way of aid, we needed to say so from the start. Perhaps the worst thing we did in Iraq was to raise the expectation of help, then do nothing. Throughout this book I've been open about the peculiar defects of character of the Iraqis as I observed them, especially how they expected to be taken care of rather than do for themselves. But nothing was gained and much was lost in catering to these sentiments of deservedness and dependency, and then turning away.

# EIGHT

# Soldiers

This is the hardest chapter to write. It's also the chapter that many of my friends asked me to think twice about setting down. All criticism—not of the war but of our warriors—is immediately taken as disloyalty to the men and women whose lives are on the line every day. As Americans, we're told, we need not support the war, but we must always support our troops. Yet the fact is that the US military has, by its actions, made winning the peace in Iraq a precarious and difficult operation.[1]

Let me not be misunderstood: There were soldiers, sailors, marines, and airmen in Iraq who were and are doing superb

---

[1]The phrase current while I was in Iraq was that the military won the war, but lost the peace. Still, through no fault of our soldiers, the fact is that the war was never won in the first place. I'm sure that the Pentagon's plan of attacking Iraq from both the north and south simultaneously was the right plan. But Turkey's intransigence in preventing us from opening up the northern front in any major way simply meant that the retreating Iraqi army had secure areas in which to retreat to and hide. The mission of defeating Saddam's forces was never accomplished; they simply left the field and waited. Then, with new allies of foreign terrorists and religious radicals as their advance men, they fought the second, current, war of sabotage and destabilization.

jobs in helping win over a hurt and puzzled country. There were military doctors, for example, who worked to save countless Iraqi civilians from death and disfigurement, who made no distinction between our soldiers and the lives of those we were sent to liberate. Some of these soldier-doctors helped us set up nursing programs, helped supply the medical schools with books and equipment, helped set up Iraq's only independent medical association. I know others who worked in the schools, who cadged computers from their companies back home to distribute to the universities, who built classrooms, who found money to fix dormitories, who propped up the veterinary schools. One colonel I knew did everything from helping to start the first agricultural extension service in Iraq to putting together fishing tournaments for Baghdad children. Some rebuilt the national museum; others managed to get TVs to women's dormitories to help increase their openness to the outside world. The list of individual good things done by our soldiers would be far longer than this book.

But most of these good things done were done by the civil affairs part of the military operation, primarily by soldiers in the Guard and Reserves, by people with a few years on them and more than a little real-world experience, and not your average enlistee.

More still needs to be said: If I had to pick the single most serious miscalculation made before the war began, it would be reliance on the thought that many Iraqis would rise up along with our troops and march with us to overthrow the people who had oppressed them for so long. We expected not only gifts of candy and flowers as we marched from Basra to Baghdad, but real help as well. Yet, whether it was because (as we were often told) the Shiite majority had memories of being double-crossed by us before, in 1990, or, more likely, because we were liberating a scared, disabled, and dysfunctional country, the fact is that we did the most difficult thing: *We liberated Iraq; we did not join the Iraqis in their own liberation.*

Consider the oddness of this: Aside from the Kurds in the North, who were more than willing to join forces with us, we liberated a people who by and large waited on the sidelines to be handed their freedom. It would be as if, for example, in the liberation of Eastern Europe from Soviet control, we did all the fighting while the Czechs, the Poles, the Latvians sat on the side, waving. In every other act of national liberation with international help, the country's nationals took the lead, and the Free World played the supporting role. Not here.

I would suggest, if a lesson needs to be learned, that we never again liberate a country *for* a people, unless we are prepared to bear all the burden, the cost, and so many of the casualties ourselves. I trust this is a lesson already understood.

That is not, however, to say that we liberated an unwilling country. Any number of the stories recounted in this book tells of the happiness of the average Iraqi at being freed from the horrors of Saddam's rule. But, as the stories also tell, the truth is that the average Iraqi was puzzled, frightened, and suspicious of our motives. Why would we really want to help them? It's not something they would have done for others; why were we doing it for them? They were a people formed so completely by a culture of fear and a culture of suspicion that they could not act; they could barely react.

It was also a culture of corruption, where for at least the last three decades nothing was done without a payoff. Saddam's soldiers would take money from families on the pretext of bringing food to their loved ones starving in prison. The food, of course, never arrived; often the loved ones were already dead. Police were paid next to nothing, so all they had was power. The government fully expected that they would enhance their meager paychecks by, for example, stopping cars at random and taking a bribe not to make an arrest. Any civic sense, any initiative, any independence of spirit and willingness to fight for one's self or country was totally beaten down by the cultures of fear, suspicion, corruption, and, as I describe elsewhere, the cultures of dependency and privilege. They were a subdued people, and this made the job of liberating them on the part of our soldiers even harder.[2]

---

[2]In a meeting I had with Paul Wolfowitz and a delegation of university and ministry officials, Mr. Wolfowitz asked, with clear exasperation, why it was

Yet, more. If warm and visible support for the soldiers liberating them was hard to find, attacks on our soldiers were behind every corner, down every road. The enemy wore no uniform and carried no flag. The enemy was indistinguishable from the friend. So our soldiers were in a situation where friends were quiet and subdued, and enemies were deadly, and there was no way to tell one from another. In a situation where, perhaps, 10 percent of the population is against you, is armed, and wishes you dead, but that 10 percent is indistinguishable from all the rest, every person you meet will soon be treated as a potential enemy rather than as a safe comrade. And, fairly quickly, this is what happened: Unable to tell friend from enemy, all Iraqis began to be treated as the enemy. The people we went to liberate soon came to be the people we were fearful of, and the soldiers treated all Iraqis from this wellspring of fear. If you cannot tell friend from foe, the only safe course is to treat everyone as the enemy.

Again, these sentiments were not universal among all the military. When I commented to the colonel who was setting up the fishing tournament for Baghdad teens that he was daring death, his answer was simple—he was there to help the Iraqis get back on their feet and take over their lives; he wasn't there to worry about saving his own. But that's not a speech the average enlistee, scared and away from home for the first time, in a strange and clearly hostile land, would be able to give. His first concern was, understandably, himself and the wellbeing of his friends. Yet, while understandable, securing his life was not the reason he was sent over.

▲▼▲

In a small way, the rhetoric that came out of the Pentagon contributed to this atmosphere of seeing Iraqis as the enemy we

---

that he met with so many Iraqis who couldn't bring themselves to say "Thank you." Whereupon, one of the university presidents gave one of the most moving and heartfelt thank-you's I had ever heard, saying that the Coalition did indeed find and destroy the most murderous weapon of mass destruction, Saddam himself, and for that his country would be grateful forever. Yet, while every word of it was sincere and true, it was an expression of gratitude that needed to be prompted. The spontaneous embrace of those who liberated them was rarely apparent.

needed to defeat rather than as friends we were sent to liberate. Consider the way the Department of Defense, indeed the whole Administration, constantly referred to the pacification of Germany and Japan after the war as the model of what we were hoping to do. There were constant references to how long our troops stayed in those places after the war was over, or how long it took to get constitutional democracies functioning there. But Germany and Japan were our sworn enemies whose people were loyal to their leaders—a situation far different from what we said was the case in Iraq.

Indeed, if comparisons had to be made, it would have been far more appropriate to look at what the Allies did in Italy after the Second World War rather than the difficulties we faced in either Japan or Germany. In Italy we had a Fascist regime not unlike the Ba'ath Party's rule in Iraq. We had a populace willing and, in places, joyful to be liberated from their Fascist overlords. We faced resistance from pockets of foreign elements, mostly German, who, as they retreated, were willing to kill the indigenous population. And you had resistance from the remnants of the former Fascist rulers. Yet we were able to bring the Italians into a status of co-belligerency with us against the Fascists and Nazis; military civil affairs officers were able to work closely with liberated Italians to rebuild their nation after devastation far worse than was inflicted on Iraq by the war; and we were able to stand up a democratic government sooner than we were able to do in the rest of the Axis nations. In looking to know what we should have done after the war in Iraq was over, we would have been much wiser to inform ourselves by studying our activity in Italy after WWII than in looking at either Germany or Japan.[3]And we would have avoided the temptation to see Iraqis, whom we went to liberate, as similar to either the Germans or the Japanese, whom we went to defeat.

▲▼▲

---

[3]I am indebted to Gordon Rudd, a military historian working in Iraq, for this insight.

Elsewhere I said that one reason we civilians went out by ourselves rather than with military escort was because we were more visible and exposed to attack if we traveled with soldiers. But the other reason was that it was too often simply unbearable. The lead humvee would often have a soldier standing armed through the roof of the car, pointing his fist, often in a black glove, at any car that dared get near. "Back off, you f****r," was the repeated refrain, as he pointed his black-gloved fist and his gun at them. These were, in almost every instance, just ordinary Iraqis going to work, going to market, minding their business. And they didn't need even the slightest command of English to know they were being pushed around and cursed on their own streets. In this way, what began as a liberation became an occupation, and became nourishment for the growing insurgency. Ever so paradoxically, the more the military tried to keep itself safe, the more it treated everyone as the enemy, the less safe it became, and we with them.[4]

▲▼▲

In many ways, the Iraqis most charitable toward the plight of the American soldier were those who worked for the CPA as translators and drivers. Suhail, for instance, would always make excuses for them—"You have to see how young they are. They're away from their mothers for the first time, they don't know who we are, and they're scared. Sure, they push us around, but it's just because they're frightened." But arrogant, scared, ignorant, and armed is often not the best combination. Even Suhail stopped defending them when once, at a checkpoint he had to pass to come to work with us, a soldier broke his cell phone to make sure it wasn't a bomb. When Suhail protested (he cried, actually) that he needed it to work, it was brand-new, and cost

---

[4]Soon after I left, the president of Al-Nahrain University was shot in the stomach and his driver killed by exactly one of these black-gloved soldiers. By all accounts, the Iraqi driver didn't move out of the way fast enough, so the car was shot up. Al-Nahrain was the former honors university that Saddam carved out of the University of Baghdad. Soon after liberation, we were in discussion with the president who was interested in renaming it the American University of Iraq in Baghdad. No longer.

him almost a week's pay, he was told, "Next time try buying a better one." Then the soldier shoved him out of the way.

These checkpoints were a special torture for Iraqi women, many of whom were raised with the view that no man should touch their bodies but their husband. Yet, rightly, no one could enter the Green Zone without a search and without being patted down. If female soldiers were available, they conducted the searches. If not, the men had to do them. Humiliation was constant. Once, when one of my senior advisor colleagues complained that her female translator was distraught at being ridiculed by the soldiers, as if she didn't understand perfectly well what was being said, the snickering response came from the soldier that he was commenting to his buddy on the size of her breast *pocket,* nothing more. I guess if you see your job as simply protecting yourself, what difference does lying make?

▲▼▲

Our office's closest contact with the military was over something that might seem minor; but it seriously undermined our relationship with the university community and was a catalyst in reversing the initial favorable student opinion towards our efforts and towards America. When the military first entered Baghdad in April of 2003, an army battalion commandeered part of a large dormitory complex that housed students from both Baghdad and Mustansiriya universities. On July 22, the night that Uday and Qusay were killed, our soldiers heard gunshots coming from a section of the dorms still used by students. Although the gunshots might actually have been celebratory fire, the military saw this as reason enough to evict the remaining students and take over all the dorms for their own use.[5]

---

[5]The students at these two universities were among the most anti-Ba'athist, anti-Saddam elements anywhere in Iraq. After the Coalition deposed the former presidents of the universities, for example, it was, I was told, three students who cooked up a ruse and gunned down the Ba'athist former president of Baghdad University after luring him out of his office.

There were thirteen buildings in the complex built to house about 1200 students. In typical Iraqi fashion, it probably housed four times that number, with students sleeping on roofs, on ledges, and on blankets thrown everywhere on the floor. Soon, the 1st Armored Division battalion occupied eleven of the buildings, as they systematically evicted those students who were there for the summer session. On July 29, an agreement was reached between the commander and the president of Mustansiriya University (Dr. Tahir al-Bakaa, who succeeded Dr. Zeiad as the Minister of all of Higher Education the following year). Under the agreement, the evictions were to stop and the remaining 325 students would be allowed to stay in the two remaining dormitories in order to finish the summer semester and take their exams. Despite the agreement, those students, too, were soon ejected.

I arrived on the scene a few weeks later, just before the start of the fall semester. The two universities desperately needed their dorms returned. The Coalition equally desperately needed as many students in class as possible, studying, and not on the streets. And the universities had no money to find alternative housing for the students, though in the end they were forced to use what few funds they had to rent hotel and apartment rooms for returning students. Still, this would be, we all assured ourselves, over soon.

But it wasn't. The battalion was renovating the dorms to suit its needs—new beds, air conditioners, refrigerators, game rooms—and they weren't about to leave. Indeed, more soldiers were invited to move in. The university presidents and the Ministry went through us and through every appropriate channel to get their legitimate property back. Through my office, Bremer became involved, and, while he probably had authority to command the soldiers to leave, he clearly had no desire to cross General Sanchez, who, in turn, had no desire to discomfort his men.[6]

---

[6]I've just said that I think Ambassador Bremer could have commanded the troops out, but I'm not certain that it's true. Crossing General Sanchez—no doubt an officer who would do anything for his men, but an icy and visibly

In order to make the transition easier for the soldiers, Lieutenant Colonel Curda managed to secure a nearby campus that was being abandoned by the Defense Ministry and that campus was offered to the troops. But, since it involved a line change on a map of about three hundred feet, and moving men who were already happily ensconced in a setting they made quite habitable for themselves, they refused. They weren't going anywhere until Sanchez ordered them to.

October semester was soon to begin, and we braced for the worst. In the face of these pressures, the other side of the American military came into view. If one part of the army occupied university property and dared the students to riot, another part would do what it could to calm the waters. Under the direction of Lieutenant Colonel John Kem, an army engineer who

---

arrogant man who displayed neither thoughtfulness nor policy sensitivity—may not have been either wise or possible. More importantly, this effective lack of a unified command was a serious liability for the whole operation. We know, for example, that Bremer told the White House that he thought more troops were needed to restore order, but he was contradicted by the military. In putting Bremer's pleas aside, the Administration spokesman said that, when it comes to a choice, the President listens to the soldiers in the field. This meant, of course, not so much that the Administration would get bad advice, but no advice at all—simply what "the soldiers in the field" think that the commander-in-chief wants to hear.

Sometimes, however, the military acts in more self-interested ways, ways contrary to the mission but agreeable to them. If Bremer is to be believed, it was the American military that worked against the arrest and trial of Muqtada al-Sadr after an Iraqi magistrate bravely issued a warrant for his arrest for the killing of the Ayatollah Khoei. In August of 2003, the marines in and around Najaf lobbied the Pentagon and campaigned within the Coalition military command against his arrest, and then pressured the Iraqi judge to forego the arrest, since it would involve their having to back up the Iraqi police in the operation. "The only explanation I could come up with," Bremer writes with strange dispassion, "was that the 1st Marine Expeditionary Force was due to rotate out of Iraq in three weeks—to be replaced by the Polish-led force—and didn't want any trouble before that."

I said at the start that no single policy and no single decision should be seen as determinative of our difficulties in Iraq, but I'd be tempted to make this the one exception. To have supported a courageous Iraqi judge at this juncture, to have stood behind the rule of law, to have shown the authority and not just the power of the Coalition, and to have nipped the threat of al-Sadr this early would have gone far to change the current situation in Iraq for the better. Instead, it seems that policy was made by soldiers who wanted to be safe rather than useful, and they were backed up in this by others up the military chain of command.

had been fixing up university property in Baghdad with money our forces found when they liberated Baghdad, the army took over the Defense Ministry campus and turned it into a dormitory complex for some of the displaced students. It wasn't as extensive as what was taken—it could house just over 700 students, not the thousands who had been displaced. And it did nothing to placate the students who had been evicted during exams nor the hundreds who still had no place to live. But it helped calm a very volatile situation, at least for a few more months.

What finally happened to the occupied dorms? The battalion stayed in them until its tour was up the following summer, then it left. The universities were promised that at least there would be some new plumbing and wiring, some fans and mattresses left behind, in small compensation for their loss. But, as soon as the soldiers were gone, brigands from the Iraqi National Guard jumped over the wall that separated their offices from the dorms, had a gunfight with the university guards who were there, and tore the place apart. Nothing of any value survived.[7] What the Americans failed to inflict on the universities, again the Iraqis did to themselves.

There were times in our relationship with the military when you didn't know whether to cry or laugh. In late Spring 2004, the army entered the campus of the Agriculture College of Baghdad University, over near Abu Ghraib. They had received word that there was "bomb-making equipment" hidden on the campus. So, without coordinating with our office, without going to the dean or any campus administrator who would have unlocked every door for the men, they entered in force, kicked in doors, broke windows and computers, and, worst of all, destroyed research projects that graduate students had been working on for the year—incubation projects and the like. The dean also reported that the antique hunting collection he had

---

[7]This was a guard unit that was being trained by the battalion that lived in the dormitories. When the head of the guard was arrested for thievery, the battalion commander, I was told, had him sprung the next day.

in a locked room next to his office—old shotguns and rifles his father had collected—were taken.

When I asked for an accounting of what had happened, I was told, proudly, that the soldiers did indeed find what they were looking for—they definitely found bomb-making equipment. I was brought some to examine. Sure enough: fertilizer. It was, after all, as I had to explain, a goddam AGRICULTURE college. What did they expect to find!? And, no, none of our guys had any idea what happened to the research projects or the antique shotguns.

▲▼▲

Still, all these were as nothing compared to the revelations of abuse at Abu Ghraib. The abuse at Abu Ghraib did immense damage to our operation. It reinforced the widespread Iraqi notion that human nature is such that given any power most people will become mini-Saddams, even the Americans with their odd protestations that they were there to help. And it gave currency to the insurgents' view that the Coalition was there to satisfy its own perverse desires, mock Islam, and humiliate and subjugate Iraqis.

Iraqis are, of course, no strangers to torture. "We are a cruel people," one of our Iraqi translators would always remind us; "it's in our DNA." So it wasn't the revelations of torture, as such, that so troubled Iraqis. Rather, it was the character and sexual nature of these abuses. Let me try to explain.

My guess is that much of Iraq had some idea about what was going on inside Abu Ghraib long before we Americans did. It soon became difficult to go onto any campus without a delegation of faculty petitioning me to free one or more of their colleagues or perhaps even a family member who had been taken in for interrogation. I always gave the same answer: If the person had done nothing wrong, the interrogation would show it and the innocent person would soon be released. If the person were guilty of something, they should be happy that he was taken into custody. And their response was always the same "You don't understand, he's been taken to *Abu Ghraib*. Please help release him." Interestingly enough, if my guess is right that they had a good idea of what was going on, no Iraqi I knew could bring himself to say in words exactly what they had heard from their neighbors—it was that humiliating.

If the first problem with our military in Iraq was that they treated Iraqis not as liberated friends but as the enemy because they had no idea how to work in a country where friend and foe all looked alike, the second problem was a face of America and Americans that some in the military sadly showed to the outside world. To many Iraqis, however, both were the two sides of a single coin, with only the following difference: The first, the abuse of ordinary Iraqis, showed our fear of and contempt for them; the second, Abu Ghraib, displayed not only Americans' abandonment to perverse sexuality, up to and including homoerotic sadism, but also the willingness of American females to be photographed sexually abusing naked men, and the joy that they all seemed to display at not only degrading Iraqis but at degrading their own natures as well. It showed, in other words, contempt for the foundations of morality and humanity. Abu Ghraib looked less like severe treatment of detainees in order to wrest important information from them as much as it seemed depraved fun and sexual games, all captured on film, and all for the pleasures of the Americans. Is there any wonder why ordinary, good-willed Iraqis are conflicted by our presence there?[8]

The American response to Abu Ghraib was, in all candor, totally insufficient. To say that these were rogue acts of improp-

---

[8]This from my friend Ali, whose desire to be an American opened the first Chapter: "[The insurgents] just want to torcher [torture] us before cutting us [down] because we work with the Americans. And the Americans only care about their safety while ours they never care for. In deed they put us in long lines with out any protection just to humiliate us & make us feel that we are the masters [Americans] & you are the slaves [Iraqis]. And the hard part is that all is going on in our lands. We can see all the nationalities passing the check points & looking with disgust to us while we are waiting our turn at the lines just like a dog waiting for his bone. After all this they tell us that we are of great value for them & with out us they wouldn't make it."

But Ali was torn between his love for democracy and the daily cruelties done in its name: "Any way, all these are better than Saddam's period. I know we have to wait. But I really don't know that I will make it & how long we will have to wait more."

erly supervised young men and women is to admit that the military put into positions of power American degenerates who, because they were unsupervised, were simply acting as they would naturally. To say that they were improperly trained implied, again, that our military need to be "trained" not to act as brutes, that this is what our soldiers do when left in their own custody. But the worst response, and perhaps the most common (though it was always said quietly, as if the sayer knew it was shameful), was that it was no big deal: "So what? Yes, men were forced to perform before strangers and before women; yes, they were sexually ridiculed and humiliated. But nobody died; nobody even really got hurt." To those for whom life and the absence of pain are paramount virtues, such an answer is sufficient. But to those for whom honor and morality are paramount, such an answer is part of the problem.

I don't want to overstate damage about the revelations of abuse at Abu Ghraib. Nor do I want to read my feelings into the feelings of all Iraqis. But I do know that what was going on at Abu Ghraib was troubling enough to our supporters and allies that the Iraqis closest to us didn't want to talk about it. Even my Kurdish friends, who would joke and tease about most anything, were silent and circumspect when it came to this.

To a people told by our enemies that modernity stands for indulgence and the loosening of all moral rules, that America is a perverse and hedonistic culture, that liberty is libertinism and anarchy, and that our secularism is really nothing but irreligion and an affront to God, Abu Ghraib was a gift to our enemies and an utter disaster for America and its friends.

▲▼▲

There are many lessons to be learned from all this, some easier, some harder. The US military is not the only group put into dangerous situations where it's hard to tell friend from enemy. Police forces worldwide are often called upon to patrol areas where criminals live and work side by side with the innocent. Some police forces handle this situation better than others, but the techniques they use for managing these situations would surely bear not simply study but application.

Second, we are all grateful that so few Americans have died in Iraq as compared to other wars. But to the extent that policy is set rather than executed by the military—even when it's set for their convenience or to avoid risk—we endanger the policy aims of the mission itself.

Third, there's a species of rhetoric that surrounds military recruiting these days that may be less than helpful: "Be all that you can be," "An army of one," and similar phrases center the demands and rewards of military service too individually. Military service is "service"—service to the country, not something self-directed. It was once considered a duty, a duty we owe our neighbors and fellow countrymen, not a kind of self-improvement or something we do to find ourselves or because we don't yet have sufficient training or education to get a good job.

Fourth, in Iraq, some of the finest people I ever met were in uniform, and others were, let us say, less than admirable.[9] No matter how desperate the military may be for soldiers to fill their ranks, it seems to me simply counterproductive to recruit the unintelligent, the poorly educated, the morally confused, or the desperate. If I were to be told that the military does its best to keep such people out, I would have to say that I saw enough and spoke to enough military police working fiercely to keep good order to consider such statements to be counterfactual. And if all this means that far different recruiting pools need to be considered, or that some semblance of a draft is in order, I would not shy away from those considerations.

I believe it to be untrue, as I've heard it said by some on the left, that war or military service brutalizes young men and makes them into bad people. Military service seems to me not to change a person's character, but to magnify it. A person of good character, brave, patriotic, eager to serve—that person

---

[9]One rather peculiar soldier told me over dinner that he had spent the day washing and waxing a vehicle he had use of, and if any Iraqi dared even to touch it, he would blow his head off. He seemed happy to be waiting for just such an occasion. All I could do was protest that sometimes I look Iraqi, so what would he do if I touched the car? To which all he could say was, "Don't be silly. You're not Iraqi."

shines. But the morally challenged, the self-centered, the unsteady—all their faults and vices seem to be underscored and to grow. If this is even partly true, then nothing, not even training, is more vital than proper and wiser recruiting.

But the whole burden cannot fall simply on the military. American colleges and universities have an obligation to encourage, not discourage, good men and women who may wish to serve. If our best institutions dishonor military life, from where will improvement come? Unless our institutions of higher learning once again recognize that producing educated and thoughtful leaders in our military is as important as producing smart lawyers or careful doctors or savvy businessmen, they will have failed in a serious part of their moral and civic mission.

In like manner, for high schools to bar recruiters from meeting with students, for high schools not to encourage their best graduates to think about military service before going on to college or career is a disservice not only to our students but also to our country.

Finally, I understand the position taken by many that the condition of today's military is simply a reflection of the current condition of American character. Sure soldiers might look out first for themselves, but who doesn't? All that the guards at Abu Ghraib were having was "fun," and isn't having fun what our culture is all about? Why hold soldiers to a higher standard than we hold anyone else? Aside from the fact that we do and must hold certain positions—like doctors, policemen, judges, and, yes, the military—to higher standards than we hold most others, the truth remains that blaming the culture is the coward's way out. There were soldiers in Iraq who were far better, both morally and in terms of service, than most ordinary Americans, and ones who were worse. I do know that we cannot look at the damage that the guards at Abu Ghraib did to the image of America, for example, and just shrug.

There is nothing in my background that makes me a military planner, and I'm the first to recognize the insufficiency of the suggestions I've made above. I only offer to those more adept at discovering possible solutions that the problem of leadership, the problem of character, and the whole problem of recruiting are not matters that will right themselves naturally. Indeed, they are cyclical, and feed upon themselves—the lower down we reach into the pool of available talent, the fewer will be those proudly willing to serve in the future; the more our institutions discourage military service because it doesn't comport with their current political ideology, the worse they will find military practice in the years to come; the more we disengage military service from real service to the country, the more will the ideal of service wither in America.

# NINE

# Reality Often Astonishes Theory: American Ideals and the Failure of Good Intentions

Let me return to Ali, the young man I wrote about at the start of first chapter, the one who wanted so desperately to be an American. As I mentioned, he signed up with the army of liberation as soon as it entered Baghdad. He gave up his career as a pharmacist to work payroll at KBR; then, knowing full well the dangers, he left KBR to work directly for the American Embassy. By now his sister was well ensconced at the university, happy in her field of computer science, though going to class was for her a triple difficulty: political fanatics shelled her campus with fair regularity, hoping to profit from a chaotic and destabilized public life; student religious zealots were mandating this and forbidding that for women students, despite the university president's vain belief that a less restrictive educational environment coupled with the internet would open up their mind and show everyone the value of liberty; and she now developed a crippling disease that made her progressively lamer and unable to get to class without Ali's help. There was no father, by the way, and Ali and his older sister, Zeena, were pretty much the sole support of the family, since their mother was lame as well.

Ali was also the one whom I quoted in the previous chapter writing so eloquently about the torture inflicted on Iraqis by the insurgency on one side, and the humiliation they suffered day to day at the hands of those on our own side.

Ali handled all this with grace and, above all, with determination. After all, the more he helped others, the more he was practicing to be a true American, and the more he helped his sister the better Muslim he was, putting family above himself. Still, despite his patience, after I returned to the States he did feel forced to write to me, with typical Iraqi fatalism, "I really don't know that I will make it."

On August 7, 2005, Ali was assassinated in his car on the streets of Baghdad—retribution for his collaborating with the Americans. Zarqawi's group claimed the credit, just as had with Jim Mollen nine months before. I met precious few Iraqis who were able to combine a love of liberty, a love of Iraq, a love of family, a transparent honesty, and determination to hold his little world together no matter what the price. Now, there is one less. Dedicating this book to him, as well as to Jim, is small recompense for everything they gave.

Dr. Jawad, our Shakespearean scholar, is faring better, but only because he managed to escape. In addition to teaching literature and Shakespeare, he started publishing the only English language weekly newspaper in Baghdad soon after I left Iraq. But sectarian fanatics firebombed his offices in an attempt to kill him, and he was forced to close the paper down. He was then driven from his teaching post at the university by radicalized students and he fled to Jordan. Happily, Duke University, which has been the most consistently helpful university to higher education in Iraq throughout this ordeal, has offered him safe haven for the immediate future. If he ever is forced to return, Sadr's Mahdi Army will assuredly kill him, thus accomplishing what even Saddam failed to do.

▲▼▲

By now it should be clear to any candid observer that things are not going well in Iraq. Success, of course, is relative to one's goals, and if you set your expectations low enough, success becomes easier to claim. And, since the end of initial hostilities, our goals have visibly been getting smaller. Now, it seems,

America will claim victory in Iraq if we can point to some sort of democratic government, no matter what its character, and if we can stand up an Iraqi defense force in sufficient numbers to allow us to pretend that they are replacements for our troops. No matter that the "democratic" government now entrenched is as sectarian and incompetent as we ever could have feared; no matter that their army and police are as corrupt as under Saddam and just as bloodthirsty. Once there is a working government, once there is any lull in the bloodletting, and once there are Iraqi men under arms in sufficient number, we will begin to disengage. But given the high goals set out in the first chapter—a free and prosperous Iraq allied with the West that served as both a bulwark against terror and as a democratic model for the rest Arab and Islamic world—I think candor now leads us towards sobriety and concern. While I am hesitant to say Operation Iraqi Freedom, as originally conceived, was a mistake, I am prepared to entertain the thought that it is fast becoming a tragedy.

I say this in full acknowledgment of the things that *did* go right, especially at the start. The war was fought so precisely, so carefully, that the only pictures of military destruction I was able to take while I was there were photos of former Ba'athist government buildings and military or communications facilities. The cities and towns were intact; homes and schools survived. To be sure, the looting after the war destroyed ever so much—but this was the marauding of Iraqis against themselves, not the depredations of an invading army. It would be hard to imagine a war fought, at the start, with greater care or with greater concern for non-combatants than Operation Iraqi Freedom.

In addition, many of the evils of war that are usually visited on civilian populations at the end of hostilities never happened. There were no outbreaks of disease, no lines of the newly homeless begging bread or water, no displaced persons and refugee camps. We should remember that the immediate predecessor to the CPA was ORHA—the Office of Reconstruction and Humanitarian Assistance. But, unlike every other war, reconstructive services and humanitarian assistance were not needed after this conflict, at least not in the usual sense. There were no war-ravaged homeless rummaging through garbage cans, killing each other for crusts. Soon, ORHA dissolved and the CPA, a governing organization, took its place.

The level of economic activity I witnessed when I arrived in Baghdad was, honestly, staggering. Sidewalks in the central business district were piled high with consumer goods: refrigerators, air conditioners, electric generators, TVs, and the ubiquitous satellite dishes. Even if electricity was sporadic (and, remember, it was much improved in the months following the war when our efforts weren't daily destroyed by the insurgents), almost every family bought its own generator since the fuel to run generators was virtually free. There were fruits and vegetables and meat in the markets, and money enough to buy what was wanted. Where it all was coming from, we weren't all that sure, but it was clear that the average Iraqi had enough money stashed away that hunger or even deprivation was hardly an issue.

Some things didn't work. The banking system was in poor shape, and despite the fact that there was a postal service issuing new stamps, postal *service* remained non-existent. Still, a new currency was introduced and immediately accepted, and the uncontrollable inflation that often followed past wars was not a problem. While the *official* unemployment figures were high, and while under-employment was definitely high, anyone who wanted ready cash always found a way of making a quick buck hustling some kind of merchandise on the streets. For the Americans there were kabobs, ice cream, purloined CDs, and rugs. For the Iraqis there were clothes, black-market gasoline that allowed you to avoid the lines, kitchenware, and, everywhere, electronics.

Over the course of two years, first the insurgency and later the rise of sectarian violence have hindered, or, more accurately, destroyed much of this. Americans no longer walk around the streets bargaining with merchants or sitting in the kabob houses. And the markets where the Iraqis shop are now targets. But it must be said that right after the war, ordinary life flourished with a determined intensity that was exciting to witness.

There were a few other notable successes there at the start. The Transitional Administrative Law (the TAL as it immediately became known) was the single most important thing to come out of the Iraqi Governing Council during its life under the CPA. It was far from being a great political document, but it did manage to establish real democratic forms and expectations in Iraq, and lay out the basis of individual rights that would give the world a benchmark by which to judge any future backsliding. This was especially true after Ambassador Bremer effectively (and I'd add courageously) took a stand against establishing Islam as *the* source of all future Iraqi legislation.

My pessimism was again surprised by the appointment of the Allawi government in June of 2004 to succeed the CPA—a secular Shiite regime that was more unified than expected in the face of the growing insurgency and that paved the way for elections and an orderly change of authority.

This was followed, however, in January of 2005 by Iraq's first elected government, that of Prime Minister al-Jaafari. It would be hard to overstate the catastrophic nature of this administration. Under it, foreign insurgents poured into Iraq, Iran's influence grew, a poorly disguised theocracy became embedded in a newly written constitution, religious militias infiltrated and controlled the police forces, revenge killings rose, and sectarian violence grew so fierce that an internal religious civil war reached the point where no ordinary Iraqi was safe whether on the streets, at work, at home, or at prayer. And today, under the government of Maliki, Jaafari's successor, life is even worse. Today, death squads are still active in Iraq, the police and army are compromised, Sadr's power is at its peak, and ordinary life is besieged by violence.[1]

---

[1]There's a rumor current in Iraq that Maliki, although he gives the impression of being a quiet and even somewhat bumbling politician, worked with Hezbollah in Lebanon in the 1980s and that he played a part in bombing the Marine base in Beirut in October of 1983. In those years, it is said, he went under the name of Abu Isra'a. (That Maliki's party, Dawa, was connected to Hezbollah in Lebanon and had a role in the bombings is even more likely.)

Iraqi rumors, as I noted before, are more often than not false. My friends at State will neither confirm nor deny this rumor, though it is sufficiently damaging to our interests that the Iraqis themselves believe it. Sorry to say, Maliki's embrace and defense of Sadr in his continuing murder of American soldiers does precious little to undermine these allegations.

What began so well and with such optimism—what began with the overthrow of a murderous regime, with widespread economic activity, and with the promise of democratic liberty—is now little more than a turbulent spectacle of corruption, revenge, sectarian barbarism, and death. To see anything that smacks of great success in this, to see a future of hope amid all this strife, is to babble the same kind of Happy Talk that kept us from acknowledging each problem as it arose, and kept us from planning accordingly from the start.

Despite a few early successes, and despite the sacrifice and struggle carried on daily by so many of our Iraqi friends, it became increasingly apparent to some of us on the ground what a nearly impossible task the Coalition set for itself. It became clear how difficult it is to build and how easy it is to destroy. To restart universities anxious to regain their liberties and restore their curricular offerings will always falter in the face of guns and fanaticism. If 90 percent of a scholarly community wants peace and freedom and 10 percent does not, and that 10 percent is armed and willing both to kill and die for its cause, then that 10 percent will win. (Sadly, the religious fanatics are now, in many places, far beyond 10 percent.) *All* institutions that depend on trust and mutual forbearance, not just schools and universities, are hard to establish and easy to subvert. Nor should it be forgotten that my time in Iraq was bounded by the killing of SPC Jeffrey Wershow on the campus of Baghdad University just before I arrived and the assassination of Jim Mollen, then Ali al-Hilfi, after I returned. We lived in Iraq knowing that, simply to survive, we had to be lucky every day, but that the enemy only had to be lucky once. Or, more particularly, we learned that the determination to live and build is often no match for the determination to kill and destroy.

It now seems that little that we accomplished even in the area of university reform survived our departure. Dr. Tahir al-Bakaa, who was outspoken and even courageous when it came to resisting the central Ministry in the name of academic freedom and university autonomy when he was a university president, could not sustain many of the reforms we worked together on when he became Minister in 2004. His successor under the Jaafari regime,

Dr. Sami al-Mudhaffer, turned out to be an even stranger disappointment. Dr. Sami, you'll remember, was the person Dr. Zeiad ousted from the presidency of Baghdad University because of what everyone whispered was a Sunni-Shiite battle over control of Iraq's premier university. Well, Mudhaffer joined Jaafari's party, was appointed Minister of all higher education, and quickly took upon himself to fire all university presidents, vice presidents, and deans who had been in office in Arab Iraq more than two years and put in their place officials of his own choosing. So all the rules for the selection and retention of university officials—*formulated in response to Dr. Sami's firing from Baghdad*—were now jettisoned by Sami himself as unsuitable in the newly re-centralized Ministry. The rule of old Iraq still rings true: trust no one, for within every Iraqi lives a mini-Saddam. Our friend I've called Mahmood, who was nearly assassinated by Sunni fanatics for his secular ways, and whom we restored to his post after Dr. Zeiad fled, was now finally removed by Dr. Sami. In Iraq, with religion, power, or patronage at stake, the center cannot hold.

Finally, in almost all the universities as of this writing, student religious fanatics rule the dormitories, the hallways, and the classrooms, sometimes backed up by the local police forces now infiltrated and controlled by militias loyal to the Sistani/Hakim branch of "moderate" Shiite ideology or attached to the even fiercer brand of zealotry of Sadr's black-shirted Mahdi army. Intimidation, beatings, and murder in the name of modesty, of orthodoxy of religious belief and interpretation, and of conformity to Islamic mores and customs are pervasive on today's university campuses. I know it's considered politically unhelpful to say it, but it is nonetheless true: there is today considerably less everyday freedom on the campuses of most Iraqi universities than there was under Saddam. Operation Iraqi Freedom unleashed the dark and despotic underside of the Iraqi soul—not of all, by any means, but of many—and all the finest institutions of Iraq are now suffering. What the criminal marauders did to the whole physical and material infrastructure of Iraq right after the war, so too are the political and especially religious extremists, both Shi'a and Sunni, doing to the spirit and heart of the Iraqi people now.

▲▼▲

I have, throughout this book, not hesitated to paint a picture of the limits of our American understanding, our understanding not only of Iraqi culture and character, but of our own democratic philosophy as well. But let me spend a few moments not on our defects, but (if I may be honest) of the limitations of the Iraqi character and culture as I experienced them.

First, I think we Americans have simply lost sight of the fact that democracy, "self-government" as we once called it, requires first and foremost the governance of the self. That is, of each individual self. Unless we are willing to have forbearance toward our neighbor, tolerate everything from his religion to his eccentricities, pay our taxes without compulsion, join together for the common defense—in brief, unless we are willing to submerge our opinions and interests for the common good, democracy will fail. John Adams once said that he could form a republic out of a band of robbers if only he could have them watch one another. I don't think that's true. No democracy survives without some willingness on the part of each citizen to want to live together, to accept political defeat without resort to violence, and to stand up for our neighbors even when we reject all they hold dear. Finally, it means a kind of self-denying patriotism—a willingness to recognize our duties to the country even if it means putting our lives, fortunes, and honor on the line.

In Iraq, I saw none of this. There's a patriotic and democratic fervor in Kurdistan, but it's directed at Kurdish independence, not the well-being of all Iraq. In Kurdistan, there are flags everywhere. But they are the Kurdish flag, not the Iraqi flag. In Arab Iraq there are flags, or, more correctly, banners—but not the banners of Iraq but the colors of the various religious factions. In the time I was in Iraq, I heard many hymns and songs, but never a song about Iraq. Iraq is the only country I've ever been in where no one sings about his country. I know there was once, before Saddam, a national anthem and some people over fifty can repeat it, but I never once heard it sung.

In the midst of all this stands the ever-present reality of corruption. For instance, Diego and Jim would often drive back to Baghdad from Amman by taxi in order to avoid the harrowing corkscrew descent into Baghdad airport. At the border on the Iraqi side were long lines of cars waiting to be searched. It might take hours to get your car cleared. But not if you put a twenty in your passport when you handed it to the Iraqi border patrol. You'd get your car cleared through very quickly, and your passport stamped and returned immediately, but, of course, sans money. There were those who claimed even a five would do. So anyone, ally or enemy or suicide bomber, could easily enter Iraq. "Sealing the border" by doubling or tripling the number of US troops might sound good in American political rhetoric, but the reality was that no number of troops could make up for Iraqi border corruption. Consider the police in the story in Chapter Three, on the kidnapping. They had nothing against the guy who was kidnapped, nor were they likely partisans of the insurgency. They were simply on the take. They have families too, as my friend who told me the story of the killing of Saddam's sons might have said.

Add to this the ever-pervasive cultures of dependency and entitlement that I discussed before—a people who expect to be rewarded because of who they are rather than because of what they do or make, and a people who expect government and society to supply them with the satisfaction of their needs and desires. It is, as Alexis de Tocqueville might remark, a kind of despotism in itself, a tyranny that does not break the body but softens the human spirit: A soft despotism that "enervates the soul and noiselessly unbends its springs of action."[2] Overlay on all of this the great cloud of fear bred by thirty-five years of unrelenting and arbitrary rule, and you hardly get a picture of a people ready for the demands of self-government. Hard as it is to say, still it must be said, that it did not seem that the majority of Iraqis had, or had yet, the souls of free people.

I am aware that such statements annoy contemporary academic multiculturalists no end. It would seem that the only

---

[2]See *Democracy in America,* Book 2, Chapter. 11.

culture an observer can safely make a negative comment about these days is American. For instance, soon after my return, I gave a talk in Washington. I mentioned that one problem in establishing the substance of democracy in Iraq is the serious inability of Iraqis to "know how to be a community," and the pervasive prevalence of self-interest over national interest. This was labeled "ugly ethnocentrism" by one of the least perceptive commentators on Iraq in the academy. But the academic preference for ideological purity over truth is an old story, and too many contemporary multiculturalists are more than happy to hint that their opponents are racist or "ethnocentric" whenever their own prejudices are undermined by alternate analyses or even just facts.[3]

Only in matters of religion and the afterlife were many ordinary Iraqis willing to make extraordinary sacrifices and step over the narrow boundaries of their private fears and concerns. This is what made Ali and Imad and Mahmood so exceptional— their willingness to go out of themselves for others, or for the good of their country. Still, given the general character of the people I met, it should have come as no surprise, as I said, that we were left to liberate Iraq on our own, they did not join with us in their own liberation. And no surprise, therefore, that democracy and liberty together might not in Iraq find the deepest soil in which to take root.

When you couple a culture of individual self-interest with the tendency of so many Iraqis to lie low and avoid danger above all, is it any wonder that we are having such a hard time standing up an army and a responsible national guard in that country? I know there are both spectacular and everyday exceptions to this rule—soldiers trained by the coalition willing to fight for Iraq; translators who still drive into the Green Zone every day to work; and, above all, Iraqi women who, often more than men, seem willing to devote their time and effort to various non-governmental organizations in support of human rights, or women's

---

[3]See Keith Watenpaugh, "Between Saddam and the American Occupation: Iraq's Academic Community Struggles for Autonomy," *Academe,* September-October 2004.

rights, or humanitarian aid. But the simple truth is that the volunteers are the exceptions that prove the rule. There are too many stories of mass desertion—five thousand from the armed services in Mosul in just one day!—or of turning in one's comrades because of payoffs from insurgents, or the sale of one's uniform for money, or joining the police in order to kill one's religious opponents, to give us great hope.

In sum, in all too many places I saw everything from hesitancy and understandable fear all the way up to mendacity, cowardice, and widespread corruption. I saw an eagerness not to take personal responsibility but to shunt the fault onto one's neighbor. I saw little common civic spirit. And despite so many protestations to the contrary, I saw few incidents that led me to think of Iraqis as naturally belonging to one country for which they would work or sacrifice, rather than as primarily tribe or sect or family or self interested.

These are the things I fear we didn't fully understand about Iraq and Iraqi culture before we began this venture. But (to shift to our own, our American, failings) there are two broad categories of things we failed to understand that are less forgivable than blindness to these weaknesses in Iraqi national character. The first is the character and preconditions of democratic freedoms. Blinded by the idea of "democracy," we forgot that there are good democracies and bad, free democracies, less free democracies, and despotic democracies. We think of our democratic revolution, followed by the Constitution; we forget that the democratic French Revolution was, for example, followed by the Terror. We forgot that the true goals of social life are liberty, prosperity, toleration, and peace—for which ends democracy has to be shaped as a means. We forgot that the noble end for which we who volunteered to go to Iraq all worked and some died was the establishment of a mild, moderate, middle-class, and liberal democracy, not a factionalized, warring, theocratic society propped up by elections.

If our first limitation as liberators and occupiers was our failure to understand the nature and preconditions of democratic society and the difference between democracy and freedom, our second limitation was a bizarre inability to understand what human nature truly is like. I say "human nature" and not the character of Iraqis in particular because, while we might be forgiven for misconceptions about Iraq or Islam, we can hardly be forgiven for misjudging the demands of a nature all humans share in common.

I'm not sure exactly what caused this misunderstanding: the success of our political and social institutions that has led us to forget what humans are like in pre-modern, pre-liberal communities? Or our history of living freely, that causes us to forget how an unremitting tyranny strips down to its essentials human character and the soul? Or Christianity, that has modified our moral horizon so that we indeed do worry about the demands of justice and proportionality, about humanitarianism and our obligations to others, even in war? All these, no doubt, have some explanatory force. What I do know first-hand is that there is a substratum of a baser human nature that Americans, and especially conservatives, seem forever eager to point out in theory, but forget about when confronted with in reality. It was this forgetting of what human nature is like in the raw, before its taming by modernity and mild religious teachings, that lay at the root of so many of our miscalculations in Iraq

▲▼▲

### The Confusion of Hope and Reality

Perhaps the trouble with the liberation, coming when it did, was that in large measure Iraq was not ready for liberation, nor were we ready to be the kind of liberating occupiers necessary to do the job right. We were unprepared to do the job both because we failed to see the driving passion of many in the region—that is, the furor of religious ideology and the psychic joys of extremism—and because we no longer have a good grasp of our own philosophic and political underpinnings, what makes them work or even what makes them defensible.

Indeed, in so far as we look at the problems of the Middle East as solvable through politics ("Have elections!" "Write a constitution!" "Get the Sunnis to the bargaining table!"), or economics, or education, or even cultural change, we will always fall short. I know full well that these four items can certainly ameliorate the situation. If that were not true, there would have been no reason to take the time to write this book. But we all have to acknowledge that the eight-hundred-pound gorilla in the room is a religious ideology that we in the Judeo-Christian West have scant notion how to confront. Or, perhaps to be clearer, we know that this ideology is largely not amenable to brute force, though we do sense that it can be tamed by the counter-growth of a more democratic, liberal, and tolerant ideology. If only we knew how to do that better than we do.

Yet, if we were myopic about particular things that were true cultural differences, we were also blind, as I said, to things that we should have understood from simple reflection on our common human natures. Even if self-understanding is hard, still the book of History is open for us to read. We all understand, or should, that there is a complex mixture of selfishness and altruism that makes up our basic natures. We all understand, or should, that some needs such as safety, security, or the protection of self and family from hunger and want are universal and tend to trump all higher wants and desires. The fact that we as Americans have by and large tamed the furor of religious extremism should not blind us to the historical and current reality of theocratic fanaticism. We find it hard to understand that, in both the war on terror and the war for the liberation of Iraq, our main antagonist is motivated by dreams of heavenly reward, of theological victory, and of religious domination. What caused us to lose sight of the notion that triumph in religious warfare is an idea that motivates more men than even the promise of gold or territory? What caused us, moreover, to lose sight of the heady joys of fanaticism, a fanaticism that touches deep springs in the human soul and invigorates a person to do and dare even the very worst? We needn't study the history of ancient tyrants and zealots to understand the vicious charms of passionate intensity—the recent history of Stalinism, Nazism, and Maoism, or the sad tales of butchery in black Africa, should suffice. But a nation that prides itself on its pragmatism, its realism, and its clear-sightedness when it comes to human behavior should not be forgiven its blindness to the baser parts of human nature, a nature we all hold in common no matter what our culture.

Neoconservatives, aware as they supposedly are to such realities, should have been the first to recognize what was necessary, and what was secondary, in dealing with Iraq. Yet, even when confronted with such patently self-aggrandizing and manipulatively self-interested characters as Ahmed Chalabi, they tended to make excuses and imagine the best, despite their vaunted knowledge of human affairs. Chalabi—friend of America, friend of Iran; defender of liberation, defender of theocracy; ally of Bush, ally of Sistani, ally of Sadr; selfless expatriate abroad, self-serving politico in Iraq, convicted criminal in Jordan—is a man whose loyalty changes in every regard except in regard to himself. In his personal desire for power and his constant re-invention to suit his audience, he is like no one more than Alcibiades, though without his charisma or physical magnificence. Again, that so many in the Administration followed him (I had not a few otherwise sensible people tell me of his many virtues) is another case of hope triumphant over rationality.

To give another example: We insisted that the Ayatollah Sistani was surely a "moderate" and a friend to civil and religious liberty despite all the hard evidence to the contrary. Let me repeat my previous observations and predictions: The Ayatollah Sistani is an Islamist bent on establishing a theocracy not far removed from that found in Iran. He is an open anti-Semite and a not-too-subtle anti-Christian. He threw his support behind democratic elections because they were the handy vehicles for imposing religious authority over all Iraq. Nor is he the only one, or even the worst, only the most prominent. Yet, while I believe the evidence is as clear here as it is in the case of Chalabi, we only see what we want to see, not what's visible. In our religious lives Hope may well be a virtue—but in foreign policy it is more often a sin, a temptation to willful blindness.

In sum, we were, from the start, far too trusting in those charlatans and demagogues who knew what we wanted to hear about liberty and democracy and had no hesitation in telling us. Despite our often-noted American cynicism, it was always the Iraqis who understood self-interest, suspicion, calculation, and the darker side of our natures far better than we. Compared to them, we were simple-minded Pollyannas.

In a similar way, I heard and read otherwise sensible people in the Administration saying that, since "all men" desire to be free, therefore Iraqis would fight for freedom as others did. In insisting that freedom is a common human desire, we overlooked the fact that, if there must be a choice, most people would first choose safety and security more readily than freedom. Indeed, without the safety and security of our persons and property, freedom is little more than a word. And, as we discovered even more to our chagrin, many others would choose being Islamic and submissive to Allah's word over being free any day.

Besides, as I've already noted, while I might be persuaded that, at some level, all men desire freedom, if History teaches anything about our natures it is that the desire for freedom is self-directed—we all might wish for freedom for ourselves, but surely not all of us wish it for our neighbors. Especially when it comes to freedom regarding the most important things—such as religious teachings and the construction of a culture that follows or rejects God's supposed will—that is where a belief in the value of freedom universally applied is sorely tested. In Iraq, as we are seeing, even how you dress is deemed a matter of God's will, and God's will needs to trump human wishes all the time.

"All men," we further convinced ourselves, desire to be self-governing, to live in a democracy. But "democracy" was, to most Iraqis, little more than a pleasantry, or a tool. While no one willingly wants to be ruled over by goons or thugs or despots, any number would happily choose to be governed by imams and ayatollahs or tribal and party leaders. Conservatives may joke that they'd rather be governed by the first hundred names in the Boston telephone directory than by all the full professors at Harvard, but many if not most Iraqis would rather be governed by religious leaders of their own sect than by their neighbors any day.

Perhaps most bizarrely, too many strong supporters of the war convinced themselves, on the basis of no evidence whatever,

that Iraqis had suffered too long under dictatorship to be anything but tolerant and respectful of the rights of all; that despite
the fervor of their beliefs, that there would be no desire to impose
one set of religious views on those who saw things differently;
and that, despite religious, political, and military ties, Iran's
influence would be kept at bay because, well, Iraqis would want
to keep up their own identity as Iraqis.[4] In the end, it was not
so much any supposed "otherness" of Iraqi culture as much as
the softness, the fuzziness, the shallowness—and the error—
of this type of American outlook that unraveled all our hopes
and will prove our undoing.

Those Americans who think there's a hunger for liberty in
every human breast, or that a respect for the rights of all is
natural and not inculcated, or that by spreading democracy we
naturally spread liberty, toleration, and moderation, well, then,
those Americans are wrong. If there are neoconservatives who
believe that in overthrowing tyrants we will call forth the better angels of our human nature, then those theorists need to

---

[4]Consider: "Even the most extreme of the Shiites and Sunnis have seen
horrific tortures under Saddam. They will not want to go backwards. They
may shout and threaten at first, for the liberty to do so has been long denied
them. But let us see how fast they cool down, once the practical work of
rebuilding civil society engages them. The vast majority of Sunni and Shiites
seem to be moderate, practical people, who want liberty and prosperity, not
irrational fantasy."

Or: "We must not allow ourselves to assume that great numbers of Muslims do not crave the best opportunities of our age or allow ourselves to
believe, wrongly, that freedom, individual dignity, equality under the law
and the rule of law are fated to belong only to Christians, Jews and
humanists.

"Islam is a religion of reward and punishment; hence, in some sense, of
personal responsibility. Islam has a long tradition of working from consulta-
tion and consensus. There are heavy religious proscriptions against taking
the lives of civilians. And in recent years currents of democratic thought,
often repressed, have begun stirring in institutes, journal articles and democratic associations."

Or: "Iraqis know that they must turn in a new and more cooperative direction. [They have the benefit of] the comparative moderation of their religious feelings, and a kind of mutual tolerance nurtured by the hardships
each of Iraq's minorities has undergone under Saddam." (See Michael Novak,
*National Review Online,* April 8 and 28, 2003 and Michael Novak, *The Wall
Street Journal,* January 7, 2005)

listen to more old-fashioned conservatives who know something about the fallenness of our natures, conservatives who
know the ease with which we war against each other when not
held in check by moderating institutions, civic virtue, and mild
rather than furious religious teachings.

▲▼▲

One final word on religion. After so many suicide bombings
and so many beheadings, I think we now have begun to understand the fundamental otherness of radicalized Islam. On one
side, we have to recognize that the shrill voices on the right
that see *all* of Islam as medieval, intolerant, and bent on world-
wide domination by any and all means are, thankfully, wrong.
There is a part of the Muslim world that is secular, progressive,
and tries to be tolerant. Still, as the religious passions unleashed
by the printing of the Danish cartoons made clear—or as the
furor directed against the poor convert from Islam to Christianity in "liberated" Afghanistan made even clearer—this liberality is hard to uncover these days.

There is, moreover, a perhaps somewhat larger segment that
is religiously observant and not secular, which believes in the
truth and universality of Koranic teachings, but which has no
interest in imposing its views on others or of spreading its tenets
by force. If that weren't true, Imad couldn't have written what he
did about Hadeel. It's because there were currents of liberality,
modernity, and secularization throughout all sectors of Iraq, but
particularly in the professional ranks, that made us think the liberation of Iraq might be a possibility. Sorry to say, in our desire
to placate the Sistanis and Hakims of Iraq, in our failure to extir-
pate the Sadrite fanatics when we could, and in our drive to
"democratize" Iraq and move power from the moderate minority to the religious majority, we handed Iraq over to exactly the
worst elements. Today, the Sattars of Iraq have fled, the Alis are
dead, and the Hasans and Mahmoods are in hiding.

But to return to religion itself: Insofar as there are those
in America who see or want to see no great divide between people unbridgeable by dialogue and understanding—insofar as
there are those who believe that all religions seek peace, all

religions preach brotherly love, or all religions have a common core of humane values—they propagate a view that is not merely fuzzy and sentimental but false and dangerous. Unless we understand that Islamic radicalism is as antagonistic to all the values the West stands for as were Fascism and Stalinism previously, our response will always be muddled and insufficient. I have no doubt that we should thoroughly study and understand the true nature of radicalized Islam—though, unlike in some other areas, I do not believe that greater understanding will lead to greater peace, only, I trust, to more effective policies.

There is a small part of the American polity that understands the relationship of radicalized religious teachings to despotism, but that thinks they see this fetal tyranny here in America, in evangelical Protestant fundamentalism or in Roman Catholicism. Such people simply have no conception of what a truly fierce religion, one that sees dissent as treason to God and punishable by death, might actually look like. The day the Mormon church starts to behead Methodists, or nuns strap bombs under their habits to blow up women and children in the marketplace is the day I'll concede that these people know anything about fierce theology and radicalized sectarianism. Their response—"but the religious right wants to impose its *values* on us"—is just about as unimpressive an insight as if the right complained that the left was breaching the wall between church and state by wanting all of us to be compassionate in our social policy towards the poor, or treat all people as equally precious and deserving of respect. Such "values" are, arguably, just as rooted in Christian teaching as the desire, say, to prevent the killing of the unborn. To equate American religious sentiment and those who want to effectuate it in public policy with the religious mayhem going on in the Middle East is both dangerous and nonsensical.[5]

---

[5]See, for example, Bill Moyers' talk "9/11 and the Sport of God," an address he gave at the Union Theological Seminary on September 9, 2005, for perhaps the most rhetorically bombastic and intellectually vapid of all such offerings.

As anyone who has followed American higher education for the last two decades will understand, turning to our colleges and universities for help in understanding the cultural problems in dealing with the Middle East is all too often a useless errand. All education must be an education in understanding other cultures, or so we are told. Yet, when it comes truly to understanding other cultures, perhaps the most important determinant of cultural difference and self-understanding—namely, a deep understanding of that culture's moral horizon and religious beliefs—always gives way to studies on gender and power relations, class conflicts, or lectures on the nasty vestiges of colonialism. So the fringe is always studied over the core, and what makes a culture truly different is often overlooked. Contemporary academic multiculturalism has become so internally confused and intellectually incapacitated—as well as fiercely politicized—as to be of virtually no help to anyone in the real world.

I have no doubt but that multiculturalism, properly understood, has a handle on the truth. Even in this chapter, I've given fairly equal weight to both what is naturally human and what is developed in our souls by the workings of culture, especially religious culture. But multiculturalism has to break the chains of old Marxist habits that put economic conflicts at the center of culture, or the chains of more contemporary interpretations that see gender or racial issues as more determinative than moral views or religious understandings, if it is ever to see the full variety of the human experience and understand the dangers we face together in the modern world. It also means putting aside the shallow sentiment that urges us to *celebrate* diversity rather than critically *understand* it.

In all, I would urge us to take seriously Pascal's aphorism that "custom"—culture—is our second nature. Rightly understood, culture is not just a modification of or an overlay on our outlook or perspective, but, truly, a second *nature*. Culture is a particular and powerful *transformation* of who we are equal in force to, and existing beside, the nature we all hold in common. That the average American rejects human slavery, will often sacrifice his own well-being for that of his neighbors, believes in equal justice and the rule of law, contributes charitably, and even goes abroad to help those he's never met, just goes to show how the combined cultures of the Enlightenment and Christianity have effected a change in our natures—how they have, indeed, become a "second nature."

Let me go out on a limb and speculate that one problem many in the Administration had in finally understanding how unprepared the Iraqi character was to have liberal democracy thrust on it so abruptly might be the academic immersion of so many neoconservatives in how they view the thought of ancient Greece. The discovery of nature by the Greeks—of what is right and just everywhere and always *by nature*—downplays the effective force of cultural particularity. While what is truly just may well be what is in accord with nature and not custom—blood sacrifice of the innocent, for instance, is wrong everywhere and at all times, no matter what one's culture teaches—still, what is *perceived* and *acted on* as just is more often determined not by nature but by culture. Thus my fellow neocons could readily imagine that the desire to live freely is natural to man, or that no one would prefer autocracy to democracy, or that civility is more human than barbarism. But in seeing others this way we may well be forgetting the force of culture in shaping understanding—and I mean both how historical culture has shaped our understanding as well as theirs.

▲▼▲

Everyone wants predictions of what will happen. The truth is, I don't know. No one really knows. There's a wide range of possibilities, though I will readily admit that, today, the odds are that the future will wind up worse than the present.

As I said in the Preface, the Administration has reduced all the great and good goals we had at the outset of this venture to two: Have the forms of democracy in place in Iraq, and stand up something we can point to as an effective army and a police force. Then we leave. And, in our wake, all the forces of Islamic radicalism, political brutality, and international terrorism will follow.

What's the best that will happen? Maybe Sunni extremists will give up their lust for regaining political control, give up their fears of Shiite domination and oppression despite the prevalence of Shiite death squads, and become a loyal opposition within a unified national government. Concomitantly, maybe both Sunni and Shiite religious extremists will begin to moderate their hatreds and their desire to impose their will on all others and allow those who wish to live differently, freely, or secularly to go about their business in peace. Maybe Iraqis will find a common civic spirit, a clear sense of patriotism—a sense of being Iraqi more than being Sunni or Shi'a or Kurd— and this civic spirit will lead them to condemn and act against every terrorist attack, reject corruption in all its forms as they put the interest of the country above self-enrichment and political gain, reject political influence and religious domination by Iran or anywhere else, and defend the rights and liberties of all their fellow citizens. Perhaps Iraq will find a strong but democratic leader, one who will unify the country, repel the insurgency, end the religious civil war now afoot, and insure some semblance of domestic tranquility. Maybe Iraq will work at overcoming its culture of entitlement and its culture of dependence, both bred by decades of socialist state control, and move towards a prosperous economy built on individual initiative and enterprise and a respect for private property. Additionally, perhaps Iraq will find ways of encouraging the growth of a solid and moderate middle class as both the engine of national prosperity as well as a guard against all the varieties of fanaticism and extremism to which they seem so easily prone. Finally, maybe Iraq will remain a people fully committed to their moral and religious culture, but without any part of that culture imposing its rites, rules, laws, customs, duties, or beliefs on those who profess differently. Maybe all the fine words about Islam being a religion of peace and toleration, one that is compatible with democracy and respectful of rights will prove themselves to be true. Maybe . . . Perhaps . . . *Inshalla* . . .

If we define the success of our venture in Iraq along these or similar lines, I think we can honestly say that the chances for good are now nil. But, sorry to say, *it was for a future exactly along these lines that we dared the venture in the first place.* Success in Iraq? If we call it "success," it's only because we've lowered the benchmark to near zero.

What would be the worst possible outcome? That the current civil/religious war is enflamed and grows; that no government lasts because of the inability of everyone to end the insurgency, control the militias, and put an end to racial cleansing; that the country breaks up into three parts—religious fundamentalists in charge of the southern third acting as an Iranian client state; the Sunnis, now fully in league with the Ba'ath remnants, in charge of the center of Iraq and allied with Syria and international Al-Qaeda; and the Kurds, independent but beleaguered by Turkey and Iran and by a growing fanatic insurgency of its own. These, or some variants, are hardly beyond the realm of possibility. In fact, this most pessimistic view is far more likely to become reality that any variant of the best-case scenario above.

Why would this be the worst outcome? Because to have fought and died to liberate a people, only to have them turn—for reasons of religion or civic breakdown—to Iranian religious oppression and foreign adventurism, or a regenerated Ba'ath tyranny, is to leave the scene to exactly those forces we sought to overcome, and to have set back the cause of Middle East progress, and future American security, for years. It will open the door for Iraq to become the new and energetic center of international terror, both Al-Qaeda/Sunni terror and Iranian/Shiite terror.

I know there are those pundits and even some US legislators who blithely talk about the breakup of Iraq into three parts as something both natural and acceptable. I'm sorry; I think they are mistaken. To have fought this war to secure Iranian hegemony over more than a third of Iraq—or perhaps all of Iraq—and hand them the Basra oilfields; or to strengthen Syria; or to put women and the more liberal elements of society under religious and political oppression more restrictive than under Saddam; or to give haven and a base of operations to fierce and fanatical international terrorists; or to continue the steady cleansing of all Christians from Islamic Arab lands while the West bites its official tongue for fear of giving offense—all this would be tragic.

▲▼▲

Were we wrong in invading and then occupying Iraq? I believed in 2003—and I still believe today—that the invasion was justifiable. Justifiable as part of the war on terror—in moving that portion of the world towards democratic liberty, toleration, and modernity. Justifiable, that is, in turning around a part of the world most dangerous to our own safety and well being. Perhaps justifiable, also, as part of America's growing understanding of its obligation to assist others in achieving freedom from murderous and tyrannical regimes. How quickly the liberal elements in this country have forgotten the mass graves of Saddam while they now berate us to do something, anything, to end the killing fields of Darfur.

An action not wrong in itself, however, can still be or become a mistake. Depending on the consequences, what started out as morally and theoretically fine can move to miscalculation, to blunder, and even to disaster. Sad to say, this looks to be the trajectory we are on. And, as I hope I have helped us understand, I'm not convinced it had to be this way.

Be that as it may, given the probability of chaos, continued corruption, renewed despotism, and fierce religious fanaticism, what should we Americans now do?

Perhaps we have finally reached a situation where no option is good. I'm reminded of Jefferson's remark regarding slavery: "we have the wolf by the ears, and we can neither hold him nor safely let him go." We cannot safely let Iraq go; we cannot simply disengage and come home. It's unclear who would then win the sure war to follow, though the greatest fear is that a war begun to end despotism and thwart terror will then have become a war to embolden Al-Qaeda, give the merchants of terror a sure foothold in Iraq, and advance the power and interests of Iran. One thing is certain: our leaving does not "give peace a chance," but, rather, its very opposite.

But our inability to accomplish even a fraction of what we had set out to do—our inability to advance liberty, protect out true friends, or even stand up a unified and brave military to fight the insurgency and quell sectarian violence—can be nothing short of sobering. In our private lives we understand the notion of cutting our losses. Why not do the same now in Iraq?

Why? Because what we can do in our private lives we cannot always do as a nation. We went to Iraq for defensible geopolitical reasons of state. Not only have those reasons not changed, they have intensified. Iraq has truly become a center of international terror, and our leaving would do nothing to change that and everything to embolden it. Insofar as there are Shiite forces willing to fight a Ba'athist resurgence and Al-Qaeda fanaticism, we need to help them in that fight. We may be unable to intervene in the internal religious killings and the torture chambers of the growing civil war, but we can continue to help Iraqis fight the foreign terrorist insurgency. Moreover, I believe we went into Iraq for moral and humanitarian reasons and I believe we now need to see it through for equally strong moral and humane reasons. Today the liberal and non-fanatical center can barely hold in Iraq; our disengagement would kill it. Insofar as the Kurds need support in preserving their free institutions, we need to be behind them. Insofar as women and professors and teachers and secularists and Christians need help in defending freedom and resisting religious intolerance, we need to speak out on their behalf. None of this can be done if we leave. Yet, given all that we did and failed to do over the last few years, and given an Administration whose desire to leave is as strong as its political opponents' (so long as we don't call it failure and pretend to do it under the banner of "victory" and "success") salvaging even a portion of our original goals becomes more difficult every day.

Everyone—the CPA, the US Government, the military, my ideological allies and neoconservative friends, the Iraqis themselves—bears some responsibility for the situation we find ourselves in. I only hope that if we do stay, or if we ever think to spread "democracy" to other unready nations, there are a few insights in this book that might keep us from continuing blindly along the same lines that brought us to where we are today.

# Acknowledgments

A number of friends from across the political spectrum, both in favor of and against the war, read over the various bits and pieces as I wrote them and gave me advice and often encouragement: Sondra and Jim Farganis, Joe Traub and Pamela McCorduck, Ed and Alice Delattre, Jim and Lisa Carey, Fred Baumann, James Pontuso, Omar Altalib, Steve Balch, Carol Iannone, Karen Zahler, Leslye Arsht, J. D. Phillips, Darab Ganji, Susan Bolotin, David Bolotin, Ron Herzman, Hugh Hewitt, Drew Erdmann, Joe Phelan, and Steve Curda. Williamson Evers and Bill Wright have kept me posted almost daily on both events in Iraq and the best analyses available.

My good friend George Ball of the Burpee Seed Company and the Burpee Foundation materially supported our efforts in Iraq and continues generously to support our on-going work there.

My sister-in-law, Mary Patricia Becker, sent me off to Iraq with a blank book to use as a journal. In that, I recorded each day's events and each day's reflections. That small book became the source of this longer one. Thank you, Patty.

I want to acknowledge my many colleagues in the CPA, from Jerry Bremer on down, who put aside their lives here in the States to help in the rebuilding of Iraq. Most of us made it through the daily fire of Iraqi fanatics and insurgents only to face the small-minded sniping of armchair critics here in America. There was much we did and, yes, much we left undone. But Iraq was worse for our leaving.

Roger Kimball, the publisher of Encounter Press, saw something in these pages even when I had my doubts; and Lauren Powers and Alexandra Mullen Kimball of Encounter worked in exceptional ways to help make this book a reality.

Perhaps above all, this book owes its life to so many of my Iraqi friends—those who worked with me at the CPA; with administrators, professors, and students at the universities; and with the men and women in the Higher Education ministry. Our conversations and letters back and forth continue to this day. Part of my deep pessimism over the future of Iraq is fueled by the descriptions of the life they now face each day. And part of the tragedy of Iraq is the unmerited dread they feel in knowing that, as we leave, there will be virtually no place for them to turn.

Finally, thanks to my wife, Cathy, who didn't stop me from going to Baghdad because she knew how much it meant to me, called me every day when I was there, and then let me work on this book for over two years in lieu of more gainful employment.

# Index

Abu Ghraib prison, 94; under
  Saddam, 78; under the CPA,
  164–167, 169
Adams, John, 178
Afghanistan, 10–11, 13, 117;
  suicide bombers from, 58–59
Ahmadinejad, xix
Al-Anbar University, 142
Al-Hikmat University (Jesuit-
  run), 75, 151
Al-Jazeera, 32, 128
Al-Mustansiriya University, 43,
  77, 83, 150, 161–162
Al-Nahrain University, 160
Al-Qaeda, xix, 10–11, 45, 116,
  192–194
Alcibiades, 184
Algeria, xix, 116
Ali, *see* Hilfi, Ali, al-
Allawi, Iyad, 87
American University of Iraq in
  Baghdad (planned), 160
American University of Iraq in
  Sulaimani (planned),
  136–137
Amin, Idi, 7

*Arabian Nights,* 44
Arizona State University, 140
Arsht, Leslye, 27
Assassins' Gate, 55–58
Australia, 12
Austria, 12
Aziz, Tariq, 66

Badr Brigade, xxi
Baghdad College (Jesuit-run), 38,
  75, 121, 137, 151
Bakaa, Tahir al-, 148, 162, 176
Barzani, Nechirvan, 135
Barzinji, Saedi, 135
Basra University, 76, 77, 146
Bent, Rodney, 27
Bill of Rights (for Iraqi educa-
  tion), *see* Declaration of Erbil,
  88
Bin Laden, Osama, 11, 45
Blondie, 38
Bosnia, 8
Bowen, Ray, 140
Bremer, Ambassador Paul,
  administration of, 3, 26–27,
  41–42, 54, 68, 81, 101, 125,

175; Administrative Order #8, 83; and educational issues, 86–87, 135, 151, 162–163; residence of, 34, 87; and the transfer of power, 102
British Council, 148
Burpee Seed Company, 148
Bush, George W., 23, 163, 184
Bush Administration, x, 99, 115, 116, 139, 159, 163, 184–185, 190, 194

Canada, 12
Capone, Al, xiii
Chalabi, Ahmed, 101, 184
Challenger disaster, 52
CNN, 127
Coalition Provision Authority (CPA), arrival of, 67, 173–176; dissolving of, 32, 82, 87; educational goals of, 2, 71, 76, 83, 87, 132, 137, 143, 146, 161–163; failures of, 80, 100–101, 107, 115, 165, 194; forces, 126; governance of, 109–111; Iraqi staff of, 38–39, 57–58, 60, 64–65; legal office, 88; management office, 147; oil prices under, 93
Communism, 12
Coor, Lattie, 140
Curda, Lt. Col. Steve, 25–26, 28–29, 41–44, 62, 83–84, 142, 145–146, 163
Czech Republic, 32

Dana (colleague), 32–33
Dawa Party, xxi, 175
Declaration of Erbil (education), 88–89, 151
Declaration of Independence, 129
Denmark, cartoons from, 187
Denton Program, 148

Diego (colleague), 32–33, 178
Duke University, 148, 172

Egypt, xix, 84
Eisenhower, Dwight D., 98
Enlightenment, the, 190
Erdmann, Andrew, 26–27, 62, 83, 86
European Union, 10
Evers, Williamson, 27

Faisal II, 98
Fallujah, 127; Battle of, 22, 37, 60
Fascism, xx, 12, 188
Fashion Channel, 39
Fatah, xix
Fatfat, Mounzer, 27, 31
France, 6, 12, 54, 140–141; lack of air conditioning in, 28; Revolution in, 181; Terror in, 181
Fulbright Program, 91–92, 94, 145, 151

Germany, 6, 12, 140–141; Nazis in, 12, 20, 159, 183
Ghougassian, Joseph, 25, 29, 92, 144–145
Godwin, Robert, 27
Great Britain, 6, 54
Gulf War, First, 31

Hadeel (colleague), 56–58
Haiti, 8
Hakim, Abdel Aziz al-, 177, 187
Halliburton, 1, 5
Hamas, xix, xxi, 99, 116
Hameed, Dr. Moshen, 84–85, 87
Harvard University, 148
Hasan (colleague), xvi–xvii, 38–39, 48–50, 51, 57, 60–61, 187
Haveman, Jim, 27

HEAD Program (Higher Education and Development), 144–145, 147
Hezbollah, xxi, 175
Hilfi, Ali al-, 1–3, 166, 171–172, 176, 180, 187; *see also* Zeena
Hitler, Adolf, 7–8, 99
Holland, Fern, 32
Hussaini, Dr. Abdul-Rahman, 140
Hussein, Qusay, 46, 161, 179
Hussein, Saddam, architectural taste of, 34–35; capture of, x, 3, 54; and democracy, 110; fall of, 10, 51, 60, 115, 149; forces of, 155; "friend of Saddam," 150; and the Kurds, 134; invasion of Kuwait, 78; Iraqi attitudes toward, 22, 29, 36, 55, 98, 158; lack of national anthem under, 178; liberation of Iraq from, xviii, 37; palace renovations of, 31; releasing prisoners, 67; reward money for, 45–47; secularism under, 7, 12–13, 103; statue toppling, 9, 22; suffering under, xii, xvii, 7–8, 35, 44–45, 157, 166, 172, 186; universities under, xvi, 72–77, 81–82, 177, 180; and weapons of mass destruction, 6; women under, 12–13
Hussein, Uday, 8, 46, 161, 179

IBM, 148
Imad (colleague), 37–39, 57–58, 180
International Monetary Fund (IMF), 141
Iran, xix, 11, 13, 192; ties to Iraq, xxi
Iraqi Governing Council, 37, 83, 85, 92, 104–105, 107, 140,
151, 175; interim constitution of, 101; rotating presidency of, 109
Iraqi Ministry of Finance, 150
Iraqi National Guard, 164
Israel, 5, 12, 13, 15
Italy, 159

Jaafari, Ibrahim al-, 175–176
Japan, 140–141, 153, 159
Jawad, Dr. Sattar, 71–73, 148, 172, 187
Jefferson, Thomas, 20, 101, 109, 129, 193; *Notes on Virginia,* 100
Jesuits, 38, 75, 121, 151
Johnson, Samuel, 80
Johnson, Susan, 27
Jordan, 112, 172, 184

Kassem, Brigadier Abdul-Karim, 98
Kellogg, Brown and Root (KBR), 1, 3, 34, 171
Kem, Lt. Col. John, 163
Kennedy, John F., 9
Khalid, Dr. Asmat, 127–133, 134
Khoei, Ayatollah, 163
Khoshnaw, Kamal, 135
Kidnapping, 66–70; under Saddam, 66
Kilmer, Joyce, "Roofs," 38
Kimmitt, General Mark, 60
Koran, 19, 53, 73, 103
Kurdish Democratic Party, 135
Kurdistan, 13, 192, 194; courage of Kurds in, 61–62, 157; Erbil, 54, 88, 116, 135–136; friends in, 167; patriotism in, 178; religion in, 103–106; resourcefulness of Kurds in, 133–134; rights of, 101; universities in, 77, 80, 86, 90, 125–128
Kuwait, 78, 141

Lebanon, xix, xxi, 31, 175
LeCroy, Jessica, 27
Le Moyne College, 132
Lincoln, Abraham, 106, 109, 110
Locke, John, *A Letter Concerning Toleration,* 19
Lowry, Representative Mike, 146–147

Madison, James, 108, 109, 129
Mahdi Army, 79, 89, 172, 177
Mahmood (colleague), 63–66, 177, 180, 187
Maliki, Nouri al-, xxi, 175
Mandela, Nelson, 134
Mao, 7
Maoism, 183
Marv (Green Beret), 48–49
Marxism, 17, 125–126, 189
Marxist-Leninism, 7
Modernity, 20–24
Mohammed, 19, 53, 117
Mollen, Jim, 26–27, 32–33, 38, 48–49, 60–61, 150, 172, 176, 178
Moyers, Bill, 188
Mudhaffer, Dr. Sami al-, 85
Museum of Natural History, 150
Musharraf, President Pervez, 116
Muslim Brotherhood, xix, 84
Mustansiriya University, *see* Al-Mustansiriya University

Nash, Admiral David, 147
National Endowment for the Humanities, 131
National Security Council, 25
Nazar (colleague), 135
Neoconservativism, 11–12, 18, 100, 184, 186–187, 194
Netanyahu, Benjamin, 13
Novak, Michael, 186

O'Brien, Gregory, 140
Office of Reconstruction and Humanitarian Assistance (ORHA), 173–174
Office of Transition Initiatives (OTI), 145–146
Oil subsidies, 93, 112
Oil for Food Program, 143
Omar (colleague), 125, 130
Operation Iraqi Freedom, 173, 177

Packer, George, xxi
Pakistan, xix, 116; suicide bombers from, 59
Palestinian Authority, xix, 116
Pascal, Blaise, 189
Pentagon, 149, 155, 158, 163
Petraeus, General David, 80, 125–126
Poland, 12
Popular Union (Kurdistan), 135
Powell, Colin, 140
Presidential Palace (Baghdad), 31, 35

Qatar, 25

Rashid Hotel, 29, 41
Roosevelt, Franklin D., 109
Roosevelt, Theodore, 109
Rubini, Daniel, 27
Rudd, Gordon, 159
Rumsfeld, Donald, 77
Russia, 6, 140–141
Rwanda, 8

Saddam University, 75
Sadik, Mohammad, 135–136
Sadr, Muqtada al-, xiii, xxi, 79, 89, 101, 163, 172, 175, 177, 184, 187
St. John's College (Santa Fe, NM), 4
Salahaddin University, 135–136

Salih, Barham, 136
Sanchez, General Ricardo,
    162–163
Saudi Arabia, xix, 84, 116
Shakespeare, William, 38, 72–73,
    172
Shock and Awe, 28
Sistani, Ayatollah al-, xii, xxi,
    101–102, 119, 177, 184, 187
South Korea, 140, 142–143
Spain, 141, 153
Sri Lanka, 141
Stalin, Josef, 7
Stalinism, xx, 84–85, 93, 95,
    183, 188
Statute of Religious Freedom
    (Virginia), 129
Stephenson, Adlai, 98
Student Union, 80
Sudan, suicide bombers from, 59
Suhail (colleague), 37–39,
    42–43, 56–58, 71, 82,
    101–102, 112, 125–126, 130,
    160–161
Sulaimani University, 134–137
Sunni Islamic Party (SIP), 84, 105
Supreme Council for the Islamic
    Revolution (SCIRI), xxi
Supreme Federal Court of Iraq,
    118–119
Syria, 10, 13, 192

Talabani, Jalal, 135
Taliban, xix, 10–11, 116
Texas A&M University, 140
Tocqueville, Alexis de, xxii,
    50–52; *Democracy in America,*
    179
Transitional Administrative Law
    (TAL), 109, 175
Turkey, 10, 155, 192

UNESCO, 149
United Iraqi Alliance, xxi

United Nations, 54, 104, 107;
    embargo to Kurdistan, 134
Union Theological Seminary,
    188
United States Agency for Inter-
    national Development
    (USAID), 80, 82, 91, 94, 133,
    144–145, 149
US Army, 47; 1st Armored Divi-
    sion, 162; 101st Airborne,
    125–126; National Guard, 28,
    156; Reserves, 156
US Congress, 80, 91, 141
US Defense Department, xi, 4,
    91, 116, 159; Project Manage-
    ment Office, 147
US Marines, 1st Marine Expedi-
    tionary Force, 163
US Secretary of Agriculture, 94
US State Department, 26, 29, 54,
    91, 116, 137, 145, 175
Universal Declaration of Human
    Rights, 117
University of Arizona, 95
University of Baghdad, xvi, 28,
    71, 74–77, 79, 84–85, 150,
    161, 176, 177; College of
    Agriculture, 94–96, 164–165;
    College of Arts and Humani-
    ties, 72, 74, 77; honors uni-
    versity, 160; Veterinary
    College, 76
University of Dohuk, 126–128,
    132–133
University of Kut, 79
University of Mosul, 79–81, 88
University of New Orleans, 140
University of Oklahoma, 142
University of Technology (Bagh-
    dad), 81, 148
University of Tikrit, 75; Law
    College, 76
University of Virginia, 129

Veneman, Anne, 94
Viet Nam, 26, 59

Wahabbism, 84, 116
War on Terror, 11–12
Washington, George, 109
Watenpaugh, Keith, 180
Wershow, SPC Jeffrey, 28–29, 176
Wolfowitz, Paul, 157–158
World Bank, 121–122, 125, 141–143
World Trade Tower attack, 25
World War II, 159

Yemen, 28; suicide bombers from, 58–59

Zangas, Robert, 32
Zarqawi, Abu Musab al-, x, 11, 172
Zeena (Ali's sister), 2–3, 171
Zeiad, Dr. Abdul Razzaq Aswad, abuse of authority of, 65–66, 84–87, 151, 177; "attack" on, 41–44; indecisiveness of, 140; relations with World Bank, 121, 142; religious affiliation of, 105–106; successor of, 148, 162; thoughts on international situation of, 152